The Pacific Northwest

Its discovery and early exploration
by sea, land, and river

Edward W. Nuffield

hancock

house

ISBN 0-88839-236-2

Cataloging in Publication Data

Nuffield, Edward W., 1914 –
   The Pacific Northwest

   Includes bibliographical references.
   ISBN 0-88839-236-2

1. Northwest, Pacific — History. 2. Northwest,
Pacific — Discovery and exploration. 3.
Northwest Coast of North America. I. Title.
F851.5.N83 1990   979.5'01   C90-091436-2

Senior Editor/Designer: Herb Bryce
Editor: Philip Atkinson
Production: Lorna Lake
John Innes' painting courtesy of the Native Sons of B.C. Post #2
Photographed by Don Waite

Printed in Hong Kong

Published simultaneously in Canada and the United States by

HANCOCK HOUSE PUBLISHERS LTD.
19313 Zero Ave., Surrey, B.C. V3S 5J9

HANCOCK HOUSE PUBLISHERS
1431 Harrison Ave., Blaine, WA 98230

Contents

Dedication 8
Acknowledgments 8
Preface 9

Part One   First Voyages to the Pacific Northwest . . 11

1   Discovery in the Atlantic Ocean 13
2   Way into the Pacific Ocean, 1520 19
3   Search for an English Passage into the Pacific 29
4   The River of the West, 1603 38
5   Changing Fortunes in the Pacific Ocean 43
6   Vitus Bering Sails into the Strait of Anian, 1728 . . . 47
7   A Russian Expedition Sights North America, 1732 . . 51
8   Russian Voyage of Discovery to America, 1741 55

Part Two   The Coast of the Pacific Northwest 60

9   Bruno de Hezeta and the "River of the West," 1775 . 62
10   The Voyage that Led the Western World to the
     Pacific Northwest, 1778 68
11   John Meares Muffs his Chance for a Place in
     History, 1788 79
12   Confrontation with Spain at Nootka Sound, 1789-90   85
13   Robert Gray, 1791-2 89
14   Captain George Vancouver, 1792 93
15   The Columbia River, 1792 99
16   Lieutenant Broughton Charts the Lower Columbia
     River, 1792 104

Part Three The Interior of the Pacific Northwest . 109

17 The la Vérendryes 113
    The Western Sea 113
    Fort la Reine — French outpost on the
      Assiniboine River, 1738 117
    The Mandans 122
    Expedition to the Western Sea, 1742-3 125
    La Vérendrye's last years 127
18 Alexander Mackenzie, First Man to Cross the North
    American Continent 130
    Alexander Mackenzie 130
    Peter Pond 135
    The voyage that started for the Pacific Ocean
      but reached the Arctic, 1789 138
    Preparations for a second attempt to find the
      Pacific Ocean, 1792 141
    Up the Peace River, May 9 - 31, 1793 146
    Across the Continental Divide to the Fraser
      River, May 31 - June 18 149
    On the Fraser River, June 18 - July 4 154
    Overland to the Pacific Ocean, July 4 - 22 . . . 158
    Mackenzie's Columbian Enterprise 162
19 David Thompson 165
    David Thompson 165
    Western Indians cross the Continental Divide to
      trade on the Saskatchewan River, 1798-1800 . 170
    First white men on the upper Columbia
      and Kootenay Rivers, 1800-01 174
    First attempt to reach the Pacific Ocean from
      the Saskatchewan River, June 1801 176
20 Lewis And Clark 178
    Thomas Jefferson 178
    Meriwether Lewis 180
    The Louisiana Purchase 182
    William Clark 185
    To the Mandan villages, May 14 - October 26,
      1804 187

Fort Mandan to the foothills, April 7 - July 22,
1805 194
Over the Continental Divide, August 12 200
Down to the mouth of the Columbia River . . . 207
Back to St. Louis, 1806 213
21 First Trading Posts West of the Rocky Mountains,
1805-07 217
Simon Fraser 219
First trading posts west of the Continental
Divide, 1806-07 221
Kootanae House — first trading post on the
Columbia River, 1807 223
22 Simon Fraser's Journey to the Pacific Ocean, 1808 . 230
First days on the Fraser River 230
Fraser puts up his canoes 235
End of journey 238
23 John Jacob Astor 242
24 The Mystery of the Columbia River is Solved . . . 246
David Thompson comes within 40 km. (25 mi.)
of the lower Columbia River, 1808-10 246
David Thompson pioneers the use of a new
pass, 1811 250
End of the search for the "River of the West" . 254

Part Four   After the Voyages 260

25 Disposition of the Pacific Northwest 261
26 "By the work one knows the workman." — La Fontaine 265
Alexander Mackenzie 265
Lewis and Clark 266
David Thompson 268
Simon Fraser 270

Notes 273
References 281
Index 285

List of Maps

Fig. 1   The discovery routes of the Norsemen 14
Fig. 2   The Line of Tordesillas 17
Fig. 3   The Spice Islands and the Philippines 20
Fig. 4   The Southwest Passage — the Strait of Magellan . .24
Fig. 5   The voyage of Magellan's ship Victoria 25
Fig. 6   The route of Spanish galleons across the Pacific . . .27
Fig. 7   Early attempts to find a Northeast /Northwest
           Passage 31
Fig. 8   Sir Francis Drake's voyage to the Northwest 34
Fig. 9   The probable tracks of Bering and Gwosdef 49
Fig. 10   The discovery of North America from Asia 57
Fig. 11   The coast of the Pacific Northwest 64
Fig. 12   The mouth of the Columbia River 66
Fig. 13   Track of Cook's voyage to America 73
Fig. 14   Early outline of the west coast of America 74
Fig. 15   Cook's map of the coast of the Pacific Northwest . .81
Fig. 16   Part of Meares's map of northwestern America . . .94
Fig. 17   Chart of the mouth of the Columbia River, 1792 . .106
Fig. 18   Map of the lower Columbia River, 1792 107
Fig. 19   European influence following Treaty of Utrecht . .115
Fig. 20   Distribution of Indian tribes 117
Fig. 21   Route used by la Vérendrye 120
Fig. 22   Search for the "River of the West" 127
Fig. 23   European influence following the Treaty of Paris . .131
Fig. 24   The "Crosse Road" between Hudson Bay and
           Lake Athabasca .133

Fig. 25   The Mackenzie River drainage basin according to
           Peter Pond, 1785 137
Fig. 26   Peter Pond's 1787 version of the Mackenzie
           River drainage system 138
Fig. 27   Alexander Mackenzie's route to the Pacific 143
Fig. 28   Mackenzie's route from the Peace to the Fraser . . 151
Fig. 29   Mackenzie's journey across the Divide 153
Fig. 30   Mackenzie's overland route from the Fraser
           River to the Pacific Ocean 158
Fig. 31   La Gasse and Le Blanc's route to the Columbia
           and Kootenay Rivers 175
Fig. 32   The route of the Lewis and Clark expedition 190
Fig. 33   Lewis and Clark portage to the Clearwater River . 199
Fig. 34   Clark's map of the mouth of the Columbia River . . 211
Fig. 35   Columbia River according to Mackenzie 218
Fig. 36   Fraser's travels between 1805 and 1807 221
Fig. 37   Thompson's route to the Columbia River, 1807 . . . 226
Fig. 38   Fraser's route to the Pacific Ocean 231
Fig. 39   Fraser's voyage down the Fraser River,
           1810-11 232
Fig. 40   Thompson's travels between 1807 and 1811 247
Fig. 41   Thompson's route to the Columbia River 253
Fig. 42   The Territory of Oregon 263

Dedication

For Islay
who grew up in Revelstoke beside the Columbia River

Acknowledgments

I am grateful to authors and publishers for permission
to quote from the references I have cited. I wish to
thank Melina Bowden and Josephine Penman-Meek
of the Northwest History Room in the Vancouver
Public Library at Burrard & Robson for their never-
failing patience and courtesy in responding to my
requests for material. I am indebted to my editors; Phil
Atkinson dealt patiently and cheerfully with the
verbiage of my manuscript and Lorna Lake fashioned
the manuscript into a book.

Preface

The term, Pacific Northwest, is generally understood to represent the northern part of North America that borders on the Pacific Ocean. It is defined here more precisely as the part of North America above California that drains into the Pacific Ocean (the California-Oregon border is a convenient east-west line for dividing the west coast into two roughly equal parts). Accordingly, the Pacific Northwest includes Washington; most of Alaska, British Columbia, Oregon and Idaho; and parts of the Yukon, Montana, Wyoming and Nevada.

The Pacific Northwest is a young region as the history of the white man's civilization goes. Two hundred years ago it was virtually unknown, in stark contrast to the eastern seaboard of the continent where several million people, immigrants from at least ten European countries, lived. The American colonists south of Nova Scotia had developed a postal system and intercolonial roads. They were served by more than twenty-five newspapers and had founded a number of universities, among them Harvard, William and Mary, and Yale. American lawyers, doctors and other professionals assessed themselves by European standards.[1] In 1776, the year the colonists declared their independence, there was not one white settlement on the west coast north of the California-Oregon border.

The history of the discovery and exploration of this region, both by sea and overland from the Atlantic, is intimately associated with rivers. The mariners, first on the scene, found much of the coastline inhospitable, offering few places where a ship could be moored in quiet waters, safe from the restless Pacific Ocean. They

9

searched for openings in the coastline, sheltered from the elements, where they could careen their ships to clean and recalk the bottoms, and for stands of timber so they could replace broken masts and spars. The mouth of a large river might provide all this and, as well, fresh water and the opportunity to meet natives from the interior and barter for meat, fish and other fresh food.

Rivers were the highways of the interior. The fur traders advanced westward across the interior in the quest for new sources of furs, principally on three river systems — the Peace, the Saskatchewan and the Missouri. When they reached the Rocky Mountain barrier and breached it, they found that one river system dominated travel west of the Rockies. The Columbia River from its source in Columbia Lake in British Columbia at an elevation of 809 m. (2,655 ft.) to Astoria at its mouth, has a length of 1,900 km. (1,200 mi.). As it flows first northwesterly, then southerly and finally westerly, its tributaries drain all of Idaho; most of Washington and Oregon; and parts of British Columbia, Montana, Wyoming and Nevada. It provided a wide network for trade, exploration and access to the sea. Its mouth proved to be the one place along the open coastline of Oregon and Washington that offered the prospect of a totally safe harbor.

Part One

First Voyages to the Pacific Northwest

The modern traveler can obtain maps that show the geographical features of remote areas. He can plan an expedition to any part of the earth and know before he sets out exactly the kind of terrain he will encounter. His undertaking is an exercise in logistics as much as an adventure and chances are he will find that someone has been there before him. Relatively few places have not been visited by man. The world has been mapped in great detail and with the advent of space travel and the positioning of satellites around the earth, a new dimension has been added. Man can see at one glance whole lakes and rivers, cities, countries, even continents — physical features on and of the earth that formerly could be visualized only from maps.

It is difficult, from this level of scientific achievement, to grasp how uneven the veneer of Europe's civilization was spread across North America just two hundred years ago. On the east coast, social development had advanced to where American colonists could create an "almost perfect document," as the Constitution of the United States has been called. The Pacific Northwest, in marked contrast, was a remote part of the globe.

The way by sea to the Pacific Northwest was around the southern tip of South America — through the often-treacherous waters of Cape Horn — or around Africa and then more than halfway round the world across the Indian and Pacific Oceans. It required a long, difficult and dangerous voyage to reach this coast, whatever the route, and there was no evidence of precious metals, spices or exotic Oriental goods to entice seafarers. The route overland was across the width of North America. It was known to

11

be a long distance — no one knew how long — and chain after chain of mountains barred the way to the Pacific Ocean.

The northwest coast was one of the last coastlines to be explored by mariners from the other continents. European navigators had charted, albeit roughly, the outline of Africa; the coastline of Asia, even where it is bordered by the Arctic Ocean; the shape of Antarctica; the east side of the Americas; and the western shores of South and Central America before the British Admiralty sent James Cook to this coast in 1776 to search for openings into the Arctic Ocean. Only a handful of mariners had sailed their ships through these waters. It was a wild and barbaric part of the world.

1

Discovery in the Atlantic Ocean

The first ventures directed purposely into the open sea from Europe and Britain are believed to have probed the North Atlantic in the first centuries A.D. In the fourth century Iceland was discovered and its position relative to Europe established well enough to allow return trips to the island. However, Iceland remained merely a place to visit until the ninth century when Irish hermits fled to the island looking for freedom to practice their way of life. Norsemen — fierce, daring and skillful mariners from the Scandinavian countries — had appeared on the Irish coast in 795. Thereafter their raids became more frequent, sometimes reaching inland. In the ninth century Norse kings occupied much of Ireland, warring against England and Scotland, and unsettling the customary life in Ireland.

The Norsemen were forerunners of a movement of Scandinavian people in search of new places to settle. Iceland became an outpost of their civilization when Ingolfur Arnarson, a Norwegian chieftain, settled there with his family and followers about 875. New settlers arrived steadily for the next fifteen years, not only from Norway, but also from Britain and from the Hebrides, and the Orkney and Shetland Islands north and west of Britain.

Inevitably, mariners sailing for Iceland missed the island when driven by capricious winds; some of them sighted land to the west. Although reports of such misadventures were heard as early as the first years of the tenth century, it was not until the year 982 that Eric the Red set out from Iceland specifically to investigate these reports. He landed on the southwest coast of Greenland and lived there for three years before returning. It seems he called

Fig. 1
The discovery routes of the Norsemen around the north end of the Atlantic Ocean.

the new land Greenland to make it sound more attractive to his countrymen and induce them to join him in forming a settlement. He sailed again in 986 with twenty-five ships, of which only fourteen reached their destination, and founded a colony on the southwest coast.

The Norwegian Bjarni Herjolfsson, came onto the coast of North America in 986 when he was driven off course while sailing from Iceland to Greenland. His voyage completed the circuit of the North Atlantic and opened the way for exploration to the south along the western edge of the ocean. Leif Ericsson, son of Eric the Red, sailed down the coast of North America early in the next century, and he and other Norwegians started settlements there. Yet exploration of the western side of the Atlantic and its adjacent lands faltered in the eleventh century and lost ground. The settlements in North America were abandoned and forgotten and in the fifteenth century, Norway actually lost contact with Greenland.

The next surge of exploration of the Atlantic began more than four centuries after the peak of Norwegian activity. It pointed toward the south and came under the influence of Henry the

Navigator (1394-1460) of Portugal. After spending his youth fighting the Moors in Morocco, Henry was appointed governor of the most southerly province of Portugal in 1419. Here, "where endeth the land and beginneth the sea" as an early Portuguese poet put it, he gathered about him a company of mathematicians, navigators, astronomers, instrument makers and cartographers. Among other tasks, they collected and scrutinized old charts, and studied accounts of early voyages. In the course of this research they came upon the histories written by Herodotus (484-425 B.C.) and the story of the voyage by Phoenicians from Egypt, clockwise around Africa into the Mediterranean Sea and back to Egypt.[1]

The substance of the report that the Phoenicians had sailed around the south end of Africa flew in the face of the generally accepted idea about the geography of this part of the earth. Maps of the day showed the southern end of Africa joined to a great antarctic continent with no water passage between the two. Henry chose to believe the Phoenicians had made the voyage — that there was a water passage around Africa, and that it might lead to new commercial ventures. At that time, the route from Europe to the Orient was overland across Asia Minor, peopled by the Islamic nations who jealously controlled the traffic between West and East. Henry became convinced that the Orient could be reached by sailing south from Portugal, keeping the mass of Africa on the left. It would be a long voyage — the Phoenicians had taken three years to circle Africa. Once his ships rounded the tip of Africa they could enter the Indian Ocean and make for the riches of India, China and the islands off mainland Asia.

Henry encouraged his sea captains to extend their voyages southward, around the western bulge of Africa. His astronomers began instructing the seamen to use the stars to navigate their ships more surely and fix the positions of rivers, promontories and islands with better accuracy. By the time he died in 1460, they had mapped the coast as far south as Sierra Leone, only about ten degrees north of the equator.

Fortunately, a vigorous and scholarly man, John II, came to the throne of Portugal in 1481 when it appeared that the bold voyages promoted by Henry were beginning to languish. John, like Henry, was fired by the ambition to find a sea route to India around Africa. His expeditions pushed ever farther south and in 1488, Bartholomew Diaz rounded the tip of the continent. The weather was foul and Diaz called the point of land the Cape of Storms. John knew he was on the verge of achieving his ambition; his mariners had found a way out of the Atlantic and the riches of India beckoned. He renamed the point the Cape of Good Hope. It had taken seventy years to win this goal.[2]

Little was known about the Atlantic Ocean late in the fifteenth century. The Portuguese, in coursing around the bulge of Africa, had ventured or been blown far enough out to sea to discover the Azores, Madeira, and the Canary and Cape Verde Islands before the middle of the century. But the thrust of their explorations was southward and not to the west. Navigation in the Atlantic was confined to a narrow strip of ocean from Iceland in the north to the Cape of Good Hope, outlining the west coasts of Europe and Africa.

The more imaginative Portuguese navigators must have wondered what lay beyond the islands and over the water for

> all the time the unknown world [beyond the horizon] was sending out signals of its existence . . . pieces of timber, curiously wrought with tools that were not iron . . . Dead bodies came ashore in the islands, with broad countenances and other signs that they were not Europeans. Dug-out canoes drifted in from the mysterious horizon, and when the north-westerly gales roared over the Azores in winter they brought great pine trunks such as western Europe could not grow.[3]

Yet no adventuresome Portuguese came forward to search for the source of the signals. After Diaz's voyage to the Cape of Good Hope in 1488, John II occupied himself with readying an expedition to reach India and its wealth. What lay to the west beyond the sea that lapped the shores of his country was of secondary concern to him. The ambition to reach India had driven him, and Henry the Navigator before him, and he would not be diverted. It was Christopher Columbus, an Italian sponsored by Ferdinand and Isabella of Spain, an inferior maritime power, who seized the moment. He sailed away from the land and onto the

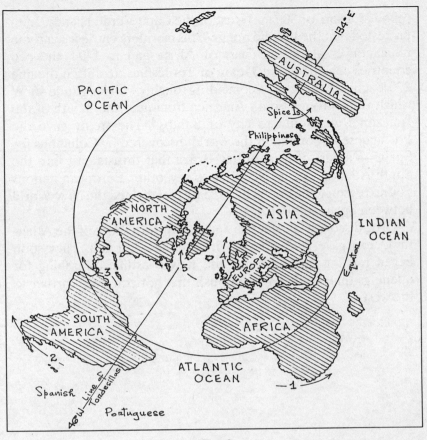

Fig. 2
The Line of Tordesillas, 1494, by which Spain and Portugal divided the "heathen" world between them, and its relation to the ways out of the Atlantic Ocean.

open Atlantic, bound for the opposite shore with visions of reaching India by another route to sustain him.

Bad weather on the return voyage forced Columbus to take shelter in Portuguese waters enabling John II to learn about the discoveries. John decided to claim the new lands on the basis of an old and obscure agreement between Spain and Portugal. Ferdinand and Isabella immediately appealed to the Spanish-born pope, Alexander VI. He responded, in 1493, by assigning to Spain all lands west of an imaginary line drawn pole to pole, 100 leagues

17

(about 500 km. or 300 mi.) west of the Cape Verde Islands. John protested that the line did not give his mariners enough sea room to maneuver along the coast of Africa and in 1494, the two countries concluded the Treaty of Tordesillas. It shifted the line 270 leagues to the west — coinciding roughly with longitude 46°W which runs through South America from near the mouth of the Amazon River south to city of Santos.[4] The treaty gave the Portuguese a foothold in the world discovered by Columbus for Spain — a part of present-day Brazil that thrusts east into the South Atlantic Ocean. Needless to say, other European nations saw no reason to be bound by a treaty that divided the New World between Spain and Portugal.

The discovery of America and the western shore of the Atlantic Ocean gave European mariners a new horizon. They soon began ranging up and down the new coastline, searching for openings that would let them push that horizon even further to the west.

2

Way into the Pacific Ocean, 1520

Bartholomew Diaz's achievement in 1488 of rounding the Cape of Good Hope was a momentous event in seafaring history. For the first time European mariners broke free of the confines of the Atlantic Ocean. The Southeast Passage, as it was called, made it possible for them to sail into the Indian and Pacific Oceans and reach every navigable coastline on the face of the earth. It was important for western commerce. Trade between the Orient and Europe had hitherto been forced to move overland, mainly through the Islamic countries of the Middle East. The Southeast Passage opened a sea lane to Asia and its riches and it broke Islamic control over the movement of goods between the continents.

The Portuguese moved to establish domination over the part of the world awarded to them by the Treaty of Tordesillas. Vasco da Gama rounded the Cape of Good Hope in 1498, entered the Indian Ocean and sailed to India. Having discovered the Southeast Passage, the Portuguese claimed control over its use and for a time were able to limit traffic between the Atlantic and Indian Oceans; it became a Portuguese passage. It gave them an enormous advantage in the competition for trade with the Orient. By 1505 they had gained enough power in India to install a viceroy and in 1511 a Portuguese naval expedition wrested control of Malacca Strait (between Malaya and Sumatra) from the Muslims. The strait was the gateway from the South China Sea into the Indian Ocean. Through it passed the wealth of the Far East, bound for the West; its capture gave the Portuguese control of the sea trade along the whole southeastern flank of Asia.

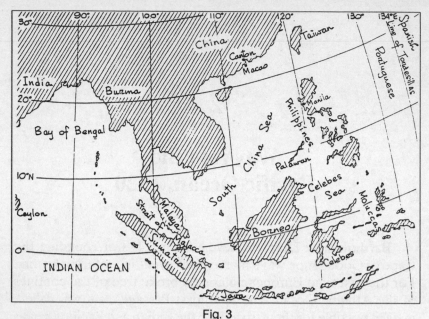

Fig. 3

The Spice (Molucca) Islands and the Philippines, and their relation to the Line of Tordesillas and the Strait of Malacca.

It was not enough for the Portuguese. They next cast covetous eyes on another jewel — the Spice Islands (the Moluccas of Indonesia) from whence came cloves and nutmeg, the spices prized most for preserving, flavoring and garnishing food. For centuries, Arabian mariners had controlled the sea trade with the islanders, carrying spices to mainland Asia and Africa. Spices destined for Europe were brought to the Persian Gulf, then shipped by caravan to ports on the eastern Mediterranean where traders acquired them for distribution throughout Europe. The trade had generated much wealth, particularly for Venice and Alexandria. The Portuguese intended to take over this trade and dominate it. Their mariners would carry spices around the Cape of Good Hope and Lisbon would become the center of the spice trade.

The Spaniards wasted no time in exploiting Columbus's discovery of America; but always they dreamed of Cathay (China) and India, and the riches these countries held for them. In subsequent voyages, Columbus sailed the Caribbean waters and the coast of the mainland between Hondurus and Panama, searching for a passage to that "other" sea that touched the shore of Cathay.

20

Some of his comrades probed the Gulf of Mexico, looking for openings to the west. They searched in vain, of course. That other sea was first seen by Vasco Balboa, one of the more notable Spanish conquistadors. He had become convinced the sea could be found by going overland through Panama. In 1513, with 100 Spaniards and 800 Indians, he drove across the isthmus and reached the Pacific Ocean, the first white man to stand on its eastern shore.

The Spaniards had watched the surge of Portuguese expansion into Indonesia with some concern. Were the Portuguese encroaching on their half of the world? When the Tordesillas line (46°W) was drawn in 1494, it was intended to divide the known (Atlantic) region of the world into Spanish and Portuguese spheres of influence. Suddenly, with the rise of interest in the Pacific, the line took on a global significance. Where would it pass in relation to the Spice Islands if it were continued around the globe into the Pacific (where it becomes 134°E)? The Spanish naturally chose to believe the islands lay east of longitude 134°E — in the part of the world over which they claimed dominion by right of the treaty. But how to prove it? It was not a matter of sailing to the islands and measuring the latitude and longitude. The earliest reliable way of finding longitude (by using Galileo's method of observing the eclipses of Jupiter's four brightest moons) would not be practicable for another century and a half.[1]

At this time mariners traced a ship's course across the open sea by dead reckoning. They plotted the direction of each leg of a course from the compass bearing steered by the helmsman, and the length of the leg by estimating the speed of the ship. Theoretically then, there *was* a way of locating the Line of Tordesillas in the Pacific. When the plot of the ship's course indicated the ship had traveled halfway around the world from the original line, the ship ought to be at longitude 134°E.

The plot of a course was subject to a number of errors and unknowns. The pilot knew how to determine latitude from the height of the midday sun and this enabled him to correct the north-south dimension of the plot. However, a significant inaccuracy lay in its east-west dimension because he could not measure longitude. The weather might have an effect — a storm

21

could upset the calculations. The size of the earth was not accurately known and for this reason it was not possible to know when the ship had passed through 180 degrees of longitude. There was another difficulty for the Spanish. Balboa had found the Pacific Ocean for them but there was little they could do about it — the Portuguese controlled the Southeast Passage and it was the only known way into the Pacific.

Ferdinand Magellan, a native of Portugal, was a veteran of the struggle for Malacca. In fighting for his king against the Moroccans, he had been wounded and this left him with a limp. He petitioned for an increase in his pension and a small rise in rank. He was refused and ordered back to Morocco. Three years later, in 1516, he petitioned again and was refused once more. Even worse, he was invited to offer his services elsewhere if he felt dissatisfied with his lot in Portugal. Utterly dismayed at this treatment, Magellan went to Spain and renounced his nationality.

Now his thoughts turned to a letter he had received two years previously from Francisco Serrao, an old comrade-at-arms. Serrao had been shipwrecked with six companions off the Moluccas in 1512. The men were welcomed as highly skilled westerners to the islands and they settled there, each marrying one of the attractive native women. Serrao was so pleased with his lot that he wrote to Magellan describing his happy life on the Spice Islands and rather exaggerating their wealth. Most important in the present context, he described the islands as being considerably further east in the Pacific than they were generally believed to be.

Magellan pondered the reference in Serrao's letter to the position of the Spice Islands. If the islands were much further east than generally supposed, they might be east of longitude 134°E and, therefore, in Spanish territory. Here was a chance to ingratiate himself with his new king and at the same time win fame and fortune. He would sail southwest from Spain, pioneer an all-Spanish route around or through the Americas into the Pacific, and establish that the Spice Islands lay on the Spanish side of longitude 134°E.

Many geographers of the day held to a belief that a vast continent, as large as Europe and Asia combined, covered the whole of the southern part of the globe. Classical scholars argued that a southern continent was necessary to balance land masses in the northern hemisphere. They reasoned that the newly discovered Americas were probably connected to this continent and Magellan's only hope of sailing into the Pacific lay in the chance existence of a channel. Since other navigators had searched in vain for it, he was not likely to succeed.

Magellan was certain he could find a channel into the Pacific and establish the position of longitude 134°E in that vast ocean. He took his proposition to King Charles of Spain, pointing to the enormous rewards that would result from a successful voyage. Magellan was convincing; the king was persuaded and agreed to sponsor him.

Magellan left Spain in September, 1519, with a fleet of five ships bound for the east coast of South America. He had trouble from the beginning. The King of Portugal was determined to stop the enterprise and he sent out two fleets to intercept the expedition. Having been informed of the danger, Magellan avoided the usual route to South America and eluded the Portuguese. His problems had barely begun. Three Spanish captains under his command bitterly resented the appointment of a Portuguese to lead a Spanish expedition. They plotted to provoke a quarrel, kill him and take over the fleet while it was still in the Atlantic. Magellan learned of the plan and easily defeated it. He relieved the ringleader of his command and placed him under arrest; but he dealt leniently with the others.

The fleet reached South America late in November and turned southwest, searching for an opening into the Pacific. Magellan came to the estuary of the Rio de la Plata in January, 1520; it looked promising but he soon realized it was only the mouth of a river.

The Spanish captains had been fomenting unrest again and on March 31, when the fleet was near Santa Cruz in latitude 50°S, they felt confident enough to mutiny. They were no match for Magellan. He had begun to show an iron will and a toughness of character as the voyage progressed. He beat down the revolt and this time the consequences for the captains were more serious. One was killed in the fighting and Magellan had another executed. He allowed the third captain to live but came to regret it, for soon

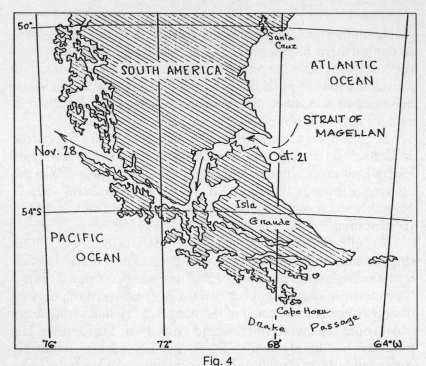

Fig. 4

The Strait of Magellan or Southwest Passage — Magellan's route, in 1520, from the Atlantic to the Pacific Ocean.

the troublemaker was plotting another mutiny. Magellan disposed of the man by marooning him on the mainland.

One of the ships was wrecked off Santa Cruz and Magellan lost a second when it was taken over by mutineers who turned it about and sailed back to Spain. He continued to probe the coast, patiently but relentlessly searching the deeply indented shoreline for the channel he must find or turn back. On October 21, 1520, in latitude 53°S, he entered the strait that was to bear his name. As the three ships penetrated ever deeper, he must have dared to hope he had found his passage.

It was November 28, almost six weeks later, before the ships burst into open water. The tough, stubborn mariner broke into tears of joy at the sight of the Pacific Ocean stretching out before him. A year had passed since the fleet had first touched the coast of South America.

24

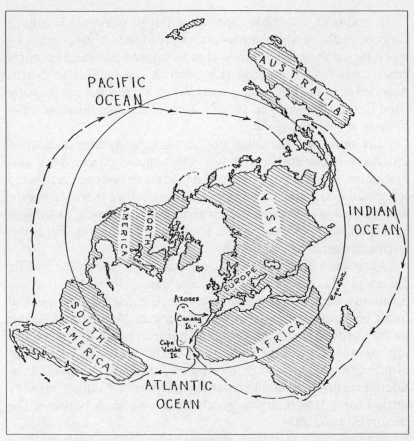

Fig. 5
The voyage of Magellan's ship *Victoria*.

Magellan never reached the Moluccas; he was killed in the Philippine Islands in a fight with natives. However, he had concluded an alliance for Spain and converted one of the local rulers to Christianity, thereby gaining an advantage over Muslim traders who regularly called there. Two of his ships visited the Moluccas though only one, leaking but laden with precious spices, completed the first circumnavigation of the globe. It rounded the Cape of Good Hope and returned to Spain on September 8, 1522. Only eighteen of the original crew of 265 men survived the three-year voyage.[2]

It had been a terrible experience but its effect on Europe's concept of the western horizon was profound. A vast ocean — much bigger than the Atlantic that Columbus had crossed thirty years earlier — separated the Spanish possessions in North America from the East Indies and Cathay. To reach these markets from Europe by Magellan's route, a traveler had to sail more than halfway around the globe.

The news that Magellan had crossed two oceans and sailed around a continent must have upset many geographers and navigators who did not believe the landmasses of the earth were separated into distinct continents. Wasn't Africa merely a southwest extension of Eurasia? They argued that America, too, might be a peninsula of the master continent, jutting out from the northeast corner of Asia.

Magellan's discovery of a Southwest Passage into the Pacific did not provide the quick and easy alternate route to Asia that the Spaniards wanted, but it did open the way for exploration and trade on the west coast of the Americas. Unfortunately, the journey around South America was hazardous and time-consuming, and this kept traffic in and out of the Pacific by way of the Strait of Magellan to a minimum. For a time the Spaniards considered cutting a channel across the isthmus of Panama but they settled for a trail, ferrying goods back and forth between the oceans by mule train.

And what of Magellan's attempt to find where the papal line of demarcation (134°E) would pass relative to the Spice Islands? His estimates of longitude, after sailing 30,000 kilometers (almost 20,000 mi.) and calculating his position by dead reckoning, placed the Philippines as well as the Moluccas *just* within Spanish territory.[3] In fact, Magellan's reckoning was in error by about fifteen degrees of longitude (about 1,600 km. or 1,000 mi.). The Philippines and the Moluccas are west of meridian 134°E — on the Portuguese side of the Line of Tordesillas.

The position of the line became of little consequence in 1529 when the two countries agreed that Portugal should have the Spice Islands and Spain the Philippines. Importantly for expansion of European trade with the Orient and the discovery of yet unknown lands (such as the Pacific Northwest), both nations

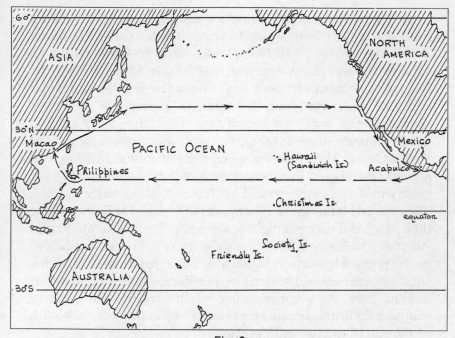

Fig. 6

The route of Spanish galleons across the Pacific, discovered late in the sixteenth century. The ships were carried west by trade winds prevailing in the latitude of Acapulco, and returned in a region of generally east-blowing winds north of the Horse latitudes.

now had a foothold on the southwestern edge of the Pacific Ocean.

The Spaniards made little headway in establishing themselves in Asia for some years after Magellan's voyage. Their access to the Philippines was from Mexico, west across the Pacific, sailing between the Tropics (between 23 1/2°N and 23 1/2°S), a region in which the winds blow constantly from the east. Getting back against these winds would take too long for this to be a practical commercial route. It would have been relatively easy to reach Spain by continuing across the Indian Ocean and rounding Africa, but this required the use of the Southeast Passage, which was controlled by the Portuguese.

In 1564 the Spaniards opened a campaign from Mexico, under the command of Miguel de Legazpi, to subjugate the Philippines.

27

In that same year Legazpi made a discovery without which a conquest of the islands would have had limited value. He found that in the vicinity of 40°N the winds blow generally, although variably, towards North America; and three of his ships made the first Asia to America crossing by Europeans along the 40th parallel.[4] The discovery gave the Spanish a practical means of communicating with Asia and after consolidating their hold on the Philippines, they developed a profitable commerce on the Pacific Ocean. Their galleons sailed from Acapulco, Mexico, with precious metals and European merchandise. Carried west by the trade winds they reached the East Indies in about three months. They visited Manila in the Philippines and Macao in China, selling their cargo and taking on spices, silk and porcelain for markets in America and Europe. Then the galleons sailed north and picked up the prevailing westerly winds which enabled them to meet the coast of America in the area of northern California about six months later. As a consequence of this traffic, the coast of southern California became reasonably well known to the Spanish by the end of the sixteenth century.

3

Search for an English
Passage into the Pacific

In the middle of the sixteenth century there were four routes to the Pacific from Europe. A traveler could go all the way by sea, either around Africa or South America, or transfer from the Atlantic to the Pacific by crossing the isthmus of Panama, or journey overland through the Middle East. It was a discouraging prospect for English, Dutch and French traders. The first and best route was controlled by the Portuguese; the second and third by the Spanish, and the last by the Islamic nations who actively opposed European contacts with the Far East. The only practical way of moving a large quantity of goods was by sea, through the Southeast and Southwest Passages. English merchantmen could expect to be harassed, turned back or captured if they were sighted by Portuguese or Spanish fighting ships in these waters.

Sebastian Cabot, son of the John Cabot who had voyaged to North America in 1497 for Henry VII, found these restrictions to travel exasperating. In his younger years, he, too, had acquired maritime experience overseas, exploring the coastline of the New World for both the English and the Spanish. It had given him a considerable knowledge of the northeast coast of North America. He retired to England and became governor of the Merchant Adventurers, a company of English merchants whose charter dated back to 1407. Their business consisted mainly of the export of woolen cloth and, to a lesser extent lead and tin, to Europe. Cabot got the merchants to look further afield to Asia, with the object of diverting some of the wealth in trade from Portuguese, Spanish, and Islamic hands to their own. Of course the lack of an unrestricted sea route was a serious obstacle to developing commerce with the Far East. One way around this was to pioneer a new route — but where?

Cabot reasoned if you could get out of the Atlantic by sailing around the south end of Africa or South America, perhaps there was a way around the north end of America — a Northwest Passage — or across the top of Europe, a Northeast Passage. Nothing was known about the north polar seas but Cabot decided, in his capacity as governor of the Adventurers, to organize an expedition to test the possibilities through these waters. Perhaps because he knew and feared the northeast coast of America, he chose to probe the seas north of Europe.

Cabot put together a fleet of three ships under the command of Sir Hugh Willoughby with Richard Chancellor as second-in-command and chief pilot. The fleet left England in May, 1553. Its immediate destination was Vardo (70°22'N, 31°06'E) on the northern tip of Norway. Vardo was an outpost of Europe; nothing was known by the British about what lay east of it.

A fierce storm off the coast of Norway scattered the fleet and Willoughby, with two ships, lost contact with Chancellor. He attempted to reach Vardo, where they had agreed to rendezvous, but he became hopelessly lost. After beating back and forth in the northern waters until late September, he took refuge for the winter on the Lapland coast in a small bay. Its waters were full of fish and game was plentiful on shore, yet not one of the sixty-three men survived the winter. They were found by Russian fishermen in the spring of 1554; all had frozen to death.

Chancellor was more fortunate. He reached Vardo, waited a week for the other ships, and then pushed on. He entered the White Sea about the middle of May and encountered a boatload of Russian fishermen who conducted the Englishmen to their village. Eventually they were taken overland to Moscow to meet Ivan (later called Ivan the Terrible) to whom they delivered letters from King Edward VI of England, carried against just such an eventuality. They were well received by Ivan and when Chancellor departed for England in the spring, he was invited to return and establish trade relations on Russian soil.

Despite this promising beginning, English and later Dutch mariners in subsequent attempts to find a Northeast Passage to

Fig. 7
Early attempts to find a Northeast and a Northwest Passage from the Atlantic to the Pacific.

the Pacific, did not get as far east as the Kara Sea; they managed to traverse barely one-sixth of the distance from Norway to Alaska. The northern coast of Russia and Siberia was a trackless, totally uncharted and utterly hostile wilderness and no one had any idea of the length of the passage, or indeed, if there was one.

The north polar voyages and the talk of a Northeast Passage created interest in a book by Marco Polo, published late in the thirteenth century. The book, describing his travels in China, had

31

been received with disbelief and little interest. Now, however, a reference in the book to a navigable passage from Japan — southwest past Taiwan to the "countries of Ania"[1] near the Gulf of Tonkin in North Vietnam — roused the imagination of European cartographers. Not hindered seriously by a shortage of dependable information and feeling free to conjecture, mapmakers chose to misinterpret Marco Polo or perhaps to correct him. They arbitrarily moved Ania to the northeast where Asia and America were thought to face each other. Marco Polo's passage became a channel between two continents on their maps and they called it the Strait of Anian. The earliest known map to show these supposed features was published in Europe in 1565.[2]

The search for a northern "English" passage to China had been fruitless. If it had any effect, it was to increase English activity in the Atlantic. Elizabeth I openly denied the pope's right to assign "heathen" lands to the Catholic kings of Spain and Portugal. She encouraged her subjects to violate Spanish attempts to regulate the use of the seas around the Americas. Freebooters and pirates responded. Mostly they worked the Gulf of Mexico and the waters around the West Indies; but they also drove ashore on the Spanish Main, attacking treasure trains and raiding settlements where goods were stacked awaiting shipment by sea.

Sir Francis Drake, best known of Elizabeth's seamen, was engaged in the slave trade before becoming the most successful of the many English freebooters raiding the Spanish Main. In 1573, while plundering along the coast of Panama, he went ashore and crossed the isthmus to a point where he could see the Pacific Ocean. It was his first sight of the "Sea of the South" and it stirred his adventurer's soul. He swore he would sail its waters.[3]

Drake's opportunity was not long in coming. A syndicate of Royal Navy men, formed with Elizabeth's knowledge if not open encouragement, arranged to finance a voyage under Drake's command to the west coast of South America. These were Spanish waters, protected from casual intrusion by the stormy seas below Cape Horn and the wide expanse of the Pacific Ocean. Spanish treasure ships plied this coastline lulled by the knowledge that enemy ships had never menaced it. The ostensible purpose of Drake's voyage was to explore the coast of what is now Chile and Peru and discuss trade with the natives. It is not difficult to believe that there was another reason for the voyage and that it related to the Spanish treasure ships. It seems unlikely that the syndicate would attempt to dictate instructions to a man of Drake's stature, temperament and experience. More probably there was an agreement that he would enter the Pacific, but what he did there and how he returned would depend on the opportunities and circumstances as he saw them.

Drake left England on the *Pelican* (100-120 tons; later called the *Golden Hind*) in December, 1577, accompanied by four smaller ships. He steered for Cape Blanco on the bulge of Africa, taking several Spanish and Portuguese prizes on the way. On the way to the Cape Verde Islands, he captured a Portuguese ship filled with fine wines, cloth and other dry goods that would be useful on the voyage into the Pacific. He began the crossing of the Atlantic in February 1578, and sighted the coast of Brazil at latitude 30°S, two months later. Stopping at intervals to go ashore, the expedition reached San Julian, in latitude 49°S, on June 20 to be met by the grim sight of the gallows on which Magellan had hanged one of his Spanish captains almost sixty years previously.

San Julian proved to be as unpleasant for Drake as it had been for Magellan.

John Doughty, one of a number of "gentlemen volunteers" on the expedition, and Drake's friend, had been undermining Drake's authority and plotting the failure of the enterprise. The ships' officers insisted he be tried before a court martial. He was found guilty and Drake was forced to punish him. He was beheaded and buried beneath the gallows.

Winter was at hand. Drake had planned to wait for summer before attempting the 584 km. (363 mi.) Strait of Magellan, but the crews were restless and Drake feared an idle six months at San Julian would breed mischief. He ordered the fleet to sea and entered the channel on August 21. Now good fortune smiled; steady northeast winds carried the ships through the strait and into the Pacific on September 6. The passage had taken only sixteen days including stopovers to take on water and kill 3,000 penguins for food.

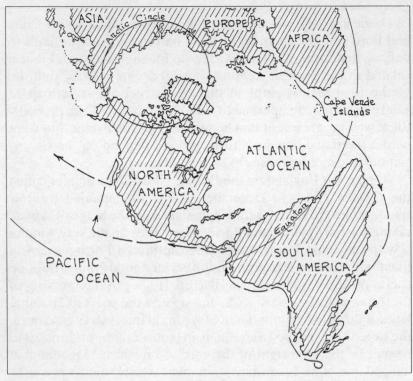

Fig. 8
Sir Francis Drake's voyage from England to the Northwest coast of North America, 1577-9.

Drake abandoned the two smallest ships and turned the other three up the coast. Now in the Pacific, the weather changed abruptly; the winds blew furiously from the north. The little fleet was driven south, and one of the ships was swept away and lost in the heavy seas while Drake watched helplessly. Finally, after battling the elements for a month, the remaining two ships found shelter in the lee of some islands and anchored. The captain of Drake's companion ship had had enough; early in October he slipped away and sailed back to England. The original fleet of five ships was reduced to the *Pelican*.

Drake found himself well south of the Strait of Magellan — in the vicinity of latitude 57°S — further south than any ship had ever ventured anywhere on earth. His situation revealed, for the first time, that there was open water between the Atlantic and Pacific oceans, that the two oceans were parts of the same great mass of sea that covers most of the earth. The belief held by some scholars, that the Americas were separated from a large southern continent only by the narrow Strait of Magellan, was evidently false. It was another forty years, however, before the first ship sailed around Cape Horn — the southern tip of South America — from one ocean into the other.

The weather improved in November and Drake was able to take the *Pelican* north. In the next six months he sailed up the coast, sacking the Spanish settlements he found, taking prisoners if it suited him, capturing merchantmen and accumulating an incredible amount of booty. The Spaniards were not equipped to resist him, not expecting anything more menacing than a native craft in this part of the world. Drake played wolf among the sheep, even seizing a treasure ship, the *Cacafuego*, off Peru in March.

He made his final raids in April, 1579. It was time to give up the escapade; the whole of the west coast below him was aroused. Indignant Spaniards, on shore and in now-well-armed ships were on the lookout, eager to make him pay for his deeds, watching for his return. Drake knew he had almost no hope of eluding them if he attempted to reach England by retracing his course through the Strait of Magellan; he would have to choose a different route home. He entered the Acapulco harbor on April 15 and took on all the provisions he could carry. Next day he left port accompanied by one small captured ship, steering for the open Pacific, the *Pelican* leaking from the weight of treasure in her hold.

Drake's official journal and charts have been lost but an account of the voyage was published in 1628 by Francis Fletcher,[4] a preacher on board the *Pelican*. According to this account, Drake kept a westerly course for five hundred leagues when, catching a favorable wind, he turned north. Apparently the westward course-setting was a ruse designed to deceive the Spaniards, who would be unlikely to pursue him if they thought he was bound for the Cape of Good Hope.

Drake was almost certainly familiar with the latest maps of the Americas and the speculation among geographers that Asia and North America were separated by the Strait of Anian.

Willoughby's quest, in 1553, for a Northeast Passage had led to nothing, but a Northwest Passage remained a possibility. Martin Frobisher had left England to search for it from the Atlantic side but had not returned by the time Drake sailed for South America in the following year.

With the indignant Spaniards at his back, Drake decided it would be wise to look for the Strait of Anian. If he found it and it opened into the Northwest Passage, he might make a quick, safe voyage home and be doubly welcomed when he arrived.

The ships were in latitude 42°N on June 3. As they ran north, the weather grew bitterly cold and the men began to complain grievously. The ships' ropes and tackle were so stiff

> that what 3. men afore were able with them to performe, now 6. men with their best strength, and uttermost endeavour, were hardly able to accomplish.[5]

The men's hands were numbed by the cold and they became reluctant to bare them, even to feed themselves.

On June 5 a wind, icy and violent, began to blow from the north and they could make no headway against it. To maintain his latitude, Drake steered for the land and anchored in a bay — the best shelter he could find along this coast. It offered little protection from strong gusts and when they died, a thick fog rolled in from the sea and obscured everything. Drake feared for the safety of his ships and finally he put to sea, hoping to find better shelter to the north and continue his search when better weather prevailed. As soon as the ships were free of the land, however, the winds took charge, forcing them south from "the height of 48. deg. in which now we were, to 38."[6]

Drake entered a well-protected bay (probably Drake's Bay just north of San Francisco) on June 17. He careened the *Pelican* to repair her leaks, replenished the fresh water supply, and had his men cure a large quantity of meat and fish in preparation for the task he faced.

He knew now he would have to cross the immense expanse of the Pacific Ocean to get back to England. The region may have reminded Drake of England for he named it Nova Albion (Albion was the Greek name for England).[7]

Drake decided he did not have enough men to work both ships across the Pacific. He abandoned the captured ship and took the *Pelican* out of the bay on July 24, 1579. He set a southwesterly course, passing to the north of the Marshall Islands, touching Palau and landing at Mindanao. He spent some time in Indonesia. He loaded a cargo of cloves in the Moluccas which later had to be jettisoned when the ship was grounded on a reef. He visited a number of islands before sailing southwest again, heading for the Cape of Good Hope. He successfully avoided the fearful loss of men suffered by Magellan by taking on fresh water and food; and he cleaned the ship's bottom again. He arrived in Plymouth, England, on September 26, 1580. It had taken more than a year to make the voyage from the California coast.

4

The "River of the West," 1603

Latitude 48°N, Drake's most northerly Pacific reach according to Fletcher, is between Cape Flattery and the mouth of the Columbia River. Fletcher's account makes Drake the first European to touch the coast of the Pacific Northwest above California. He may have seen the Columbia River as he cruised along the coast but it is doubtful; we know from later accounts the river was difficult to perceive from offshore.

Drake's audacious pirating along the west coast of the Americas may have been an early sign that Spanish maritime strength in the Pacific was ripe for a serious challenge. Nevertheless, Spain was still a formidable opponent in these waters. The coast of the Pacific Northwest remained a Spanish preserve well into the eighteenth century but this was due more to its isolation than Spain's might. It was a long distance from Europe via sailing ship no matter by what route the traveler chose to reach it.

Drake's escapade was only one irritant Spain suffered. Another was the persistent probing of Arctic waters on the east coast of North America by English navigators (Martin Frobisher, John Davis, George Weymouth, Henry Hudson and William Baffin). In the decades spanning the end of the sixteenth century and the beginning of the next they searched for a Northwest Passage. It forced Spain to take an interest in a northern route into the Pacific, if only to gain control of its western entrance and keep the English out of the Pacific.

Claims that the Strait of Anian had been found soon began surfacing. The most celebrated had its origin in a chance meeting in Venice in 1596 between an English merchant named Michael

Lock and Apostolos Valerianos, a sixty-year-old Greek. The old man, who called himself Juan de Fuca, claimed the Viceroy of Mexico had sent him to discover and fortify the Strait of Anian against passage by the English. De Fuca said he sailed from Mexico in 1592, following the trend of the coastline, first northwest, then north, and finally northeast. Between 47 and 48°N, the coastline opened into a broad inlet whose entrance was marked on the northwest side by a great headland or island with a high pinnacle on it. The inlet bore first east and southeast and then assumed a generally northerly direction. He said he passed many islands and after twenty days emerged in the "North Sea" (by which he meant the Arctic Ocean). Then, believing he had satisfactorily completed his assignment, de Fuca returned to Mexico. He was not rewarded as promised and he fled to Europe, hoping to find some way of profiting from his knowledge.

The old man's description is reasonably close to the geography of Vancouver Island, the Strait of Juan de Fuca (which however, is between 48 and 49°N) and the Strait of Georgia. No corroboration of the claim has been found in the Spanish literature of the time but it gained for Juan de Fuca a permanent if questionable niche in history.[1]

One of the more extravagantly fictitious claims was made by Lorenzo Maldonado in 1609. Maldonado described in detail a route from Spain across the Atlantic Ocean, through Davis Strait into a northwest-trending basin he called the Strait of Labrador, to latitude 75°N. Thereafter the route turned south until, in latitude 60°N, it passed through the Strait of Anian with Asia on one side and America on the other. Maldonado said that while he lay at anchor inside the entrance, a ship passed through the strait from the Pacific, and turned west, bound for its home port of Archangel on the north coast of Russia.[2]

The rumors of a Northwest Passage and the possibility that its discovery would bring European traders into the Pacific worried Philip II of Spain. He ordered the Viceroy of Mexico to make a proper survey of the coast in the region of the reported discoveries and turn fancy into fact. The viceroy dispatched an expedition in 1596 but it did not get beyond the Gulf of California. The lack of progress was apparently of little concern to the viceroy for he could see no immediate profit in mapping this remote coastline. It was difficult to believe the region would ever yield anything to compare with the riches that were there for the taking in Mexico and Central America. Since he was expected to bear the cost of the surveys, he was only too willing to allow the project to languish.

When Philip III ascended the Spanish throne in 1598, one of his first acts was to insist that the coastal surveys be completed. In consequence, the new viceroy outfitted two large ships and a small one for a long voyage of discovery. He appointed Sebastian Vizcaino to command the expedition; Martin de Aguilar would have charge of the small vessel.

The expedition put to sea from Acapulco early in May, 1602, and rendezvoused in a small bay on the southern tip of the California peninsula to make final preparations. It sailed on July 5 and almost from the first day it was bedevilled by its "chief enemy, the north-west wind."[3] The enemy, it was said, was motivated "by the foe of the human race, in order to prevent the advance of the ships, and to delay the discovery of those countries, and the conversion of their inhabitants to the Catholic faith."[4]

Vizcaino surveyed the coastline as far north as Cape Conception in latitude 37°N (just below San Francisco Bay) by the middle of December. However, scurvy had cost the lives of sixteen seamen and many more were unfit to work. Vizcaino decided to send one of the large ships back to Acapulco with the sick; he and Aguilar would continue the survey. The two mariners left their anchorage on January 3, 1603, steering northwestward. Out in the open water they encountered their chief enemy again; this time the northwest wind blew with such a fury that the ships were separated and lost to each other. Vizcaino reached and named Cape San Sebastian in latitude 42°N (at the Oregon border) on January 20. By this time only a few of his men were fit to work; the weather had turned cold and stormy and his provisions were low. It was time to assess his situation. Vizcaino consulted his officers and they were unanimous in their advice to come about and sail back to Mexico. They arrived in Acapulco on March 21. The expedition had stopped well short of the supposed location of the Strait of Anian, frustrated by sickness and the weather.

Aguilar, in the small ship, continued northward when the storm abated, hoping to catch up with his commander. He sailed close alongside the shore and on January 19 came onto a prominent headland which the pilot found to be in latitude 43°N. Aguilar named it Cape Blanco. Above the cape the coastline turned northwestward "and near it was discovered a rapid and abundant river . . . which they endeavored to enter, but could not, from the force of the current."[5]

How near is "near?" The nearest major river is the Columbia River in latitude 46°N (about 350 km. or 215 mi. above Cape Blanco). Was the "rapid and abundant river" the Columbia?

Aguilar had already reached a higher latitude than his orders stipulated. Many of his men were sick and became a factor in limiting his freedom of action. The crew was anxious to be home. Not troubling to explore the river from the shore, or fix its latitude, Aguilar terminated the voyage and sailed for Mexico. The little vessel reached Acapulco about the same time as Vizcaino brought his ship into the port but not before Aguilar, the pilot and most of the crew, had sickened and died.

Aguilar's river was variously interpreted by geographers. It was taken by some to be the Strait of Anian and the entrance to a passage to the "North Sea." Others thought it was the western end of a channel that separated California from the mainland (it was some years before it was proved that California was not an island). Some geographers showed Aguilar's discovery as a great river flowing into the Pacific Ocean from deep in the continent.[6] It earned the name "River of the West" on a few maps.

The surveys begun by Vizcaino and Aguilar were not carried north of the California-Oregon boundary. Vizcaino realized it was necessary to have settlements along the coast where discovery ships could call for fresh food and water, and give their sick an opportunity to recover. He made a proposal for colonizing the coast but the Viceroy of Mexico was not interested and he got nowhere with his plans. The viceroys were expected to bear the cost of initiatives and this discouraged exploration of the Pacific Northwest.

In truth, all was not well with Spain. Prices had begun to rise all over Europe, fueled by the glut of silver extracted from the

41

Latin American colonies. By 1610, the economic expansion of the sixteenth century had been succeeded by a depression. It left little desire to finance expeditions north of California — along a coastline that as yet had paid no dividends nor given any indication that it would in the future. The fine resolve of Philip III to map the west coast of North America was allowed to lapse.

5

Changing Fortunes
in the Pacific Ocean

The Portuguese built up a lucrative trade with their colonial empire in the Indian Ocean during the first half of the sixteenth century, but the newfound wealth was not used to develop a sound economy at home. Farming was not given a proper priority. In time poultry and dairy products, and other basic food stuffs — even cured fish — had to be imported in large quantities. There was no fundamental strength in the country and in 1580, near the height of Spanish power in Europe, Philip II of Spain occupied Portugal and had himself crowned.

During the occupation, the Spaniards closed Portuguese ports to foreigners. Lisbon had been an international port where European traders came to buy spices and other exotic products brought into the Atlantic by Portuguese merchantmen. Dutch, English and other nationals, suddenly deprived of these items of trade, began to enter the Indian Ocean to procure them at their sources. The Portuguese, burdened by the Spanish occupation of their country and internal economic problems, could not mount an effective threat against the intruders. Dutch traders reached the Moluccas in 1600 and within a few seasons the Portuguese monopoly of the spice trade was destroyed.

Portuguese influence in the Far East continued to decline. By 1635 the Dutch were intercepting Portuguese shipping through the Malacca Strait, effectively stopping a rich flow of revenue to the Portuguese economy. The frustration of the Portuguese people boiled over in 1640; they rose and drove the Spanish, weakened by internal revolt and by war with France, from their country. It did nothing to halt the Dutch aggression. By 1656 they had wrested control of Ceylon from the Portuguese and in 1662 they occupied the Moluccas. The Portuguese were left with some posts along the west coast of India and they held Macao (the "Portuguese Hong Kong") and a string of islands reaching south towards Australia. It was a ghost of their former empire. The glory days were over — Portugal entered the eighteenth century as an insignificant maritime power. The bold pioneering days, when Portuguese mariners led the world into the unknown, were a part of the past.

Spanish fortunes, too, were in a state of change. The Latin American colonies had sent prodigious amounts of wealth in the form of silver to Spain in the sixteenth century. As in Portugal, very little of the revenue from these shipments had been invested in Spain to modernize and expand economic production. Spain remained a basically poor country. The wealth had gone to pay for imports, to support Spanish armies fighting abroad and to service the government's debt to foreign bankers.

The sixteenth century had been a period of expanded activity but the inflow of enormous capital from Latin America, the neglect of the internal economy and the dependence on imports carried a penalty. Prices began to rise in Spain and elsewhere and even before the flow of silver had peaked in 1595, Europe was in the grip of inflation. In 1621, when expenditures were far in excess of income in Spain, the king devalued the currency thereby increasing the cost of imports. Meanwhile, men and money were being drained away as Spanish forces took part in the seemingly endless struggle in Europe to decide the balance of power on the continent.

The Dutch attacked Spanish shipping in the western Pacific while they were gobbling up the Portuguese colonial empire. But after they occupied the Moluccas in 1662, the Dutch set about consolidating their gains and their attacks around the Philippines lessened. For the remainder of the seventeenth century, the Spanish were not seriously hindered in the Philippines and their trans-Pacific trade between Mexico and Asia prospered.

The Dutch grasp at Portugal's overseas empire had netted them trade posts from the Cape of Good Hope to the islands of Indonesia. To extract maximum benefit for themselves, they created a hostile environment for other traders, trying to exclude them from the commerce in the Indian Ocean and the Far East. If the Dutch thought they would be permitted to control the seas they were mistaken. In the middle of the seventeenth century, English and Dutch fleets clashed in several naval battles in the Atlantic. Soon English and French were openly and vigorously competing with the Dutch, Spanish and Portuguese for trade in the Indian and Pacific Oceans. The Spanish may have wondered how soon the nations of the world would be drawn across the Pacific to threaten their domination of the west coast of the Americas.

The unproductive wars, the mismanagement of foreign affairs and the economy, and the excesses eventually took their toll of Spain. Her power was greatly diminished by the turn into the eighteenth century; the British were now distinctly superior in naval strength in the Pacific. In 1743 the Spanish lost a prized advantage when the British captured a galleon out of Manila and found in the master's cabin his sailing instructions. They revealed the closely guarded secret of using the region of 40°N, with its easterly trending winds, to sail from Asia across the Pacific Ocean to America.

While Europeans fought in the sixteenth and seventeenth centuries for control of the southeast shores of Asia and the water lanes to reach them, an equally momentous struggle by Europeans was under way to dominate the northern territories of Asia. The aggressors were Cossacks, a Christian people from eastern Europe. The Cossacks were a mixture of the persecuted and the rebellious, of criminals and religious zealots, wanderers who had drifted east and west to the southern steppes of Europe. Dominant among them were the Ukrainian Cossacks from the Dnieper River, and the Don Cossacks from the Don River. These nomadic tribes were slowly absorbed into the Russian Imperial service and used against the Mongolian nomads, first to the south of Russia and then to the east.

Late in the sixteenth century small bands of Cossacks began moving into Siberia. They established control of the Ob, Yenisei and Lena river systems in the north, thrust east and towards the inhabited centers in the south, and fortified strategic positions.

They reached the Sea of Okhotsk in 1649. Fifty years later, in the reign of Peter the Great, the Russians annexed the Kamchatka Peninsula.[1] They had gained a coastline on the Pacific Ocean and the stage was set for Europeans to make the relatively short voyage across the Bering Sea and discover the northwest coast of North America.

6

Vitus Bering Sails into the Strait of Anian, 1728

The Russians encountered many hostile peoples in their invasion of Siberia but none more warlike than the natives that lived in the Chukchi Peninsula, the remote northeast corner of Asia. In the course of attempting to subdue them in 1711, Peter Popoff, a Cossack, learned that there was land to the east of the peninsula. The Chukchi said an island was visible on clear days and that it could be reached in a day by boat in summer or on foot over the ice in winter. The natives said it was part of the "Large Country" but exactly what they meant by that term Popoff did not discover.[1]

The Russians had heard similar reports in the past. They had no reason to associate the island with America; in fact, they had only a vague idea concerning the position of the peninsula on the face of the earth. Moreover, geographers could only speculate at this time that North America extended northwest towards the polar regions of Siberia. Not surprisingly then, no special significance was attached to Popoff's report on the Large Country when it was read by the authorities in St. Petersburg.

There is no reason to believe Popoff's report had any bearing on Peter the Great's decision to send an expedition to explore the coastline of the Chukchi Peninsula. English and Dutch mariners had tried unsuccessfully for almost two centuries to force a passage east from Europe along the north coast of Russia and Siberia. A navigable Northeast Passage could be extremely valuable to Russia. It would connect Archangel in the European Arctic with the new ports on the Siberian-Pacific coast and the markets in China and India.[2] Peter reasoned that there was no point in struggling to find a Northeast Passage or, for that matter, a Northwest Passage unless Asia and America were separate. He decided to settle first the question cartographers had been debating for more than a century — the existence of a strait — the fabled Strait of Anian. He chose Vitus Bering, a Dane serving with the Russian Navy, to lead his expedition. Apparently he had little if any faith in the existence of a strait, for Bering was instructed to build one or two boats on the Kamchatka Peninsula and sail north along the coast and "search for that [place] where it is joined with America."[3]

Kamchatka was several thousand of the coldest, most inhospitable and trackless miles from St. Petersburg. Those shipbuilding materials which could not be cut in the forests along the Pacific coast had to be transported there — by packtrain, river barges built on the way, sleds and, as it turned out, on the backs of men. It required several hundred men and twice that number of horses to move materials and the provisions to keep men and animals fed. Bering got his goods moving out of Russia in January, 1725. It was March, 1728, before he had assembled everything near the mouth of the Kamchatka River[4] and begun building the *St. Gabriel*, a ship measuring 18 m. (60 ft.) in length. She was ready in July.

Bering took the *Gabriel* out of her anchorage on July 13, 1728, with forty-six men including lieutenants Martin Spangberg and Alexei Chirikov on board. He set a course northward, following the coast, going ashore several times to search for fresh water. The landing parties saw signs of habitation but no people.

On August 8, in the Gulf of Anadyr along the south shore of the Chukchi Peninsula, they encountered a leather boat with eight men in it. Bering beckoned to them but the natives refused to bring their craft close. Finally one jumped into the sea and with the help of large, inflated seal bladders, swam across to the *Gabriel* and went aboard. Bering learned from the man that he and his companions were Chukchi living on the mainland. He informed Bering that the coastline swung around to the west, to the mouth of a large river (the Kolyma River?), and that the sea there always had ice in it. Some of his people occasionally visited the mouth of the river but always by deer sled and never by water. Bering considered the information to be good evidence that the

48

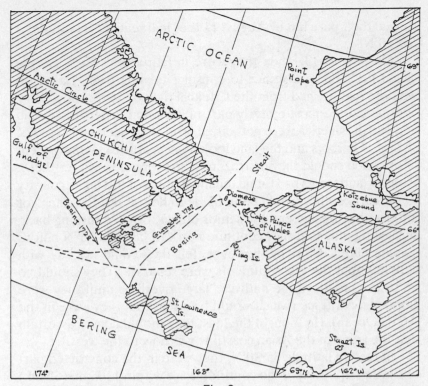

Fig. 9

The first probes by Europeans of the waters east of the Chukchi Peninsula: the probable tracks of Bering (1728) and Gwosdef (1732).

continents of Asia and North America were separate and that he was now near the eastern extremity of Asia.

Bering also learned from the native that not far ahead, in a southeasterly direction, they would come to an island. Two days later, on August 10, they located the island; Bering named it St. Lawrence Island for San Lorenzo whose martyrdom was celebrated on that day. He sent men ashore but the only evidence of life consisted of a few huts.

Bering set a northerly course from the island, sailing through drizzly weather that often drastically reduced the range of their vision. They dared not cruise near the shore for fear of running aground so they moved the ship well out to sea — and generally, out of sight of the Asian mainland. They faced headwinds which slowed their pace but by August 11 they had reached a latitude of 64° 20'N.

On August 13, when they were in latitude 65°30'N, Bering called his officers together to consider turning back. Based on what he had learned from the Chukchi native, he reckoned they had passed the most easterly part of Asia and proved that Asia and North America were not joined. The coast seemed devoid of sheltered harbors and the land looked incapable of keeping them in firewood should they be frozen in and forced to winter there. Russian land forces had found the inhabitants of this bleak country to be warlike; they would be unlikely to help if the Russians got into trouble. Spangberg, the senior officer, favored turning back, suggesting only that they continue north to latitude 66°N before coming about. Chirikov, however, felt they could not say with certainty that the two continents were separate. They should go on to the mouth of the native's "large river" or until they were stopped by drift ice (which would be a sign that they were in the Arctic Ocean). He thought the least they should do was ascertain that the trend of the Asian coastline was now to the west.[5]

In fact, in latitude 65°30'N, they were in the constricted part of Bering Strait where the continents are within 110 km. (65 mi.) but on account of a thick fog they did not see the coast of America. Bering decided to sail on until August 16 and in the afternoon of that day, in latitude 67°18'N with no land in sight, he terminated the voyage. The course had been steadily northeast for the last day and a half. They were crossing the entrance to Kotzebue Sound and approaching Point Hope on the American mainland but all the time fog obscured their vision and they did not see the land. Had Bering been able to cling to the Chukchi shoreline he would have found, in latitude 66°N, that the coastline swings to the northwest — an indication of a separate Asia. Had he continued on his northeasterly course for another day or two, he would have come to the continent on his right and discovered North America.

The weather was still foggy as they came back through Bering Strait and they neither saw nor heard anything to suggest the presence of land to the east. The discovery of the Pacific Northwest from Asia would come another day.

7

A Russian Expedition
Sights North America, 1732

The stubborn resistance of the Chukchi people was a continuing source of annoyance to the Russian authorities and a challenge to their military strategists. The prospect of a gainful campaign was a temptation that Afanase Shestakof, a Cossack, could not resist. He petitioned the Russian Senate to give him command of a force for the purpose of subduing, finally, the northeast corner of Asia. In March, 1727, while Bering was in the final year of preparing for his voyage, the Senate authorized Shestakof to lead an expedition to subdue the Chukchi and govern their country. He was given fifteen hundred fighting men, a dozen sailors and pilots to transport them along the Siberian coast, four fireworks specialists to frighten the Chukchi once the battle was joined, and two mineral-resource experts to assess the mining worth of the country after it was subdued. Dimitri Pavlutski, a captain of dragoons, was appointed co-leader.

It was 1729 before Shestakof reached the Sea of Okhotsk and began the campaign, driving northeast into the interior. He intended to engage the natives in a conventional, European-style battle, but the Chukchi were elusive. They enticed him deep into their country, leaving him only a tenuous connection with his base at the head of the Sea of Okhotsk. Finally, in March 1730, they turned on the Russians and easily defeated them. Shestakof received an arrow in the throat. He tried to escape on a convenient enemy sled but the reindeer drew the unfortunate Cossack into the Chukchi camp and he was quickly killed.

Pavlutski, wintering in the interior, was now in sole charge. He sent orders to move men and provisions to the mouth of the

51

Anadyr River and prepare to open a new front. This occupied the summers of 1730 and 1731. As part of the general offensive to gain control of the Chukchi, he decided to follow up on the Popoff report about the "Large Country" and the island off the Chukchi Peninsula. It seemed the right kind of project and the pilots could undertake it without him. He sent word to the chief pilot that as soon as the navigation season opened in 1732, he should seek out the "Large Country" and gather tribute from the natives.

When the time came to sail, the chief pilot was so ill he had to be left behind. Even the assistant pilot, Ivan Federov, was ill and had to be carried aboard. As a consequence, most of the direction of the expedition fell to Michael Gwosdef, one of the mineral-resource specialists. Fortunately, Federov recovered sufficiently during the voyage to take an active if minor role in guiding the ship.

Gwosdef put to sea in the *Gabriel* from Kamchatka, in the Sea of Okhotsk, on July 23, 1732, steering directly for St. Lawrence Island. On August 3 he estimated the ship was in the vicinity of the island and they sailed back and forth for two days without finding it. Their maneuvering brought them to the southeastern tip of the Chukchi Peninsula and they remained there for more than a week, replenishing their fresh water supply and exploring inland. The few natives they saw acted afraid or unfriendly and refused any contact with the Europeans. Gwosdef's hunters shot two deer for meat from a herd of a hundred and fifty guarded by two natives who fled at sight of the Russians. It was the only tribute the Russians could collect in this unfriendly land.

Gwosdef got the *Gabriel* under way towards the north on August 15 and two days later they sighted an island (probably one of the Diomede Islands in Bering Strait). Unfavorable winds and the unfriendly natives who greeted them with a shower of arrows prevented a landing for several days. Eventually Gwosdef did get ashore but he learned little from its inhabitants and none would pay tribute.

They found a second island to the east (probably another Diomede) on August 20 but decided not to risk a landing — an obviously hostile reception had formed up on shore when the *Gabriel* approached. There was more land visible in the east and after a stay offshore of about a day, they sailed eastward again. They reached land on August 21 and anchored some distance from the shore to wait for favorable winds and to consider their situation.

The Russians must have been thoroughly confused by this time. The Popoff report had led them to think they would encounter only one island in their search for the "Large Country" east of the Chukchi Peninsula. Was this a third island? Eventually they raised the anchor and approached what appeared to be the southwestern tip of the shore. Presently they could see huts but the water began to shoal and an offshore wind sprang up, making it dangerous to take the ship in close for a good view. They turned southward, cruising for the remainder of that day and part of the next, always with the sight of the unbroken shore on their left. Never suspecting they were sailing down the coast of mainland North America, Gwosdef concluded they were alongside a big island — big enough to be the "Large Country."

If Gwosdef had any ideas about finding a place to land, he abandoned them when a brisk wind built up from the northwest, threatening to drive them aground. They had to stand well out to sea to protect themselves. That day they sighted what Gwosdef called a "fourth" island (it was probably King Island). The wind was strong when the *Gabriel* came up to the island; so strong in fact, that the sails gave way. In this furious weather, the Russians were astounded to see a native put out to the ship from the island in a one-man, skin-covered craft. He sat in a small opening which was so well protected from the sea that when a large wave broke over the boat, there seemed no danger that it would swamp.

The native informed Gwosdef that the land on the eastern horizon was indeed the "Large Country" and it was inhabited by Chukchi. It had forests and streams and wild animals that could be killed for their meat and skins. Altogether, it was a fine country.

The strength of the wind had the feel of winter storms and it made the crew apprehensive. They drew up a petition asking their officers to turn back and this brought the expedition to an early end.[1]

Gwosdef and Federov did not speculate in their report to Pavlutski, and had no reason to think that any of the lands they had seen were part of North America. As far as they knew, all the natives they had encountered were Chukchi and the Chukchi homeland was believed to be the northeast corner of Asia. Pavlutski took no action on the report; apparently he never knew how close he came to the discovery of America from Asia. The Russian authorities showed no interest in the "Large Country" until 1741 — after Bering's voyage to Alaska. It prompted them to order Gwosdef (Federov had died from his illness) to present an enlarged account of the 1732 voyage.

8

Russian Voyage of Discovery to America, 1741

Bering returned to St. Petersburg in 1730 to learn that his interpretation of the geography of northeastern Asia was questioned by members of the Academy of Sciences. This body, newly formed, was staffed in large part by young German and French scientists who had yet to make their mark. To convince them, he devised a plan to sail to North America from Kamchatka, explore and map its northwestern coastline, and establish its position relative to Asia. The Empress Anna gave her approval to this plan in 1732 and ordered the Russian Senate to see to its details.[1]

Bering was easily the most outstanding European expert on Siberia. Instead of giving him a free hand, the Senate chose to set him an incredible series of additional tasks which bore little or no relation to the proposed voyage. He was ordered to oversee the survey of the coastline of the Sea of Okhotsk, the Kurile Islands, Sakhalin Island and Japan. Then they added the Arctic coastline from the Dvina River on the west, across Russia and Siberia, and into the Pacific in the east. They wanted the coast of this largely unknown territory mapped, its harbors and estuaries explored, the country described and its natural resources studied. The islands in the Arctic off the mouth of the Kolyma River were to be included. Furthermore, they wanted his first voyage repeated because the academy was not satisfied with the information from that expedition.[2]

By 1740, after almost a decade of struggling with a terrible climate in a primitive country, and working by sled from the land when the sea was impassable, Bering had the Arctic coast all but mapped. The Kurile and other islands had been charted and

Bering had built a small fleet of ships and gathered them in the Sea of Okhotsk. They included the *St. Peter* and the *St. Paul*, which were intended for the voyage to the American continent. The years of toil and the strain of dealing with the Russian bureaucracy had taxed Bering; his vigor had begun to decline.

Bering and his officers were convinced (correctly) that the shortest route to America lay in sailing northeast from Kamchatka. The Russian Senate, however, chose to give more credence to foreign appointees of the Academy of Sciences, particularly the brothers Delisle from France. Louis Delisle (who had assumed his mother's name, La Croyère) was appointed astronomer although his academic training had been confined to theology, and Bering was ordered to consult him concerning the route. La Croyère produced a fanciful map drawn by his brother Joseph, based on what Peter Lauridsen, the historian, has described as "unreliable accounts and the cartographic distortions of several generations."[3] It rejected recent Russian explorations and reports, and conjectured that land lay a few days' sail to the southeast. La Croyère insisted that Bering set a southeasterly course to intercept this land. A modern globe shows that a southeasterly course would carry them parallel to the coast of the Americas to an eventual landfall in Antarctica.

The expedition put to sea on June 4, 1741. Two ships carried a crew of about seventy-five men and provisions for five and a half months. Bering, on the *St. Peter*, had with him a German named George Steller who had studied medicine and botany. He would be responsible for the health of the crews and, when they went ashore, of examining the mineral and animal resources of the new world. Alexei Chirikov, in command of the *St. Paul*, carried the "astronomer" La Croyère.

They sailed on La Croyère's southeasterly course and carried steadily towards the southern tip of South America, until June 12 when Bering reckoned they had gone about 1,000 km. (600 mi.). They were now in latitude 46°N, well beyond the land shown on Delisle's map. Bering had had enough. He took the two ships about and set a north-northeasterly course. He held this bearing until June 20 when, in latitude 491/2°N, the ships were separated in a storm and lost to each other in the ensuing fog. He used two

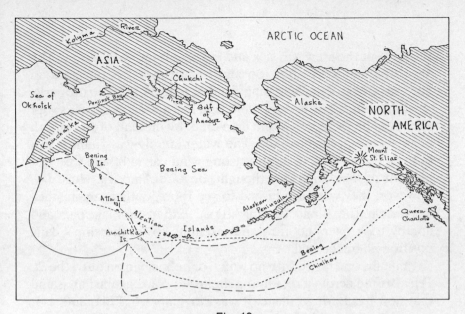

Fig. 10

The discovery of North America from Asia: generalized tracks of the voyages of Bering and Chirikov in 1741 (after E. P. Bertholf in F. A. Golder: *Bering's Voyages*, vol. 1. Amer. Geog. Soc., New York, 1922).

days to search for the *St. Paul*; then, inexplicably, sailed south again to make certain that Delisle's land did not exist. Thereafter he turned northeast, sailing during the next four weeks along the south side of the Aleutian Islands without seeing them.

Bering and his men sighted land on July 16 in latitude 53°14'N (in the Alaska Panhandle). As they approached they saw a rock-bound coastline, girded with islands. Inland, a snow-covered mountain (Mount St. Elias) rose into the clouds.

Bering's health, already affected by the years of struggle to accomplish everything expected of him, deteriorated even more now from an attack of scurvy. He was confined to his cabin and his officers took charge of moving the ship slowly up the coast, surveying the shoreline from aboard ship. They crept along in thick fog and rain, unpredictable currents and violent winds; moving southwest out along the Alaska Peninsula. The winds were worse when they reached the islands beyond the peninsula. No cooking was possible for days at a time as seas pitched the ship unmercifully and threatened to wreck them on the rocky shore. Half the crew was sick and incapacitated with scurvy. The "healthy" men were often too confused from lack of proper food and the effects of the harassing weather to work the ship properly.

In October it turned very cold, and hail and snow storms swept the ship. On October 19 one man died; by the end of the month deaths were occurring daily. The water supply was running low but when they tried to land, a strong wind carried them west out of sight of land and, they thought, beyond America. Next day, however, they were astonished to see the Aleutians again (they were near the island of Amchitka). Exhaustion, despair and apathy took over the crew and attempts to fix the ship's daily position all but ceased.

Finally, one night, with no watch or helmsman on duty, the *St. Peter* drifted across a reef into a sheltered place against an island that now has Bering's name. It was November 6, 1741, and, as it turned out, the end of the voyage for the *St. Peter*.

Bering Island measured 38 by 5.5 km. (23.5 by 3.5 mi.) and was high and rocky. There was driftwood for fuel and the island abounded in animal life — Arctic fox, sea otter and seals. This was fortunate for the survivors' store of food had dwindled to a small quantity of groats and some two-year-old flour, stored in leather sacks, that had become soaked in sea water.

Steller, the scientist, took charge of preparations to spend the winter on the island. For shelters, he had pits dug in the sand near a stream and roofed with driftwood and clothing. They covered the cracks with the carcasses of foxes, which were so unafraid that they could be killed with clubs. The sick overwhelmed the camp with their helplessness. Their gums were like brown sponges, swollen to cover their teeth, making it difficult to take the vegetable nourishment prepared to relieve the effects of scurvy. The men continued to die.

Hope that they would leave the island in the spring on the *St. Peter* was dashed on November 25 when she was driven ashore in a storm, her keel firmly buried in the sand.

The plight of his men and the unsatisfactory conclusion to his expedition weighed on Bering and aggravated the problems with his health. He lay in his sandpit, hungry, cold and heartsick — a broken old man. The sand dribbled down the sides of the pit on top of him. At first his men cleared it away but then he asked them to leave it — it gave him some comfort from the biting cold wind that swept up from the North Pacific Ocean. Eventually the sand covered his legs and part of his body. He died there on December 8, 1741, half buried in the sand. His men had to dig him free to give him a proper burial.

Forty-four of the seventy-seven men who had sailed on the *St. Peter* reached Kamchatka in August, 1742, in a boat constructed of timbers taken from the wrecked ship. They had wintered barely 200 km. (125 mi.) from their home port and the warmth, food and medical attention that would have saved many lives.

The *St. Paul* fared rather better. When Chirikov became separated from the *St. Peter* on June 20, 1741, he searched the seas for several days. Then with the general agreement of his officers, he sailed on a course slightly east of north, reaching for the American coast. They sighted land on July 16 in latitude 56°15'N. Bering and his men were getting their first look at America on the same day, about two degrees of latitude to the north. Had Bering lingered at his landfall, he might have heard Chirikov's cannon, fired to guide a shore party back to the ship.

Chirikov did not tarry long on the coast of America but turned his ship towards Kamchatka. The scarcity of safe anchorage close to shore and the ferocity of the natives prevented them from replenishing their water supplies. They attempted to distil sea water but it retained a bitter taste. Two of the officers died and Chirikov was confined to his cabin from July 21. The men became so weak they could barely handle the ship. They reached Kamchatka on October 8, 1741; twenty-one men including La Croyère, died on the voyage.[4]

Part Two

The Coast of
the Pacific Northwest

Vitus Bering's voyage to North America had ended in tragedy for this brave and dedicated man but it was not without important consequences. In his wake came Russians eager to trade utensils, hunting knives, trinkets and other items to American natives for the skins of the plentiful sea otters. They were followed in the 1770s by surveyors who began charting the American shoreline. Reports of these activities began reaching Spain and from there they were carried to Mexico.

In the years between 1603 when Aguilar reached Cape Blanco from Mexico, and 1741 when Bering crossed the North Pacific to Alaska, the northwest coast of North America was probably not visited by Europeans. The viceroys of Mexico, distracted by the troubles in Spain and her decline from the ranks of Europe's most powerful nations, saw no purpose in exploring this frontier of Spanish America.

The conclusion of the Seven Years War in 1763 and the cessation of fighting between Britain, France, Spain and Portugal in the Pacific made exploration voyaging in the Pacific safer. Improvements in navigational aids began to tell towards the end of the century and voyages could be planned and performed more effectively. Well-equipped non-military British and French ships, under able navigators, became common in the Pacific. The results of their investigations were published as maps and in journals and quickly became available to others; the Spanish tended to withhold such information, even from their own nationals.

The British with their growing maritime strength and interest in the Pacific, and the Russian traders and surveyors from Asia, became a threat to Spanish control of the Pacific Northwest. The viceroys had neglected this coast but they were not about to relinquish their claim to the territory. Spain had lost power in the Pacific; but she was still dominant in Mexico, Central and South America, and maintained military bases and a fleet in the Americas. It gave her an advantage over other nations whose ships had to sail great distances to reach this remote region. It was time to exploit the advantage and take a more aggressive stance on the northwest coast.

9

Bruno de Hezeta and the "River of the West," 1775

It was comparatively easy for the Spanish to keep an eye on the British because their ships would come up the coast from the south. It was another matter with the Russians. They came across the misty waters of the far north where no Spaniard had ever sailed.

What were the Russians doing? Had they established settlements in Alaska and were they moving south into territory which the Spaniards claimed as their own? In 1774, the viceroy decided to show them the flag. He dispatched Juan Pérez in the frigate *Santiago* to explore the coast and take formal possession of the mainland as far north as the Russian posts (if there were any). Apparently he was willing to concede that Alaska was Russian by right of discovery.

Pérez reached the northern tip of the Queen Charlotte Islands, in latitude 55°N, by midsummer but unfavorable winds and fog prevented him from landing at any time on the voyage. Still, he was the first European to see the coast of what's now British Columbia.

Not satisfied that Pérez had made a proper exhibition of the Spanish claim to the coast, the viceroy dispatched another expedition north the next year. It consisted of two ships — the *Santiago* again, this time with Bruno de Hezeta as captain and Pérez second-in-command, and the smaller *Sonora* under Juan Francisco de la Bodega y Quadra. They sailed from Mexico on March 16, 1775.

The winds blew mainly from the northwest and slowed Hezeta's progress to the north. In the second week in May, after barely two months at sea, two men showed signs of scurvy. It was time for a change of food. Hezeta found a safe harbor in latitude

41°N (just below the California-Oregon border) early in June, in a region inhabited by friendly natives. He decided to stop there to give his men a chance to recover and to replenish their water, meat and firewood.

Hezeta remained for ten days. Before leaving he had a cross erected on a high point overlooking the bay and he went through the motions of taking possession of the land. Back at sea, it was July 1 before the winds favored them and they could move the ships north past Cape Blanco.

They next anchored on July 13, in latitude 47°25'N, midway between Grays Harbor and Cape Flattery. This time their landfall had tragic consequences. Quadra allowed seven men to accept an invitation to go ashore to eat and drink with the natives. The men had barely stepped out of the longboat before a horde of Indians swarmed out of the dense wood. They dragged the boat out of the surf and set about hacking the men to pieces. As the men on the *Sonora* watched, helplessly, the Indians worked off their fury by smashing the boat. Then, gathering up the dismembered bodies of the sailors and every scrap of iron from the broken boat, they disappeared into the wood.

Seemingly not yet satisfied, the Indians soon approached the *Sonora* in nine dugouts, ringing the ship, readying their bows and putting on protective hides. Yet all the while they made signs of friendship, inviting the watching Spaniards to come ashore. The sailors lured them closer, holding up gifts of glass beads, giving the impression that the ship was manned by only half a dozen men. Finally one dugout, its occupants more bold than the others, moved in to arms' length and Quadra took his revenge. His waiting gunners turned their swivel gun on it and fired a broadside, riddling it from bow to stern. The noise of the gun, the devastation it caused and the screams of the wounded was too much for the other Indians. They broke for the shore, howling their rage and fear.

Hezeta went ashore to make a formal declaration of sovereignty over the territory, taking with him twenty heavily armed men. The party was not menaced.

They put to sea on July 14, only to be frustrated by northerly winds against which they could make no headway. Meanwhile, the number of men afflicted with scurvy and other illnesses increased

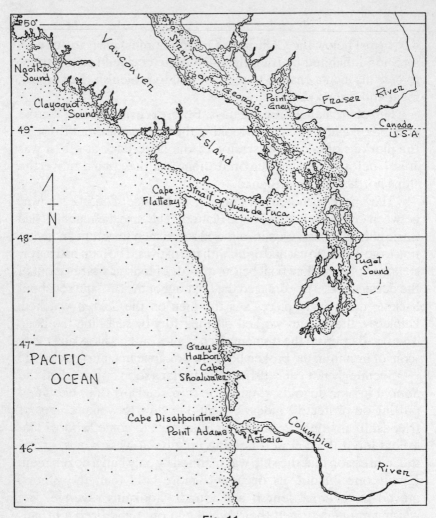

Fig. 11
The coast of the Pacific Northwest between latitude 50°N and the Columbia River.

daily. Officers urged Hezeta to turn about and head for home, but they were still well short of their objective and Hezeta decided he must keep going for a time.

On the morning of July 31, when Hezeta came on deck, the *Sonora* was lost to view in weather thick with fog and rain. Although he kept the *Santiago* in the vicinity for a week, the ships did not reestablish contact.

In the second week in August, the winds changed and Hezeta was able to move the ship northeast again. On August 10, in latitude 49°17'N, they sighted the mountains of Vancouver Island. The health of the crew had reached a critical level. Father Campa, the chaplain aboard the ship, noted in his diary:

> Today, the petty officers again stated in writing to the Commander that, efforts toward carrying out the orders of His Excellency the Viceroy to reach 65° north latitude notwithstanding, they wished to report the sad condition of the crew, for it was hardly possible to assemble three men for each watch . . . and if a storm should strike we would be in danger of perishing. Hence he ought to make a careful decision.[1]

Hezeta decided to accede to his officers' wishes. He came about and set a course for Mexico, and during the next week they coasted easily south before a northwest wind through mist and rain. August 17 dawned clear and they steered southeast to get close to the shore so they could examine it. Father Campa noted that at

> noon we took an observation: 46°11'. All the land that could be seen today was lowlying. About 5 p.m. we discovered a beautiful large bay, to which we gave the name de la Asuncion [for the Feast of Assumption on August 15]. Of the capes that form its entrance, the one that bore to the north we called Cape San Roque; the one to the south, Cape Frondoso, from the abundance of trees. Having come opposite, we noticed that the sea's eastward horizon was far extended, whence it was concluded that there must be some great river or that the bay was deeply indented. The mouth or entrance is about one and one-half leagues wide. We were a little more than a league and a half from land . . .[2]

Hezeta had difficulty maneuvering the ship between the capes for here the sea was roiled by currents and eddies that were so strong, he too was convinced this

> place is the mouth of some great river, or of some passage to another sea.
> Had I not been certain of the latitude of this bay, from my observations of the same day, I might easily have believed it to be the passage discovered by Juan de Fuca, in 1592, which

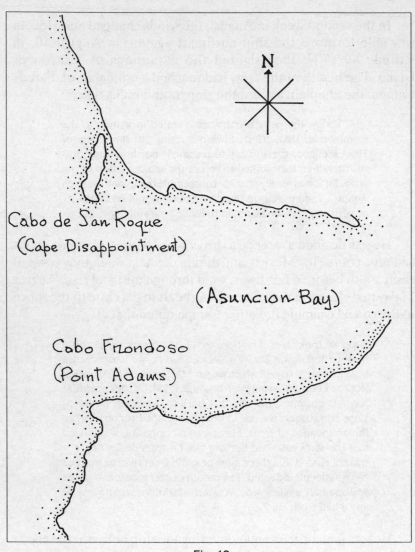

N

Cabo de San Roque
(Cape Disappointment)

(Asuncion Bay)

Cabo Frondoso
(Point Adams)

Fig. 12
The mouth of the Columbia River according to Bruno Hezeta, 1775
(modified: from *A Journal of Exploration Northward along the coast from
Monterey in the year 1775* edited by John Galvin, John Howell, San
Francisco, 1964).

is placed on the charts between the 47th and the 48th degrees;
where I am certain that no such strait exists.[3]

Hezeta wanted to enter the bay and anchor but

having consulted the second captain, Don Juan Pérez, and the
pilot, Don Christoval Revilla, they insisted that I ought not to
attempt it, as, if we let go the anchor, we should not have men
enough to get it up, and to attend to the other operations
which would be thereby rendered necessary. Considering this,
and also that, in order to reach the anchorage, I should be
obliged to lower my long-boat, (the only boat that I had,) and
to man it with at least fourteen of the crew, as I could not
manage with fewer, and also that it was then late in the day, I
resolved to put out: and at the distance of three or four
leagues I lay to. In the course of the night, I experienced heavy
currents to the south-west, which made it impossible for me
to enter the bay on the following morning, as I was far to
leeward.

These currents, however, convinced me that a great
quantity of water rushed from this bay on the ebb of the tide.[4]

The description of the bay and the promontories at its
entrance, and the measurement of latitude, leave little doubt that
the *Santiago* was opposite the entrance of the Columbia River.
Cape San Roque is the present Cape Disappointment and Cape
Frondoso is Point Adams. Hezeta had rediscovered Aguilar's
"rapid and abundant river" — the "River of the West." The
discovery was probably a piece of luck. The opening between the
capes was difficult to see from the ocean except when it was
approached directly from the west.

The *Santiago* arrived back in Monterey on August 31. Of the
ninety-two officers and men who had shipped out in March,
twelve were dead and another passed away as he was being
brought ashore, thirty-six were suffering from scurvy and fourteen
from other illnesses — leaving twenty-nine healthy men.

Captain Quadra had been more successful in moving the
Sonora north. After losing the *Santiago* on July 30, he sailed west
until August 5 when he caught a wind from the southwest. He
reckoned he was about 170 leagues from the land at this time and
in latitude 46°30'N. He sailed north to latitude 58°N (in the
Alaska Panhandle), making two landings in the northern latitudes
but seeing no evidence of Russian occupation. He brought his
ship into Monterey on October 7 with many sick on board.

10

The Voyage that Led the Western World to the Pacific Northwest, 1778

Even while the Spaniards were attempting to assert exclusive rights to the northwest coast of America in 1774 and 1775, the British Admiralty was plotting a voyage to that coast to search for a northern passage to the Atlantic Ocean. They chose Captain James Cook to lead a force of two ships — the *Resolution* (462 tons), and the *Discovery* (298 tons) which Charles Clerke would command.

Early in his career, Cook had taken part in the capture of Louisberg and Quebec, charted the St. Lawrence River from Quebec City to the open Atlantic, surveyed the harbor of Halifax and mapped parts of the coast of Newfoundland. Between 1768 and 1771, in the first of two voyages around the earth, he explored the South Pacific, touching New Zealand and Australia. In 1772, the Admiralty commissioned him to settle the question of the existence of an Antarctic continent. When he encountered solid ice below Africa, he traced its extent by circling the globe, returning to England after three years. Cook was probably better qualified as a surveyor, navigator and explorer than any other British seaman of the day.

Cook had distinguished himself, as well, in the field of nutrition on the two global voyages. The invention of Hadley's sextant[1] in 1731 and Harrison's chronometer[2] in 1759 had made it possible to take accurate navigational observations at sea. But these devices did not in themselves guarantee the success of exploration in remote areas. Extended voyages still depended on the health of the ordinary seaman. Commonly the crew was so weakened by living conditions aboard ship, and by disease, that the master had no choice but to turn for home before completing his mission.

Life on a sailing ship was harsh. The crew lived in cramped quarters in the bow of the ship immediately below the maindeck, their hammocks slung in close array. When the sea broke over the bow, it filtered through the maindeck and wet the men. If the weather was foul over an extended period the men and their bedding remained damp because the ship was not heated. In rough weather the kitchen fires were not lit because fire was always a danger on wooden ships. Then there was not even the small comfort of cooked hot food. The ship had no bathroom facilities; the men emptied their bowels directly into the sea perched on a slatted contraption slung over the ship's side. In a heavy sea they were repeatedly doused as they crouched there and performed their bodily functions.

The ship generally carried live pigs, cows, goats and chickens for food since facilities for refrigerating fresh meat did not exist. This livestock was kept on deck. Excrement and urine mixed with seawater fouled the ship as it leaked from the deck into the bilge to collect in the well from where it was pumped into the sea. The mixture generated poisonous gases; before a seaman ventured near the well he would lower a lighted lantern to see if the air contained enough oxygen to sustain life. The ships stank, some more than others, causing the masters to choose their anchorages in port with care.

It was a hard, wasting life that arrested physical development (the average height of a seaman in the eighteenth century was less than 1.7 m. or about 5 1/2 ft.). It aged seamen before their time and sapped their resistance to disease.

Typhus and dysentry were the shore diseases of Europe, and in the tropics the seamen got malaria, yellow fever, hookworm and typhus. Lice and fleas were taken for granted, and lice carried typhus. Venereal diseases were considered an occupational ailment with sailors and in the 18th century treatment was ineffective. In port sailors were frequently not allowed on shore for fear of desertions, but boat-loads of prostitutes were ferried to the ship; the scene below deck can be imagined.[3]

The disease that scourged men at sea was scurvy. It was well known in the eighteenth century that scurvy was due to the ships' inadequate fare: salted beef, pork or fat (and some raisins and sugar to mix with the fat to make it more edible), "ship biscuit" usually crawling with maggots (the practice was to rap the biscuit on the table to knock them out), dried peas, oil and vinegar. Seamen knew that fresh food would cure as well as prevent the disease. Other remedies were known; Sir Hugh Palliser had shown in 1748, on a voyage to India, that dosing with lemon juice was an effective preventative but how lemons could be kept fresh at sea was another matter.[4]

The British Admiralty was in an experimental phase when it provisioned Cook's first expedition to the Pacific in 1768. In addition to the usual food, the Victualling Board sent him almost four tons of "sour krout" (the German sauerkraut), half a ton of "portable soup" (cakes of meat essence that could be boiled with peas or oatmeal), "wort" (an extract formed by boiling malt) and syrups made by boiling lemons and oranges (which destroyed all the vitamin C). He was ordered to report "how he found the same to answer"[5] on his return.

The Admiralty had standing orders regarding cleanliness on board ship. Cook differed from most navy captains in that he took these orders seriously. He insisted that the men keep clean, personally inspecting their hands. He provided them with clean, dry and well-ventilated quarters. He was equally scrupulous about their diet, methodically adding the Admiralty's special foods to their meals. He tricked them into eating food, however unpalatable they found it at first:

> The Sour Krout the Men at first would not eate untill I put into practice a Method I never once knew to fail with seamen, and this was to have some of it dress'd every Day for the Cabbin Table, and permitted all the Officers without exception to make use of it and left it to the option of the Men either to take as much as they pleased or none atall; but this practice was not continued above a week before I found it necessary to put every one on board to an Allowance . . . the Moment they see their Superiors set a Value upon it, it becomes the finest stuff in the World and the inventer a damn'd honest fellow.[6]

Cook added fresh food to the diet whenever he could: fish, walrus, seal, penguin (which some of the men could barely stomach), wild fowl, "scurvy grass" and other wild greens, and berries. Ashore, he had the men brew beer from "wort," molasses and the leaves and branches of spruce trees. To get them to drink it, he withheld the daily ration of spirits until the beer was consumed.

Cook ate what he asked the men to eat and he was willing to experiment upon himself. It provoked the remark that "his stomach bore, without difficulty, the coarsest and most ungrateful food."[7] The men got into the habit, on shore, of eating "almost Every Herb plant Root and kinds of Fruit they Could Possibly Light upon,"[8] convinced by Cook it was good for them. On the first voyage, Cook noted after eight months at sea that there was no scurvy on board. He attributed this to the sauerkraut, "portable soup" and "wort" (he used the latter for symptoms of scurvy).[9]

The accomplishments that derived from Cook's two circumnavigations were truly remarkable. The "Method of Lunar Distances"[10] for finding longitude and John Harrison's chronometer for keeping accurate time received their first extended sea trials on these voyages. Cook established that longitude could be found at sea — that a navigator could find his position anywhere on earth, whether on land or at sea. It marked the beginning of practical, scientific navigation. Cook's success in keeping his men healthy during the long voyages demonstrated that proper dietary practice could eliminate the specter that haunted ocean voyages of even a few months, duration — the dead and dying men, struck down by scurvy and other diseases.[11]

The manner in which Cook navigated the seas and provided for his men was not the norm for British naval ships and contrasted sharply with practice on most ocean-going ships. Cook had shown that if a mariner took advantage of the advances in navigation and looked to the welfare of his men, he could sail with confidence, if not comfort, anywhere on the oceans and accurately chart his course and the coastlines he touched. The British Admiralty now proposed to use this technology to explore the most remote and least known coastline washed by open water — the coast of the Pacific Northwest — and settle the old question of the existence of a Northwest Passage.

71

The Admiralty's timetable called for Cook to round Africa by the first of November, 1776, pass through the Society Islands early in February, 1777, and then sail directly for North America. He was instructed to avoid Spanish possessions along the southern coast and to be civil and friendly with any Europeans he should meet. He should not "lose time in exploring rivers or inlets,"[12] but proceed directly north to latitude 65°N and there begin to search for and explore openings "pointing towards Hudson's or Baffin's Bays."[13]

News of Cook's proposed voyage caused alarm in Spain and the Viceroy of Mexico was instructed to seize and imprison Cook when he arrived off the coast of California. Apparently the viceroy decided to ignore the order for there is no record that Spanish ships were sent out to intercept Cook, who left England blissfully unaware of the threat. He sailed from Plymouth on July 12, 1776. In addition to the usual stores, he carried a variety of livestock — horses, cattle, sheep, pigs and rabbits — for distribution on the islands he would touch in the Pacific. There was hardly room for the animals, much less for the food to keep them alive, and some of the horses had to be stabled in a cabin.

Cook discovered that the *Resolution* had been poorly refitted for she began to leak within a few days of his departure. He reached the Cape of Good Hope well within his timetable but the ships had to be overhauled and he was a month late leaving the cape. He lost more time in the Indian Ocean, and it was February 25 before he began crossing the Pacific from New Zealand, steering north-northeast for the Sandwich (Hawaiian) Islands. Presently they entered the latitudes where the winds, at this time of year, blow gently from the northeast and then veer to the southeast, and are interspersed with calms. Cook could make little if any headway to the north and none to the east. It was soon obvious he could not reach North America and search the coast above 65°N before the bitter autumn storms would drive him south to wait out the winter.

Cook "wintered" in the South Pacific. He sailed for North America on February 2, 1778, and at daybreak on March 7 after an uneventful crossing, "the long looked for Coast of New Albion was seen."[14] The ship's position was determined at noon to be

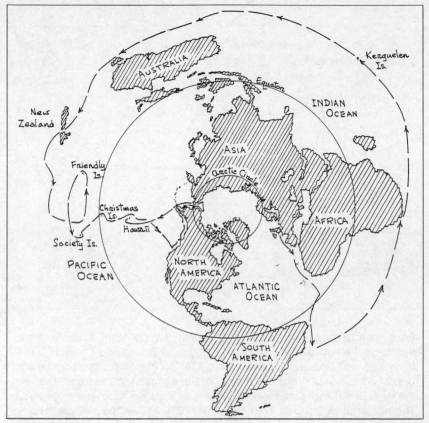

Fig. 13
Generalized track of Captain James Cook's voyage to North America and back to the Sandwich (Hawaiian) Islands (after J. C. Beaglehole: *The Life of Captain James Cook.* Adam & Charles Black, London, 1974).

44°33'N, 124°40'W — on the Oregon coast about 160 km. (100 mi.) below the Washington-Oregon boundary.

The most informative map of the northwest coast of North America at the time of Cook's voyage had been compiled by S. Muller of the Royal Academy of St. Petersburg. First published in Russia in 1754, the map had been translated into English and printed in London in 1761.[15] It gave, with good accuracy, the locations of the Russian-sponsored landings of Gwosdef, Bering and Chirikov. Muller's interpretation of the intervening coastline, down to latitude 49°N, was, however, pure conjecture and bears only a passing resemblance to a modern map. Muller had rounded

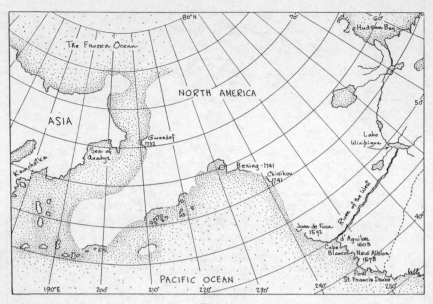

Fig. 14
Early interpretation of the outline of the west coast of North America. It was based on the voyages of Gwosdef (1732), and Bering and Chirikov (1741) from Asia and Spanish explorers from Mexico (modified; the original was published as part of S. Muller's *History of Russia*, 1754. It was translated from the High Dutch and published in English as *Voyages from Asia to America*. Thomas Jefferys, London, 1761, sec. ed. 1764). As was the practice in some meridian systems, Muller based longitude on Ferro, the most westerly of the Canary Islands and long the most westerly land known to Europeans. To convert Muller's longitudes to read west of Greenwich, add 18 degrees to the values on the map.

out his map by adding the Spanish claims of discovery on the coastline that lay before Cook. The Strait of Juan de Fuca showed as a broad opening between 47° and 48°N, and Aguilar's "River of the West" as a prominent stream entering the Pacific at 45°N.

Cook had a copy of Muller's map on board but the news that Hezeta had seen the entrance to Aguilar's river in 1775 had not reached England by the time he had sailed for America. He had read an English translation of a history of California, published in Madrid in 1757, setting out the Spanish discoveries to that time. Cook noted this in his journal on March 11:

It is worth observing that, in the very latitude where we now were, geographers have been pleased to place a large entrance or strait, the discovery of which they ascribe to the same navigator [Aguilar]; whereas nothing more is mentioned in the account of his voyage, than his having seen in this situation, a large river, which he would have entered, but this was prevented by the currents."[16]

If Cook had any intention of searching for Aguilar's river, the weather did not cooperate. The winds continued to blow from the northwest, building to squalls with hail and sleet and sometimes snow, piling up a heavy onshore swell of water. It was impossible to chart the coast under these conditions and nowhere could he find a sheltered cove to drop anchor and explore the country on foot. He had to stand out to sea where he was slowly pushed to the south and out of sight of the land. On March 21, finally, the wind veered and blew from the southwest. Cook, now some distance offshore, steered northeast, looking to fall in with the land somewhere above latitude 44 1/2°N.

At 8:00 A.M. on the morning of March 22, they saw the land again but they struck the coast in latitude 47°N, well above their last landfall. Cook, skeptical of the Spanish claim of discovery and the validity of Muller's map, had no intention of turning back to search for Aguilar's "River of the West." Besides, he had been instructed to lose no time in exploring rivers. He continued to stand to the north and so he missed the Columbia River.

In the evening, about 7:00 P.M., Cook saw a small opening on the coastal horizon. Hoping it was a protected cove, he took the ships in, only to find it was merely a low stretch of the coast. Adjoining it to the north was a high point of land which he named Cape Flattery to mark the region's unfounded promise of a safe haven for his ships.

Cook moved his ships out to sea for the night, intending to come in to the land at daylight to continue his examination of the shoreline. Before dawn broke, however, the wind came up and blew a hard onshore gale laden with rain. During the next few days the ships were battered by successive storms, veering from the northwest to the southwest and back again. Cook kept well clear of the coast, fearing the rocky shore. When the winds finally moderated, he was far out to sea and out of sight of land. He steered northeast and in the morning of March 29, the mountains of Vancouver Island were seen rising out of the sea. Cook had missed the Strait of Juan de Fuca.

It is probable that Cook planned a short search for the legendary strait which was still a mystery almost two hundred years after its supposed discovery. De Fuca's claim that he had sailed through it into the North Sea (the Arctic Ocean) had not been disproved. Cook would have discovered the strait on March 22 had it not been dusk when he approached Cape Flattery (the strait's southern portal), or on the following day had the weather remained calm. He shrugged off the lost opportunity with the entry in his journal that "it is in this very latitude where we now were, that geographers have placed the pretended Strait of Juan de Fuca. But we saw nothing like it; nor is there the least probability that ever any such thing existed."[17]

Cook made his first landfall in North America on March 29, in Nootka Sound on Vancouver Island, in a small but safe anchorage which provided fresh water, firewood and stands of timber for masts. There was much work to be done — the *Resolution* was leaking again and in need of caulking and the astronomers wished to go ashore to make accurate observations for longitude and to check the chronometer.

They stayed almost a month. It was April 26 before Cook put to sea again, reaching north towards latitude 65°N where the real work of the expedition would begin. Almost as soon as they left Nootka, a storm struck the ships and drove them north and well out to sea. When next they sighted land they were in latitude 55°N, above the Queen Charlotte Islands. Thereafter Cook crawled up the coast, attempting to find and identify the landings and observations of Bering and Chirikov.

On May 9, in latitude 59½°N, the coastline began to trend to the west and they feared it would not lead them to latitude 65°N. On May 26, however, the shoreline turned abruptly to the north and soon they were sailing northeast into a great opening. Cook dared hope this was a passage to Hudson's Bay but after four days he began to suspect that the water was less salty to the taste at low tide and that this was not a strait connecting two oceans, but a large river. Nevertheless he persisted, spending ten fruitless days in this arm of the sea (Cook Inlet) that stretches more than 300 km. (185 mi.) into the interior of Alaska. Fifteen years later Cook's River as the inlet was called at the time, figured prominently in Alexander Mackenzie's plans to reach the Pacific Ocean by canoe from the interior.

The natives along the coast were clothed in the skins of animals — fox, marten and, not uncommonly, sea otter (it was also called the sea beaver) which Cook recognized as a superior fur. He concluded that Russian traders had not been this far east "for if they did they [the natives] would hardly be cloathed in such valuable skins as those of the Sea beaver; the Russians would find some means or other to get them all from them."[18] The natives had glass beads, and spears and knives made of iron, but Cook assumed they had been obtained from natives living further west, who had been in contact with the Russians.

Past Cook Inlet the coastline changed direction, trending southwest, where the Alaska Peninsula thrusts into the sea. They followed its rugged shore, finding it difficult to distinguish the mainland from islands in weather that varied monotonously from rain to fog.

On June 25, three weeks after emerging from Cook Inlet, they turned northwest into a large opening. For all Cook knew or could make out in the heavy weather, it was just another inlet. Nevertheless, he pushed on, cautiously picking his way in fog that limited vision to less than a hundred meters (a hundred yards), while battling a fierce race of water rushing through the opening. They were favored by the wind, however, and on June 28, the *Resolution* broke free and Cook noted that "the land, on one side, was found to trend West and South West and on the other side to trend North. This gave us great reason to hope, that the continent had here taken a new direction, which was much in our favour."[19] Indeed, he had come through Unimak Pass — with the Alaska Peninsula on the right and the chain of Aleutian Islands on the left. They were in the Bering Sea and the way to latitude 65°N was open again.

The expedition moved north again, groping through weather that was generally so thick with fog they had to fire guns, beat drums and ring bells to keep the ships in touch. The possibility of encountering ice seems not to have occurred to Cook. Bering had not mentioned it in the report of his voyage.

They passed the 65th parallel of latitude on August 5 and three days later they glimpsed a point of land in 65°37'N, 168°06'W, jutting into the sea. Cook judged, correctly, that it was the most westerly extremity of mainland North America; he named it Cape Prince of Wales. It was also the continent's closest approach to Asia. They were now in the Arctic Ocean.

Cook moved his ships northeast, round the northwest angle of America. At noon on August 17, when he was near the most northerly part of the coastline, he perceived a brightness in the northern horizon. It reminded him of the Antarctic — the reflection in the sky of an ice field. An hour later he saw the ice; it extended as far as the eye could see and it was impenetrable. They were in latitude 70°44'N and it was the end of the quest for the Northwest Passage — at least for that year.

Cook was not ready to close out the season and give up the search for a northern passage into the Atlantic. He came about and steered west, intending to see if the way across the top of Siberia and Europe was open. Steadily, relentlessly, the ice moved down, forcing him south until on August 29 he was near the mainland of Asia a short distance west of the Chukchi Peninsula. The way to the west — the Northeast Passage — was also blocked by ice. His ships were in dangerous shallow water which daily was becoming more clogged with drifting ice. The arctic winter was closing in, threatening to grip and hold the expedition in an environment that offered little chance for survival. It was time to acknowledge defeat. He changed course and ran for Bering Strait.[20]

The expedition retired to the Sandwich Islands to wait out the winter and to prepare for another attempt at finding a northern passage when the arctic ice would be in retreat. Cook never made a second voyage through Bering Strait. He was killed by natives in February, 1779, while attempting to recover the *Discovery's* stolen cutter.

11

John Meares Muffs his Chance
for a Place in History, 1788

Cook's voyage to the Pacific Northwest soon led western traders to that remote coastline. During the voyage, members of his crew traded anything that was loose on the ships for whatever the American natives had to offer — be it food, local art or the favor of women. On the coast of Alaska they had acquired fur clothes off the natives' backs, mainly to protect themselves against the cold chill winds that blew off the North Pacific Ocean. Although many of the garments were well worn, ragged and filthy, and all were lousy, the seamen were astonished to find a ready market for them in Canton on the way back to England. Eager Chinese paid well for sea otter skins that the seamen had obtained in exchange for a hatchet, knife or saw. When the official account of the voyage was published in 1784, the reference to the value of sea otter skins aroused the interest of British merchants. In little more than a year the first trading ships sailed into Nootka Sound and a new era had begun for the Pacific Northwest. By 1786, at least five British ships were operating along the coast and by 1792 more than twenty ships, under various flags, were trading with the natives and selling the furs in the Orient.

John Meares, one of the earliest of the British traders and a colorful character, became well known as the result of a book he wrote about his voyages and explorations. His introduction to North America came in 1786 when he naively decided to winter in Prince William Sound in Alaska to trade with the Indians. His vessel became frozen fast in the ice. Totally unprepared for the cold and unable to hunt for fresh food in the hostile environment, the crew suffered terribly from scurvy. They could not stomach the nauseating whale oil the local Indians drank to ward off the disease, or chew pine branches and swallow the juice as the first officer did to cure himself when he appeared certain to die. They were soon reduced to existing on "ship biscuit," rice, flour, and salt beef and pork. Occasionally they managed to kill a bird.

> A crow or a sea-gull were rare delicacies, and an eagle, one or two of which we killed, when they seemed to be hovering about, as if they would feed upon us, instead of furnishing us with food, was a feast indeed.[1]

The tiny carcass gave each man little more than a taste.

Meares got away in June, 1787, when two British ships happened by, and sailed for China with only twenty-four men — twenty-three, including the surgeon and pilot, had died during the winter.

Charles Barkley was another of the early British traders who followed Cook to the Pacific Northwest. He reached the west coast of Vancouver Island in his ship *Imperial Eagle* in 1787, at the age of twenty-five with a seventeen-year-old bride. He enjoyed considerable success trading below Nootka Sound. While sailing southward along shore from Clayoquot Sound (on Vancouver Island),

> to the astonishment of all on board a large opening with a clear easterly horizon presented itself. The entrance appeared to be about four leagues wide and remained about that width as far as the eye could see. Barkley at once recognized it as the long lost strait of Juan de Fuca [although its location was about a degree of latitude north of where de Fuca said he had entered it], the existence of which Captain Cook, in 1778, had so emphatically contradicted. Barkley placed the opening on his chart, naming it Juan de Fuca.[2]

Barkley was the first European, other than possibly Juan de Fuca, to see the strait. He chose not to explore it and continued to the south.

Below Cape Flattery he anchored the ship near a small island in latitude 47° 43'N to trade. Six men who rowed up a small river

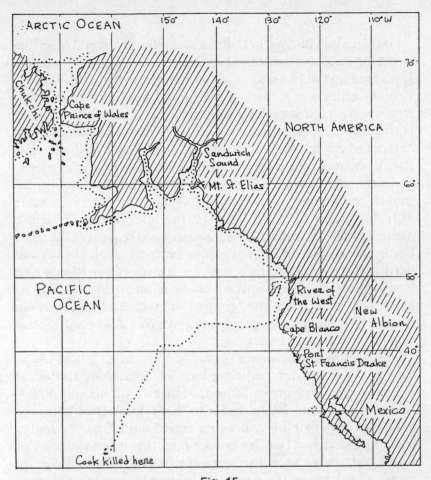

Fig. 15
Captain James Cook's interpretation of the coast of the Pacific Northwest
(modified; after *Journal of Captain Cook's Last Voyage to the Pacific
Ocean on Discovery, 1776-1779.* E. Newberry, London, 1781).

(the Hoh River?) to find the natives were never seen again. A
heavily armed shore party searched for them next day but
recovered only bloodied bits of clothing. Barkley named the island
Destruction Island.[3] It was near the place where Captain Quadra
of the Spanish ship *Sonora* lost seven men in a similar incident in
1775. Barkley decided to close out the season — he crossed the
Pacific, reaching Canton in November with a large cargo of
furs.

81

Meares met Barkley in Canton that fall and learned from him about the discovery (or rediscovery) of the Strait of Juan de Fuca. It pointed up the fact that much of the northwest coast was still virtually unknown. It intrigued him and he decided he would combine trading and exploration on his next venture in the Pacific Northwest. The coastline must be indented with safe natural harbors where he could moor his ship out of reach of the restless Pacific and trade at leisure with the natives. The protected mouth of a large river would serve him well for here he could enlarge his trade by establishing contact with Indians in the interior. Rivers were the means of travel between the interior and the coast. Meares decided to concentrate his search on the parts of the coast Cook had missed on his way up to latitude 65°N. He wanted particularly to examine the coast for a river called Rio de San Roque shown on recent Spanish charts to empty into the Pacific in latitude 46°N. It was the "great river" visualized by Hezeta in August 1775, as he sailed past a bay and gazed at a broad depression extending far inland.

Meares reached the west coast of Vancouver Island in the spring of 1788. After getting a base of operations started at Friendly Cove in Nootka Sound, Meares took his ship *Felice* south and on June 29, he came to "an inlet, whose entrance appeared very extensive, bearing East South East."[4] Meares was convinced, like Barkley before him, that it was the body of water said to have been discovered by Juan de Fuca in 1592. He intended to explore the strait and looked for a safe anchorage near Cape Flattery, but he was so menaced by Indians "of a much more savage appearance than any we had hitherto seen"[5] that he continued down the coast.

The crew found the shore below Cape Flattery

> wild in the extreme . . . immense forests covered the whole of it within our sight, down to the very beach, which was lofty and cragged, and against which the sea dashed with fearful rage. The shore was lined with rocks and rocky islets, nor could we perceive any bay or inlet that seemed to promise the least security to the smallest vessel . . . As we steered along, the force of southerly storms was evident to every eye; large and extensive woods being laid flat by their power.[6]

The seamen were acutely aware that along this stretch of coast the crew of the *Imperial Eagle's* longboat had been massacred by natives in the previous year and they reflected on the possibility of suffering a similar fate.

On July 5, they came to a low point of land in latitude 46°47'N at the north end of a broad bay (it was Willapa Bay) that seemed to promise a safe anchorage. As they approached, the water shoaled to six fathoms and the sea could be seen breaking across the full width of the entrance. It appeared too shallow and, because it was late in the day, Meares decided to stand out to sea and have another look in the morning. A strong wind pushed them about three leagues south in the night and, as they ran in from this angle, they had a perfect view of the bay. It was plain that it offered no prospect for a harbor. Meares named the point of land above it Cape Shoalwater as a warning to ships seeking shelter.

They were now very close to the location, on Spanish charts, of the Rio de San Roque. Looking south, they could see a bold promontory about 40 km. (25 mi.) to the south and Meares steered for it, hoping he would find a harbor between it and Cape Shoalwater. The coast, however, ran unbroken to the promontory but as they rounded it, the shoreline began to recede.

Meares noted the sight in his journal:

> we pleased ourselves with the expectation of its being Cape Saint Roc of the Spaniards, near which they are said to have found a good port . . .
>
> After we had rounded the promontory, a large bay, as we had imagined, opened to our view, that bore a very promising appearance, and into which we steered with every encouraging expectation.
>
> The high land that formed the boundaries of the bay, was at a great distance, and a flat level country occupied the intervening space: the bay itself took rather a westerly direction. As we steered in, the water shoaled to nine, eight, and seven fathoms, when breakers were seen from the deck, right a-head: and, from the mast-head, they were observed to extend across the bay. We therefore hauled out, and directed our course to the opposite shore, to see if there was any channel, or if we could discover any port.[7]

Meares could not detect an opening in the reef or any indication that the water inside the reef was deep enough to float his ship. He was certain this was the bay shown on Spanish charts — his measurement of 46°10'N agreed well with Hezeta's value of 46°11'N. Despite the evidence of the Spanish charts, or perhaps because they were Spanish, he quickly lost interest. Not troubling to wait for high tide, or send a longboat to take soundings in the bay and search its shoreline for the mouth of the "great river" he sailed on.

He noted in his journal that "we can now with safety assert, that . . . no such river as that of Saint Roc exists, as laid down in the Spanish charts"[8] and to commemorate his feelings, he named the promontory Cape Disappointment (which it retains to this day) and the bay, Deception Bay.

So Meares missed the chance to be the first European to enter the mouth of the Columbia River. It would have given Britain a solid claim to the coast of what is now Oregon and Washington.

12

Confrontation with Spain at Nootka Sound, 1789-90

The account of Cook's voyage to the Pacific Northwest did not go unnoticed by New England merchants. In 1787, six Boston "gentlemen," having foreseen profit in the fur trade, purchased and outfitted the *Columbia Rediviva* (212 tons) and the *Lady Washington* (90 tons) at a cost of $50,000. They gave command of the *Columbia* and direction of the enterprise to John Kendrick; the *Washington* would act as tender, with Robert Gray as master.

Kendrick was born in Massachusetts in 1740 and went to sea at an early age. He served on a whaler in the Gulf of St. Lawrence and later performed successfully as master of various merchant ships on the east coast. During the Revolutionary War he commanded ships sailing under letters of marque, raiding British shipping. He was forty-seven when he accepted command of the first American expedition to the west coast.

Gray was born in Rhode Island in 1755. He began a life at sea in his early twenties, perhaps in the United States Navy during the Revolutionary War. After the war he succeeded to the command of a small merchant ship, working the east coast for two Boston businessmen. This led to his appointment as master of the *Washington* when the two men and their associates decided to engage in the fur trade on the west coast. Gray was thirty-three at the time.

The Americans sailed from Boston on September 30, 1787, and rounded Cape Horn early in April, 1788. They reached Nootka Sound in September, the first American traders in the Pacific Northwest.

85

Late in 1788, the Spaniard Don Estaban José Martinez, returning from a voyage to Alaska to check on the Russians, was astonished to find Nootka Sound a busy trading depot. He carried disturbing news to the Viceroy of Mexico — he had found reason to suspect the Russians were planning to send a powerful force from Asia to occupy Nootka Sound. Now he would have to add the news that the British and others, including Americans, were openly trading out of Nootka.

The viceroy reacted strongly to the account of Martinez's voyage. It seems he was willing to concede that the Russians had rights to Alaska west of Prince William Sound (west of about 147°W longitude). However, he claimed exclusive Spanish sovereignty over the coastline south of the Sound, principally on two premises: that it was Spanish by right of discovery, and that it was a natural continuation of Spanish possessions in Mexico and California.

Early in 1789, he sent Martinez with the *Princesa* (26 guns) and the *San Carlos* (16 guns) to occupy Nootka — to forestall the Russians and to assert Spain's exclusive right to trade along the coast.

Martinez had orders to avoid being harsh with European traders but he was, by nature, aggressive and hot tempered, and he soon had the anchorage in an uproar. It set the stage for the so-called "Nootka Incident" which took Britain and Spain to the point of war. When Meares's newly built sloop, the *North West America*, came into the sound laden with furs, he seized her, reconditioned and renamed her the *Santa Saturnina* and sent her to explore and trade in the recently discovered Strait of Juan de Fuca under the Spanish flag.

Meares, in Canton, was unaware of the new Spanish presence at Nootka. Concerned with the increasing competition for furs, he and other British traders agreed to band together as the Associated Merchants of London and India — to avoid competing with each other and to beat other traders. Their two ships, the *Argonaut* and the *Princess Royal*, were already on the high seas when Martinez arrived at Nootka. They entered the harbor in July and Martinez promptly seized them, sending ships and crew to Mexico as prizes.

Gray was stopped at sea with a shot across his bow but when queried about his business, he coolly told Martinez he had no interest in the fur trade; he said he was after barrel staves. The Spanish had no serious quarrel with the Americans; they regarded the British as their chief rivals in these waters. Martinez let Gray go on his way and Gray continued the business that had brought him to the northwest coast, bartering with natives from the Strait of Juan de Fuca to Alaska.

Gray returned to Nootka Sound in midsummer to find Kendrick still there. He had not moved the *Columbia* out of the anchorage in search of trade and now, in his capacity as commander of the enterprise, he had Gray's furs transferred to the *Columbia*. He ordered Gray to take her to China, sell the furs, purchase Oriental goods with the receipts from the sale, and carry them back to Boston around the Cape of Good Hope. Then he "sold" himself the *Washington*, severed his connections with the enterprise, and sailed for the Queen Charlotte Islands as a private trader.

When Martinez learned that Gray was bound for the Orient, he persuaded the American to take the crew of the captured *North West America* to China and free the men there. It was only after Gray reached Canton that Meares became aware of the loss of his three ships to the Spanish.

Later that summer Martinez received orders from the viceroy that must have baffled and infuriated him — he was instructed to destroy the Spanish installations at Nootka and abandon the harbor. Martinez carried out the orders and was back in Mexico by the end of 1789. Meanwhile, Meares had gone to England to complain to the British Parliament about the seizure of his ships and the treatment of his men. Spain and Britain had not been on good terms for some years and this incident brought their simmering dispute to a boil.

The decision to yield Nootka had been taken just prior to the viceroy's retirement. His successor strongly disagreed. Never suspecting that his government would not assert its sovereignty over Nootka, he sent Don Francisco de Eliza north with three ships in February, 1790, to reoccupy the sound and hold it for Spain.

In May, 1790, British Parliament voted £1 million to mobilize men and materials and make war against Spain. The Spaniards appealed for assistance from the French but the French Revolution had begun and there was no help to be had there. The Spaniards capitulated in October, agreeing to compensate Meares and allow British subjects to conduct commerce anywhere except within ten leagues of a Spanish Settlement. It was agreed that a British emissary would go to Nootka to discuss reparations with Eliza.

Eliza had no intention of sitting on his hands at Nootka, waiting for someone from Britain to arrive. He reasoned that he could strengthen the Spanish presence in the Pacific Northwest by continuing the program of mapping begun by Martinez. In this way he hoped to establish the Strait if Juan de Fuca and all the coastline below it as Spanish territory. Thus, early in 1791, Eliza, aboard the *San Carlos* and accompanied by José Maria Narvaez commanding the *Santa Saturnina,* entered the Strait of Georgia by way of the Strait of Juan de Fuca, and began tracing its shoreline south of Texada Island. Narvaez dropped anchor one night off the mainland between Point Roberts and Point Atkinson and observed that though he was fully 3 km. (2 mi.) offshore, the ship swung in a strong current streaming out to sea. He collected and drank of the water and found it to be nearly fresh. Eliza noted in his journal that the volume and force of the flowing water must indicate the presence on shore of a "very copious river."[1] Narvaez could not land and search for the river next day on account of bad weather and the expedition moved on. It was Europe's first contact with the Fraser River.

13

Robert Gray, 1791-2

Gray sailed the *Columbia* into Boston early in August, 1790; the first American to circumnavigate the globe. The enterprise had not been a financial success but because it was due mainly to the inertia and questionable tactics of Kendrick, its backers decided to finance another voyage, with Gray in charge. He left Boston late in September, 1790, after less than two months in port and made a speedy passage around South America and up the west coast. He arrived in Nootka on June 4, 1791, in time to get in a full season's trading.

The number of traders on the northwest coast continued to increase and brought fierce competition for furs. The Indians soon learned they could ask for more than nails and beads in exchange for their skins and began demanding arms and ammunition, blankets, knives and other useful goods. The traders who were new to the game paid what the Indians asked but the hardened veterans forced the natives into accepting lower value by taking hostages. If this failed, they were not above burning and bombarding villages.

The tactics employed by the unscrupulous traders earned them a savage hatred. According to John Boit, Gray's fifth mate, the Indians around Clayoquot Sound where Gray spent the 1791-2 winter building a sloop he called the *Adventure*, were "only waiting an opportunity to Massacre the whole of us in cold blood."[1] The Indians thought that opportunity had come early in January, 1792. Gray had moored the *Columbia* alongside a natural wharf of rock, and landed cannon and stores in preparation for hauling the ship onto the beach to clean and caulk her bottom.

His men were thinly spread, guarding the *Columbia* and the material on the wharf, the unfinished *Adventure* and a log block-house. The situation favored the Indians and, to improve their odds, they persuaded a young Sandwich Islander in Gray's service to assist them. The boy's part was to wet the gunpowder in the muskets that were kept ready. When the attack came he was to come over to their side to avoid being killed accidentally. The Indians promised to make him a great chief in exchange for his help.

Fortunately for the Americans, the boy had second thoughts about betraying the whites. He confessed the plot and Gray was able to rearrange the work schedule and deploy his men so effectively that, although the Indians attacked after midnight with "a most hideous hooping,"[2] they eventually retreated "lamenting their hard luck that the Cruell plan was so completely frustrated."[3] Strangely, Gray continued to trade with the Indians and relations between natives and Americans were much as they had been before the incident. He was watchful, however, and gave his hosts no opportunity to surprise him.

The crew kept healthy and free of scurvy throughout the winter by eating a variety of food. The men picked berries that grew wild on shore and ate them in puddings. They kept a supply of spruce beer on hand and drank at breakfast a tea prepared by boiling spruce boughs, then sweetened with molasses. They avoided salt beef and pork, substituting wild fowl, deer and fish.

The *Adventure* (about 45 tons) was launched in March and Gray sent her north under command of Robert Haswell, the first mate, with a crew of ten to trade in the Queen Charlotte Islands. Late in March, before leaving his winter mooring, Gray exacted his revenge on the Indians for their attempt to corrupt the Islander and slaughter his company. He sent John Boit and a party of heavily armed men to raze the nearby Indian village. Having accomplished this, Gray took the *Columbia* out to sea on April 2, and steered southward.[4]

What kind of man was Robert Gray to be capable of such an act? He has been described by the historian, F. W. Howay, as having "a kind and affable disposition, but subject to quick and sudden outburts of temper."[5] The destruction of the village was a premeditated act, probably planned over a period of time. It was executed with military precision to leave a lasting impression on the Indians — hardly the work of a kind and affable man. Howay wrote that Gray was "resolute, self-reliant, and determined."[6] This was likely true but Howay added that "he was, above all, a consummate seaman, and knew how to win and control his crew."[7] John Hoskins, a clerk placed on board the *Columbia* by its Boston owners to watch over their interests, had less flattering comments:

> Captain Gray, whom I must do credit to say, although he cruis'd the coast more [than John Kendrick], and appear'd to be, more persevering, to obtain skins, yet his principles were no better, his abilities less, and his knowledge of the coast, from his former voyage, circumscribed within very narrow limits.[8]

Hoskins complained bitterly about Gray's temper, saying it affected the profitability of dealing with the natives.

During the first two weeks in April, Gray traded along the coast below Cape Flattery, reaching as far south as Cape Blanco in Oregon. The sea along this coastline was often rough, forcing ships well out to sea; Indians, in their unstable, rudely fashioned canoes, were confined to the shoreline. This time, however, the weather was exceptionally fine and Gray was able to heave-to near shore, enabling the Indians to paddle out to the ship. They viewed the *Columbia* with astonishment, suggesting she was the first European ship many of them had seen close up.

Gray acquired a good quantity of furs on the southward voyage, exchanging mainly copper and iron objects for the skins. He felt he could afford to spend time on the northward passage to search for anchorages that would be safe in any weather. He was familiar with Spanish claims for the existence of the San Roque River in latitude 46°11'N and he knew that in 1788 John Meares had named Deception Bay to signify his conviction that this river did not exist. Gray decided to see for himself; if the bay offered a safe anchorage, he was determined to find it.

When Gray turned northward in the second week in April the fine weather gave way to squalls. He saw openings in the coast with the appearance of good harbors and towards the third week in April, in the vicinity of latitude 46°N, the ship's movement was affected by a strong current flowing southward. However, contrary winds, heavy surf and the force of the current combined to make it dangerous if not impossible to maneuver the *Columbia* close in for a proper examination. Gray stood out to sea, hoping the weather would moderate; determined to find the mouth of the river that he now felt sure was the source of the currents. Finally, after beating along the coast for days with no sign of a change in weather, he put off the search for another time and he resumed sailing to the north.

It was April 27, in latitude 48°N, before the sea was calm enough to permit Gray to drop anchor abreast an Indian village and begin trading again. It was a short respite; the weather soon became unsettled and he had to up anchor and move out to sea where the ship could ride it out.

14

Captain George Vancouver, 1792

The voyage of Captain James Cook up the west coast of North America in 1778 had been intended to settle once and for all the question of a navigable Northwest Passage. Cook thought he had proved to the naval world that no such passage existed below 60°N; that the Arctic Ocean was the only water link between the North Pacific and Atlantic Oceans, and it was blocked by pack ice, possibly the year round.

Ten years later it was generally realized that Cook's map of the coast below 60°N was an inaccurate sketch of the true coastline. The British Admiralty had ordered him to begin his search for openings into the continent above 60°N and in the course of reaching that latitude he had not examined hundreds of miles of shoreline. The fur traders, many of them on leave from the Royal Navy, began reporting that much of this coastline was deeply indented. One of these inlets might lead northeasterly into the Arctic Ocean and provide the long-sought short route to England.

One of the more influential of these reports came from John Meares, who considered that his voyage in 1788 had given him an insight into the regional geography. He compiled several versions of a map of the coast and interior and published them in 1790.[1] Like many cartographers of the day he used conjecture, hearsay and perhaps wishful thinking to flesh out those parts of his map for which precise data were lacking. Barkley's discovery of the Strait of Juan de Fuca had convinced Meares that de Fuca's claim of entering the "North Sea" (the Arctic Ocean?) after twenty days of sailing in the strait was true. Meares was certain the strait was

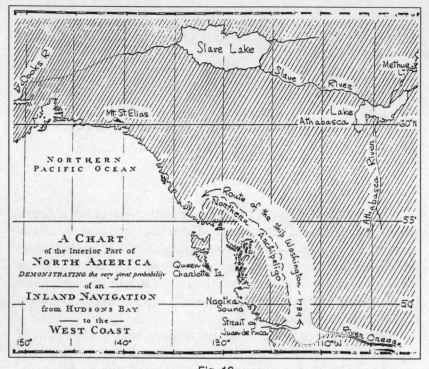

Fig. 16
Part of a John Meares map of northwestern North America
(modified; from John Meares: *Voyages made in the years
1788 and 1789 from China to the North West coast of America.*
Logographic Press, London, 1790).

the entrance to the Northwest Passage and he drew his maps to
demonstrate his belief in the existence of an inland navigation
route between Hudson's Bay and the west coast. To support this
contention he showed a large river (he called it River Oregan)
flowing into the strait from the east.

In another flight of imagination Meares visualized a huge
archipelago of islands extending north from the strait to well
above the Queen Charlotte Islands and separated from the mainland by a broad arm of the sea. It was the first intimation on an
English-language map that Vancouver Island was not part of
mainland North America. By way of proving the existence of this
feature, he claimed that the American ship *Washington*

> entered the Straits of John de Fuca [in 1789], the knowledge
> of which she had received from us; and, penetrating up them,
> entered into an extensive sea, where she steered to the
> Northward and Eastward. . . . The track of this vessel is
> marked on the map, and is of great moment, as it now
> completely ascertains that Nootka Sound, and the parts
> adjacent, are islands.[2]

The British Admiralty, paying heed to the reports of un-mapped coastline, began preparing for another expedition, commissioning the construction of the *Discovery* (340 tons) and the refit of the smaller *Chatham*. The preparations were interrupted by the threat of war with Spain but, in November, 1790, with the crisis past, thirty-three-year-old George Vancouver was named to lead the expedition. Vancouver had shipped with James Cook on the last of that great seaman's voyages (which included the voyage to the Pacific Northwest), earning the rank of lieutenant. He was given instructions to survey the mainland coast of America between 30° and 60°N, and

> to pay particular attention to the examination of the supposed
> straits of Juan de Fuca, said to lead to an opening through
> which the sloop *Washington* is reported to have passed in
> 1789, and to have come out again in the northward of Nootka.
> The discovery of a near communication between any such
> seas or strait, and any river running into it, or from the lake
> of the woods, would be particularly useful.[3]

Also, while he was in the vicinity, he should call at Nootka and accept restitution from Eliza for the injuries inflicted on the British by Martinez in 1789. To comply with these orders, Vancouver began taking on supplies and equipment in anticipation of a spring sailing.

Vancouver left England in April, 1791, steering for the southern tip of Africa. The *Discovery* carried 100 officers and men, the armed tender *Chatham* a complement of forty-five. The expedition spent the 1791-2 winter in the Sandwich Islands and put to sea again on March 18, 1792, on the final leg of the voyage to the American continent. They sighted land on April 17 through a thick haze of rain, the surf breaking with great violence near the shore; they were in latitude 391/2°N.

Vancouver worked his way up the coast in the next few days, fixing the location of headlands, trying to identify the points noted by Meares and Cook on their voyages. On April 27, at noon, they came to a conspicuous point of land comprising hummocks dropping steeply into the sea, their tops thinly covered with trees. The south side of this promontory, as Vancouver described it in his journal, had

> the appearance of an inlet, or small river, the land behind not indicating it to be of any great extent; nor did it seem accessible for vessels of our burthen. . . . On reference to Mr. Mears's description of the coast south of this promontory, I was at first induced to believe it to be cape Shoalwater, but on ascertaining its latitude, I presumed it to be that which he calls cape Disappointment; and the opening to the south of it, Deception bay. This Cape was found to be in latitude 46°19', longitude 236°6' [i.e., 123°54'W].
>
> The sea had now changed from its natural, to river coloured water; the probable consequence of some stream falling into the bay, or into the ocean to the north of it, through the low land. Not considering this opening worthy of more attention, I continued our pursuit to the N.W.[4]

So Vancouver passed by the Columbia River, dismissing Spanish reports almost two hundred years old that a great river emptied into the bay, ascribing the river-colored sea outside the bay to "some stream." Existing accounts of voyages, both Spanish and British, had made it abundantly clear that the most intriguing coastal geography below Cape Flattery lay near latitude 46°N — that this was the place to look for a major river and a water passage into the interior. Yet from well out at sea, Vancouver made the assessment that the bay was not worth exploring, motivated, perhaps, by confidence in fellow countryman Meares's judgment that "no such river . . . exists."[5]

Vancouver may have become convinced from a study of Meares's maps, that the most important and urgent part of his mission lay in the Strait of Juan de Fuca. Whatever the reason for giving the bay short shrift, this proved to be the last opportunity for a British subject to be first to land at the mouth of the Columbia River.

At 4:00 A.M. on April 29, two days after Vancouver cleared Cape Disappointment, the crew of the *Discovery* sighted a sail. As the ships drew together, the stranger ran up an American flag and fired a gun in greeting. At 6:00 A.M. it was close enough to hail and Vancouver learned it was the *Columbia* commanded by Robert Gray, waiting for better weather to anchor off the village in latitude 48°N and resume trading. It was a fortunate meeting for Vancouver. Gray had been master of the *Washington* in 1789, when, according to Meares, she had "entered the Straits of John de Fuca . . . and penetrating up them, entered an extensive sea."[6] Vancouver sent his lieutenant, Peter Puget, to the *Columbia* to question Gray about his voyage in the strait and likely places to search for openings into a Northwest Passage. Puget returned to the *Discovery* with the news that neither Gray nor Kendrick had ever been more than 80 km. (50 mi.) up the strait.

Vancouver must have been shaken by Meares's undiluted impudence in fabricating evidence for his map, perhaps entertaining the thought that no part of Meares's map or report was reliable. However, he had been ordered to "pay particular attention to . . . Juan de Fuca" and to Meares's intriguing conjecture about an inland passage from the strait to Hudson Bay. Thus when Gray volunteered the information that ten days previously he had been "off the mouth of a river in the latitude of 46°10', where the outlet, or reflux, was so strong as to prevent his entering for nine days,"[7] Vancouver expressed no interest and shrugged it off with the entry that "this was, probably, the opening passed by us on the forenoon of the 27th; and was, apparently, inaccessible, not from the current, but from the breakers that extended across it."[8] In other words, he chose to believe there was no strong current and therefore, no major river.

Later, Vancouver wrote in his journal that he "was thoroughly convinced, as were also most persons of observation on board, that we could not possibly have passed any safe navigable opening, harbour, or place of security for shipping on this coast."[9] Having concluded the short and disappointing meeting with Gray, Vancouver resumed his northward course.

Vancouver began his survey of mainland North America in the Strait of Juan de Fuca. He used boats that could be rowed, if the wind failed, to reach into narrow inlets and shallow bays that were too dangerous for the ocean-going *Discovery* and *Chatham*. He explored Puget Sound — which he named after Peter Puget — and then moved into the Strait of Georgia.

Unknown to Vancouver, Eliza, still representing Spain at Nootka Sound, had sent the *Sutil* and the *Mexicana* under Captains Dionisio Alcala Galiano and Cayetano Valdes, to continue exploring the Strait of Georgia. They, like Narvaez in the previous year, found evidence of the Fraser River:

> At 5 in the afternoon we saw ahead a line where the color of the water changed, the part towards the land being very turbid. As soon as we had gone about half a mile we saw that the current was carrying us rapidly away from the shore to westward and to midchannel. We took to the oars and endeavored to overcome the current with them, but the efforts of the sailors were useless as they were very tired with the labors of the preceding day.[10]

Vancouver's rowboats crossed the muddy waters of the Fraser River where it flows from its several arms into the Strait of Georgia between Point Roberts and Point Grey, and he went ashore at Point Grey, named for Vancouver's friend, Captain George Grey of the British Navy. He noted that the space between the two points was occupied by low land, "apparently a swampy flat . . . very much inundated"[11] but he did not realize he had crossed the mouth of a mighty river. He continued north and surveyed Burrard Inlet, Howe Sound and Jervis Inlet before turning back to rejoin the *Discovery*. At Spanish Banks, on the north shore of Point Grey, he came upon the *Sutil* and the *Mexicana* and went on board to exchange information with Captains Galiano and Valdes. That night he wrote in his journal, that when he showed the Spaniards the charts he had drawn from his surveys, "they seemed much surpized that we had not found a river said to exist in the region we had been exploring."[12] Vancouver would not believe the Fraser River existed and did not show it on the map that was published after his return to England.

15

The Columbia River, 1792

The chance meeting with the *Discovery* below Cape Flattery on April 30 had left Robert Gray wondering if Vancouver's stated intention to explore the Strait of Juan de Fuca was a ruse to hide another objective. He followed Vancouver north, watched him enter the strait and waited some hours until he had satisfied himself that Vancouver was not planning to deceive him. Then he turned back and managed two days of trading before the weather drove him out to sea again. The time wasted in beating to and fro, and waiting for seas gentle enough to anchor along this exposed coast, must have convinced Gray, if convincing he needed, of the value of an all-weather anchorage.

Gray left the vicinity of the strait on May 4, intending to make another swing to the south to pick up the trade he had missed in his earlier voyage down the coast. The ship was in latitude 47°N on May 7 when he saw a promising looking bay guarded by a reef across its entrance. Not daring to take the *Columbia* too close to the bar, plainly marked by a line of breakers for all on deck to see, Gray sent a crew in the ship's cutter to take a closer look at the bay. The men reported back that the bay appeared to offer good anchorage but they could see no break in the bar through which the ship might pass.

Gray was determined to enter the bay. Following closely in the *Columbia*, he sent the cutter towards the bar with a man in her bow to sound the depth of water and give warning if it became too shallow. Moving cautiously in this manner, he got the *Columbia* close to the bar where the lookout, from high on the mast, spied an opening between the sandbars and directed the

99

helmsman to it. It was courageous and enterprising seamanship. John Boit recorded the events in his journal:

> at half-past 3, [we] bore away, and run in. . . . At 5 P.M. came to in five fathoms [30 feet] water, sandy bottom, in a safe harbor, well sheltered from the sea by long sand-bars and spits.[1]

This was clearly not Deception Bay — it was too far north by more than half a degree of latitude. Gray named it Bullfinch's Harbor for Charles Bullfinch, one of the ship's owners. Today it is called Grays Harbor.

The entrance of the *Columbia* had evidently been watched, for as soon as she came to she was surrounded by canoes filled with Indians, anxious to trade their many furs. From their reaction to the Americans, Boit surmised that the *Columbia* was the first European ship to enter the harbor. Trade continued harmoniously next day but at night the scene turned ugly. The ship's company became alarmed when they perceived many canoes around the ship. The Indians in them acted in a bold, menacing and provocative manner and took no notice when they were warned away. Soon a canoe with more than twenty Indians was within pistol range. It was too close for Gray; if the Indians chose to rush and board the ship from several quarters, the seamen might be overwhelmed. He decided he had to act and

> with a Nine pounder, loaded with langerege and about 10 Musketts, loaded with Buckshot, we dash'd her [the canoe] all to peices, and no doubt kill'd every soul in her. The rest soon made a retreat.[2]

The incident seemed to have no ill-effect on trade the next day; Gray surmised the warlike night visitors might have come from another part of the coast.

In the evening of May 11, Gray abruptly quit the bay, clearing the sandbars without difficulty. He sailed southward all night and, according to the ship's log, "at 4 A.M. saw the entrance of our desired port."[3] He was off Deception Bay which he had tried unsuccessfully to enter three weeks earlier. The manner of his leaving and the reference to "our desired port" suggest that he had learned something from the Indians at Grays Harbor that he was impatient to investigate — something to support the conviction he had gained on his previous visit that the strong currents outside the bay marked it as the mouth of a major river.

This day there would be no waiting outside the bar. Gray recorded the historic events that followed in the laconic language typical of the ship's log:

> At eight, A.M., being a little to windward of the entrance of the Harbor, bore away, and ran in east-northeast between the breakers, having from five to seven fathoms of water. When we were over the bar, we found this to be a large river of fresh water, up which we steered, Many canoes came alongside.[4]

Gray had rediscovered Hezeta's Rio de San Roque — the "River of the West." But more than that, he had crossed the bar and entered the river. He put his imprint on it by naming it "Columbia's River" for the first American ship to sail its waters.

Gray stayed at anchor for two days, trading with the many natives that came to the ship from a village on the north shore. He took the opportunity to empty the salt water from the ship's casks and fill them with fresh water from the river. On May 14 he took the *Columbia* upstream but she ran aground on a sandbar near the middle of what is now called Grays Bay, about 25 km. (15 mi.) from the entrance. She soon came off without assistance but thereafter Gray explored the shore with the jollyboat. On May 16, he dropped the ship down to an anchorage near the river's mouth. She remained there until the eighteenth, and Gray kept the men occupied with caulking the pinnace and tarring the *Columbia's* sides while they awaited their opportunity to get out to sea. It was the twentieth before wind and tides combined favorably. They cleared the bay, through seas breaking over the bar, by beating against a fresh wind blowing off the ocean. It took two hours to get free of the breakers but at 5:00 P.M., with a breeze from the south to fill the sails, they bore away to the north.

The elements favored Gray in 1792. Fifty years later (in December 1841), after a trip down the Columbia River, Sir George Simpson had a wait of seventeen days in Bakers Bay before "the bar became sufficiently tranquil"[5] to let them get out to sea. He was told that "during the winter, vessels often lie in Baker's Bay from three to seven weeks, for the indispensable conjunction of fair wind and smooth water."[6] It was more difficult to enter the bay than leave it because "a vessel cannot so snugly watch her opportunity in the open ocean as in Baker's Bay."[7] The entrance earned a reputation for being a hazardous passage — "its unenviable trophies consisting of three ships wrecked and several others damaged, to say nothing of boats swamped with all their crews."[8] Even when wind and water favored them, skippers were apprehensive about negotiating the narrow, shallow and intricate passage; their ships were in constant danger of being driven aground by the capricious winds. Robert Gray was fortunate on May 12, 1792. The day dawned clear and calm and he sailed across the bar and into the pages of history.

The rediscovery of the Columbia River had important consequences for the United States for it became the foundation of the American claim to the Oregon Territory. It may have been a dubious claim to so much territory but it helped to win the region for them. Spanish authorities had neglected this northern extension of their possessions and the British had done little to build on Francis Drake's claim to New Albion. Cook, and more particularly Meares and Vancouver, had opportunity and incentive to discover the river and strengthen the British claim. Their actions when they were opposite its mouth were uninspired and in unflattering contrast to the persistence displayed by Robert Gray.

Gray made contact with the *Adventure* off Vancouver Island in June. Later that month, while cruising around the southern tip of the Queen Charlotte Islands, the *Columbia* struck a pinnacle of rock in water at least 125 m. (400 ft.) deep. The water poured in, the pumps just managing to keep the ship from swamping. To make matters worse, a hard gale came up in the night, making it difficult to control her. The ships fired their cannons throughout the night to keep in touch but when day dawned on a thick fog, the *Columbia* was alone on the surface of the sea. Gray got her to the Queen Charlotte Islands where he found shelter enough to fother her hull with a topsail. It reduced the leak by half and he was able to sail her to a protected cove known to him, near the north end of Vancouver Island. After removing the cannons and other loose equipment, the crew hauled the ship onto the beach and now Gray could see the extent of the damage. It was worse than he had anticipated — the lower part of the ship's stem had been torn away and her keel was split. They would have to take her to Nootka to make her sound.

The ship was still difficult to maneuver even after they had done what they could to make her seaworthy and they overshot the entrance to Nootka. They had to fire a signal gun to call for help from the Spaniards stationed there to get her into the harbor. It was July 24 before the ship's crew was ready to start repairs.

The *Columbia* was whole again and fit for the sea late in August. Gray sold the *Adventure* to the Spaniards for seventy-two prime otter skins and began preparing for the homeward voyage. He left Nootka Sound, for the last time, on October 3, bound for China where he sold his furs and took on a cargo of Oriental goods. He arrived in Boston on July 29, 1793; the voyage to the Pacific Northwest had occupied almost three years.

Gray never returned to the Pacific coast, confining himself to the command of east coast merchantmen until 1799 when he became master of a privateer (twelve guns and twenty-five men), preying on French shipping. After the trouble with France had ended, he again commanded merchantmen, voyaging to the southern states and occasionally to England. He died in obscurity — it is thought about 1806, of yellow fever — leaving a wife and four daughters. The *Columbia* was scrapped in 1801.

16

Lieutenant Broughton Charts
the Lower Columbia River, 1792

Vancouver sailed into Nootka Sound with the *Discovery* and the *Chatham* late in August while Gray was making final preparations for leaving the Pacific Northwest. He had surveyed the Strait of Georgia (Meares's "extensive sea") and, when he reentered the Pacific Ocean, he had turned south to accept reparations from the Spanish. He had not found a Northwest Passage, of course, and he must have been chagrined to learn, at Nootka, that Gray had discovered a "river and a harbour . . . between the 46th and the 47th degrees of north latitude"[1] which he had decided did not exist.

He left Nootka Sound within ten days of Gray's departure. It had become incumbent on him to reexamine the coast of New Albion and particularly the newly discovered Columbia's River. Before leaving, he received on board two young Sandwich Island women who were stranded on the Northwest coast. They had been carried, mysteriously, to Nootka on the ship *Jenny* out of Bristol, England, "not only very contrary to their wishes and inclinations, but totally without the knowledge or consent of their friends or relations."[2] Vancouver agreed to ferry them back to their families.

Vancouver reached the vicinity of latitude 46°N near midnight on October 18 after a voyage of less than a week. He anchored his ships and at daylight observed that he lay about 3 km. (2 mi.) from the breakers marking the entrance to the bay that he had passed by on April 27. He moved in, the two ships coasting alongside the bar while he searched for a place to cross it. By 4:00 P.M., when most of the length of the bar had been examined and they were approaching Cape Disappointment on the north, they saw a likely looking channel. Vancouver decided it was this or nothing and with the smaller *Chatham* leading the way, they entered the channel and moved towards the land. The water shoaled rapidly and when it reached 5 1/2 m. (18 ft.), Vancouver hauled the *Discovery* to windward, dropping the ship back down channel and anchoring in 18 m. (60 ft.) of water. Seeing this, Lieutenant William Broughton in the *Chatham* anchored his ship too, although he did not seem to be in any difficulty.

They lay there through the night and next morning, in a calm sea, Broughton sailed the *Chatham* over the bar and into the bay. It was plain to see on the western horizon that the fine weather would soon come to an end. Vancouver, worried that his ship might suffer a heavy pounding in a storm in the exposed bay, abruptly took the *Discovery* out to sea. Soon a gale was blowing and they were in a "boisterous" sea. They had to take in sail to save it from being ripped free by the wind. Vancouver began to have doubts about his plan to enter the bay with the *Discovery*. The season was well advanced and winter storms were in the offing; he felt it was time to seek a gentler environment. He had no way of communicating with the *Chatham* but he consoled himself with the thought that Broughton could look after himself and his crew and make the necessary surveys. Vancouver turned the *Discovery* and ran southward towards Monterey where he intended to have the ship refitted.

Broughton, meanwhile, had found a cove just inside the bar, well protected from storms at sea by the bulk of Cape Disappointment on the west and south. He was surprised to find the *Jenny* moored there; her master, Mr. Baker, had found the cove on an earlier visit (it is not known if the visit was earlier than Gray's). The chance meeting influenced Broughton to identify the bay as Bakers Bay on his charts. The bay proved to be about as far upstream as the larger ocean-going ships could safely sail; breakers above this cove sometimes made travel hazardous. It afforded good and secure anchorage and was a convenient place to replenish supplies of wood and fresh water. Also, the fishing was good and Broughton found the natives living around Cape Disappointment friendly.

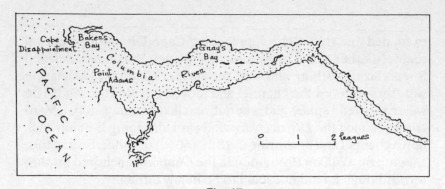

Fig. 17
Lieutenant W. R. Broughton's chart of the mouth of the Columbia River, 1792 (modified; after T. C. Elliott: *The Log of H.M.S. "Chatham."* Oregon Hist. Soc. Quarterly, 18, 231, 1917).

In the next few days Broughton took the *Chatham* up current for a distance of about 25 km. (15 mi.) to Grays Bay (where Gray had run aground with the *Columbia*), examining Cape Disappointment and Point Adams by rowboat, and charting the channel. Broughton was interested in the nature of the river and he wanted to see if it was navigable upstream. Using the cutter packed with a ten-day supply of provisions, he traveled for seven days, reaching inland another 150 km. (a hundred miles) past the site of today's Vancouver, Washington, before turning back.

Broughton returned to the *Chatham* twelve days after he had parted with Vancouver. He had acquired much information and in the process found the Columbia to be a great river although not navigable at that time for ocean-going ships. Broughton claimed the river and the surrounding country for Britain by reason of his seven-day journey upstream. He declared that Gray had never seen or been on the river — that its mouth was 25 km. (15 mi.) above Grays Bay which was about as far as Gray had gone inland. Gray deserved better; Broughton's own charts show that Grays Bay is at least 15 km. (10 mi.) above the line of the coast.

It was early November — time to leave the Columbia River and rejoin Vancouver and the *Discovery*. First they had to get the *Chatham* downstream to where she could be moored until the wind and seas were right to take her across the bar. It was several days before the weather was favorable. They found the *Jenny* still

106

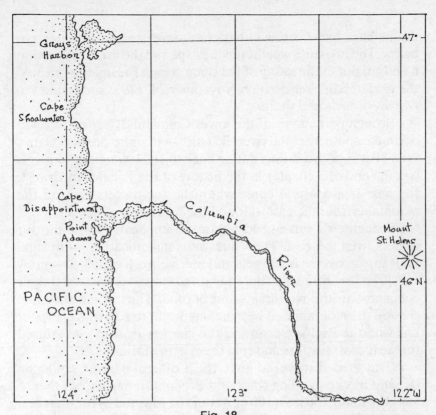

Fig. 18

Broughton's map of the lower Columbia River, 1792 (modified; from George Vancouver: *Voyage of Discovery to the North Pacific Ocean and Round the World*. G. G. & J. Robinson, London, 1798).

anchored in Bakers Bay, her master awaiting the opportunity to get his ship out to sea.

On November 10, a week after they had started the *Chatham* downstream, the wind changed into a favoring breeze and the water in the bay looked calm enough to attempt the bar. Led by the smaller *Jenny* and her more experienced master, Broughton headed for the entrance. The *Jenny* cleared the bar into a violent sea that pitched and tossed her so much the wind was spilled from her sails and for a time, she rolled helplessly in the heavy breakers. The *Chatham*, not so nimble, followed. The waves broke over her repeatedly, from bow to stern, but in anticipation of rough sea, the hatches had been well battened down and little water got below. The two ships weathered the cape and the breakers beyond it and got out to the safety of the open ocean. Broughton reached the port of San Francisco on November 24, 1792, and found the *Discovery* anchored there.

Broughton's survey of the lower Columbia River established beyond dispute, that the river did exist — that the Spanish claims for a "River of the West," dating back to 1603, were authentic. It was the end of a chapter in the history of the Pacific Northwest; the next phase would come when the fur traders crossed the mountains from the east to found their network of posts.

Broughton's survey had important implications for the fur traders from the east. Their lines of communication — to send their furs to overseas markets and receive fresh supplies — grew steadily more difficult as they advanced westward to extend their commerce to the mountains and beyond. Thus, when they had crossed the mountains, it became important to search for a water link with the Pacific Ocean and the mariner-traders who cruised the west coast for furs and sold them in the Orient.

Gray had discovered that the Columbia River could be entered by ocean-going ships and Broughton had shown that at least the lower 150 km. (100 mi.) could be traveled by fur brigades. It seemed desirable to investigate the river as a route to the Western Sea; its mouth might serve as the base for a Pacific seaport. Broughton's determination of its geographical co-ordinates (see Fig. 18) became doubly important. A trader, exploring the interior for a connecting river, need only compare the latitude and longitude of his location with Broughton's co-ordinates to know accurately his own direction and distance from the river's mouth.

Part Three

The Interior of
the Pacific Northwest

Just as the sea otter drew mariners to the Pacific Northwest, so the beaver enticed Europeans to penetrate the interior of the continent from the eastern seaboard. They were lured by the profit to be earned in bartering guns and ammunition, whiskey, kettles and knives, tobacco, blankets and articles of clothing, and trinkets for animal skins and principally the beaver.

Another great objective drew men westward. Ever since 1603 when Martin de Aguilar had discovered an "abundant river" entering the Pacific Ocean near Cape Blanco, geographers had speculated that it would provide access to the interior of the continent. They called it the "River of the West." The French, in Montreal and Quebec, visualized how such a river could expand New France and they searched for it west of the Great Lakes. Later, after Robert Gray sailed into Aguilar's river (and named it Columbia's River) in 1792, it was generally assumed that its source was on the western slope of the Rockies. When the fur traders crossed the mountain barrier, they looked for it, thinking it would be the principal navigable river down to the Pacific Ocean.

The interior was an uncharted, trackless wilderness. Europeans found their way by questioning the Indians, getting them to draw their crude maps of ancient canoe routes and hiring them as guides and interpreters. The drive to the west progressed essentially along the three great river systems that drain the eastern slopes of the Rockies — the Missouri, the Saskatchewan and the Peace. The traders built posts at favorable locations along an expanding network of routes. To gain a perspective view of the trade and travel areas, they traced the course of rivers, located lakes and other features, and showed them on maps. Some of these maps were mere sketches but others were accurately drawn by surveyors (usually called "astronomers" for their practice of observing celestial bodies to locate their positions). Accurate maps saved travel time and sometimes suggested where to search for a shorter route.

Travel in the interior was strenuous. In the course of a voyage, men journeyed from dawn to dusk — paddling, poling or dragging the boats as conditions dictated. When the craft could not be moved by these means, the men carried them on their shoulders. They worked in all kinds of weather — through rain showers, in the heat of the summer sun and with snow stinging their faces in early spring and late fall. They endured swarms of flies in spring; and they were frequently hungry, sometimes for days at a time, so that they learned to relish what the land provided, including pemmican.

Pemmican was made by Indian women. They spent weeks drying thin strips of buffalo meat over fires. When the meat was completely dry it was spread on a buffalo hide or in a hollow log and pounded to powder. Bags, made from buffalo hides sewn together, hair side out, were three-quarters filled with the powder and topped off with melted fat. If wild berries were at hand, they were added. That was pemmican. It kept well through the heat of summer and was light to carry for the amount of nourishment it provided.[1] Some said that pemmican, well made and fresh, was delicious; others who may have seen it made on a none-too-clean buffalo hide, had a different opinion.[2] The Earl of Southesk, after his travels in the west in 1859-60, described it as follows:

> Take scrapings from the driest outside corner of a very stale piece of cold roast beef, add to it lumps of tallowy rancid fat, then garnish all with long human hairs . . . and short hairs of oxen, or dogs, or both, — and you have a fair imitation of common pemmican, though I should rather suppose it to be less nasty.
>
> Pemmican is most endurable when uncooked. My men used to fry it with grease, sometimes stirring-in flour, and making a flabby mess, called "rubaboo," which I found almost uneatable.[3]

The explorers and their men lived with danger and the fear it created. Sometimes they feared violence from the native Indians who always greatly outnumbered them; they were a few white men in an alien world. At other times the threat came from a turbulent and unfamiliar river. What would they do, miles from home, if the canoe turned them bag and baggage into the water? Without arms, they could not forage for food and protect themselves against hostile natives. The men became uneasy as the distance from their home base increased and when a misfortune befell them, they were inclined to talk about turning back. These times tested the qualities of leadership in the explorer. The men had to be convinced to go on and he had no hold over them beyond the force of his personality.

Most of the traders who worked on the edge of the white man's civilization left no public account of their lives, limiting the description of their activities to brief business reports. Much of what is written on the history of the discovery and exploration of the northwest interior is based on the journals, accounts and letters of a few traders and explorers. Their literacy and gifts of rhetoric varied enormously. In some instances the writing is so cryptic that the events and circumstances the author attempted to describe cannot be satisfactorily understood. Some of the accounts were written immediately after the events occurred; others were begun years later when the writer had only his field notes to jog his memory. Some accounts were prepared for the literary market with the help of professional writers and one suspects that history was sometimes embellished to make the narrative more readable or flattering to the author. Not surprisingly then, historians have found the material on some events and subjects vague and incomplete, or contradictory and of questionable accuracy. It is unlikely though, that any great achievements of exploration have gone unnoticed.

History has been unable to give proper credit for the pioneering work performed by some of the "ordinary" men who accompanied the explorers and traders — the voyageurs and woodsmen, usually of mixed blood, and soldiers. They were an essential part of the operations, expected to work the canoes, backpack over portages, handle horses, kill and butcher animals, erect log structures, do rough blacksmithing, and fight Indians if it came to that. Some of these men were outstandingly brave and resourceful and were singled out for special duties. They often moved or lived in advance of the main party and scouted out the route for the explorer. Most were illiterate, incapable of writing a coherent account. Their exploits received, at best, a line in the explorer's journal or a mention in a letter.

The search for a route across the continent to the Pacific Northwest was dominated by Alexander Mackenzie and Simon Fraser in the north, by Pierre de la Vérendrye, Meriwether Lewis and William Clark in the south and by David Thompson on the Saskatchewan River. Their efforts were often phenomenal acts of courage, perseverance and practical ingenuity that revealed unusual qualities of leadership. They thrust deep into the wilderness of the Northwest — the first white men in a vast, often unfriendly land. The period of their exploits, particularly the final years from 1789 to 1811, was a time of remarkable vitality and accomplishment that deserves a special place in the history of North America.

17

The la Vérendryes

The Western Sea

The seventeenth century opened with three European countries — Spain, England and France — dominant in mainland North America and attempting to expand their influence on the continent. In the south the Spanish, although much occupied in South America, had by 1600 consolidated their hold on Mexico and taken control of Florida.

The English established Jamestown in 1607 and then proceeded to settle the Atlantic coast from Maine to Georgia, developing the region in the ensuing century and a half into thirteen prosperous colonies. They also gained a foothold in the northern part of the continent when Henry Hudson explored Hudson Bay in 1610-11.

The Frenchman, Jacques Cartier, had begun exploring the St. Lawrence River in 1534 but the bleak countryside failed to attract the French and interest in the interior flagged. The French found good fishing in the Gulf of St. Lawrence, however, and their fishermen came in increasing numbers and on the side they began acquiring furs from the natives. The trade proved so profitable that merchants soon took part. They founded Quebec City in 1608, made it the center of this trade, then began moving up the St. Lawrence River to the source of the furs in the interior. By midcentury the French had gained a general knowledge of the St. Lawrence River and the Great Lakes — a water system that was to give them an entry into the deep interior of the continent and access to a vast and potentially rich trading area.

A serious threat to the French monopolization of the fur trade in the interior began in 1670 when Charles II of England granted the Hudson's Bay Company an exclusive charter to occupy and trade on the shores of Hudson Bay and all the land drained by rivers emptying into the bay. The west coast of the bay borders an inland territory characterized by extensive waterways and long cold winters, the ingredients for producing a rich harvest of thick and lustrous furs. The company built a number of forts on the bay and in little more than a decade was diverting a large portion of the furs taken in North American to England.

Meanwhile, the French pursued a bold exploration program, reaching the extremities of Lake Superior and Lake Michigan and examining the country to the south. In 1673, the explorer Louis Jolliet crossed from Lake Michigan to the Mississippi River and descended to the Arkansas River. In 1682, the Sieur de La Salle completed the descent of the river; he reached New Orleans, thereby linking the St. Lawrence River-Great Lakes region with the Gulf of Mexico.

The sudden rapid expansion of New France south to the Gulf of Mexico alarmed the English settlers along the east coast. When war broke out in Europe after William and Mary ascended the English throne in 1689, it quickly spread to North America. Both the English and the French enlisted Indians and staged ruthless raids on exposed settlements. In the north, the French captured the English forts on Hudson Bay. The fighting continued with brief interruptions for twenty-five years, until 1713, when the Treaty of Utrecht was signed. It concluded the War of the Spanish Succession in Europe — the struggle to determine the fate of the Spanish Empire.

The treaty marked the first permanent losses for France in North America. The Hudson's Bay Company regained its posts on the bay and the French were forced to acknowledge British sovereignty, not only of the Hudson Bay region, but of Newfoundland and Nova Scotia as well. Spain retained its possessions in America.

Still, the treaty left the French with a corridor through the heart of the continent — from Labrador, along the St. Lawrence River, through the Great Lakes and down the Mississippi River to the Gulf of Mexico. Much of it marked the extremity of

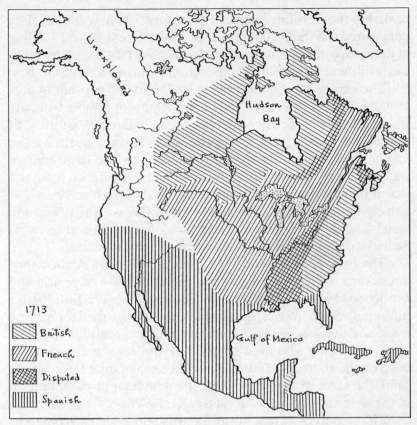

Fig. 19
European spheres of influence in North America following the Treaty of
Utrecht, 1713.

Europe's advance west towards the Pacific Ocean. Thus, although
excluded from the Hudson Bay region by the treaty, the French
were well placed to expand fur trading operations west and southwest into the interior. A disadvantage lay in the long and difficult
journeys to supply their outposts on the Great Lakes from
seaports on the St. Lawrence. The English could land supplies at
their posts on Hudson Bay directly from ocean-going ships and,
as a consequence, offer high quality goods at relatively low prices.
It made them complacent and they adopted a policy of waiting for
the Indians to come to their posts to trade. The French soon

115

realized they could compete on more even terms if they penetrated the Indian country beyond the Great Lakes. Trading at the source of the furs made it so convenient for the natives that many of them were willing to forego the journey to Hudson Bay.

The expansion of New France westward had another important objective. The French had heard persistent rumors from the Indians, even before the beginning of the eighteenth century, of the existence of a great sea to the west. The sea might be the Pacific Ocean but it was generally believed to be a large body of water connected to the Pacific by a channel. The French reasoned that if there were large areas of water to the south and north — namely the Gulf of Mexico and Hudson Bay — why not to the west? The thought of discovering an all-French inland sea connected with the Pacific Ocean was extremely attractive.

The French had no concept of the size of North America nor any inkling of the existence of the broad expanse of prairie and the Rocky Mountains beyond it. The Indians were little better informed and, moreover, did not have the background for making a quantitative assessment about geographical features they had seen. An Indian who lived on the Ottawa River and had never been on the shores of Hudson Bay or seen the Great Lakes might think the Lake of the Woods was the dominant physical feature in the west and call it the Great Sea of the West.

The rumors of a great western sea had no evidence to support them but the French government took them seriously. In 1721, Francois-Xavier Charlevoix, a Jesuit priest, was sent out from France to investigate and report on the matter. Father Charlevoix interviewed missionaries who lived among the Sioux Indians and he went down the Mississippi River to New Orleans, questioning voyageurs who had been on the Missouri River. The stories he garnered were full of contradictions but they convinced him there was a sea far to the west, possibly in the same latitudes as the Great Lakes. Indians told him they knew of rivers flowing westward, one of which had its source in the uplands where the Missouri began its southeasterly journey to join the Mississippi. Charlevoix concluded that the way to the Western Sea was up the Missouri to its source, across the divide, and down the westerly flowing river — directions, in fact, for reaching the Pacific Ocean.[1]

116

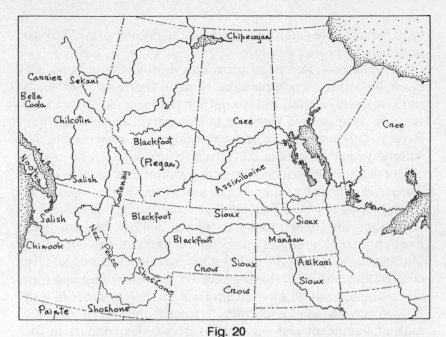

Fig. 20

The approximate distribution of Indian tribes at the time Europeans first penetrated the western part of North America. The map shows the three rivers — the Peace, Saskatchewan and Missouri — along which trader/explorers looked for a route to the Pacific Ocean.

Fort la Reine — French outpost on the Assiniboine River, 1738

Charlevoix's report must have been favorably received for the Marquis de Beauharnois, newly appointed Governor of New France, arrived in 1726 with orders from the Comte de Maurepas, Minister of Marine and Colonies, to find the Western Sea. Instead of a purposeful drive over the route suggested by Charlevoix to reach the sea, he proposed to move in stages. First he would establish a post in the country of the Sioux (Minnesota, North and South Dakota) to gather additional information from them and any more westerly tribes that might be encountered.[2]

Beauharnois sent a party to Lake Pepin (on the border between Wisconsin and Minnesota) to found the post. It was a failure — not only was the site flooded in the spring but also the

117

local Indians were determined to drive the French away. The post was abandoned after a year.

Beauharnois decided to proceed even more cautiously. He began by building a post on Lake Nipigon (north of Lake Superior), mainly to expand and strengthen the fur trade. To lead the venture, he appointed Pierre de la Vérendrye, a native of Three Rivers, Quebec — a man of considerable experience. La Vérendrye had enlisted in the Three Rivers militia at the age of twelve to fight the Iroquois who periodically menaced the settlers. Three years later he took part in a brief expedition against an English village in New England. He served in Newfoundland in 1705 when the French took St. John's. In 1707, he joined the French forces massing in Europe against the Duke of Marlborough. He fought in Flanders in 1709, and was left for dead on the battlefield, having received a musket shot and four sabre wounds, but he survived and was made a prisoner of war. Fifteen months later he returned to Canada; he had attained the rank of lieutenant and was cited for valorous conduct in the fighting.

Back in Three Rivers, la Vérendrye married and began farming and fur-trading with the Indians, and he prospered. The fur business put him in contact with traders who had been in the interior and their stories stirred the spirit that had taken him overseas to fight in Europe. When Beauharnois offered to put him in charge in the Northwest, he accepted with alacrity. He was forty-two years old when he set out with three of his four sons for Lake Nipigon in 1727.[3]

La Vérendrye was soon caught up in the speculation about the Western Sea, carried along by Indian stories intended to please the white listener by telling him what he wanted to hear. The talk concentrated on the fabled "River of the West," said to flow from the interior southwesterly all the way to the Pacific Ocean. When the French heard that a large river (the Winnipeg River) flowed west and emptied into a great lake (Lake Winnipeg), they wondered if it was part of the "River of the West" water system. They were wrong, of course; those waters pour into Hudson Bay. The Pacific drainage basin was more than 1,300 km. (800 mi.) to the west.

Of more immediate interest to la Vérendrye was the story, often repeated, of a tribe called the Mandans. They lived in the plains country southwest of the Lake of the Woods and grew grain and vegetables, and raised livestock for food and for barter with less sedentary people. They were said to resemble the French in that they were white and tall, and the men grew beards. Of particular interest was the intimation that they lived on the upper reaches of a south-southwesterly flowing river so wide it was difficult to distinguish a man on the opposite shore. Could this be the "River of the West"?

La Vérendrye was convinced that somewhere in the interior there was a large river flowing down to the Pacific Ocean. He argued that such a river was necessary to balance the enormous drainage of the continent to the south and east by the Mississippi and St. Lawrence Rivers and keep the Atlantic and Pacific Oceans at the same level. The Mandans's river must be that river. He proposed to Beauharnois that he be authorized to build a fort on Lake Winnipeg as an outpost for a dash to the Western Sea by way of this river. He thought the sea must be quite close and that a journey of ten days should bring him to it. Beauharnois agreed to the request but said la Vérendrye would have to finance the journey out of the profits from the fur trade; he could spare only enough money to buy presents for the Indians that la Vérendrye would meet on the way.

Not everyone was willing to believe the Indian stories of a race of Whites living in the unknown interior of North America. A missionary, Father Nau, was moved by his experience in the New World to write: "One is apt to doubt the sincerity of the Canadians who brought back this tale, for there is no country in the world where there is so much lying as in Canada."[4]

La Vérendrye began building posts in 1731 — Fort St. Pierre on Rainy Lake and Fort St. Charles on the Lake of the Woods — approaching Lake Winnipeg. He cemented relations with the Indians and persuaded them to trade with him rather than the English on Hudson Bay. Just when he was ready to profit from these efforts and get on with building the fort on Lake Winnipeg, he had trouble stocking the posts. His trade goods were late in arriving and were of poor quality, and many Indians refused to

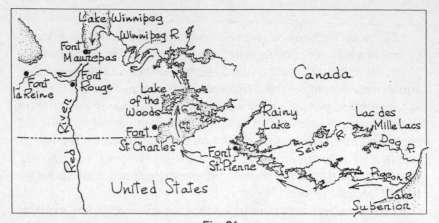

Fig. 21
Route used by la Vérendrye to travel from Lake Superior to his most
westerly outpost — Fort la Reine on the Assiniboine River.

deal with him. As a consequence he could not pay his creditors
and he had to find new financing. Finally, in March of 1734, his
financial and business matters under control, he sent his son,
Pierre, to choose a site for the fort. It was built, not on the lake,
but a short distance south of it on the Red River. La Vérendrye
named it Fort Maurepas.

The various Indian nations were constantly quarreling. Early
in 1734, their disagreements took on a more serious nature and
they began staging raids against one another. The Cree insisted
that la Vérendrye attach one of his sons to a war party planning
to move against the Sioux. Reluctantly, la Vérendrye agreed that
Jean-Baptiste, his eldest son who was eager for the adventure,
should accompany them. The party never did make contact with
the enemy but the Sioux were incensed by this act of alignment
and in June, when they happened on Jean-Baptiste and a small
party of Frenchmen camped on an island, they took their revenge.
All of the Frenchmen, including a priest whose body was found in
a kneeling position, were killed or drowned while attempting to
escape. They scalped the dead men, then severed the heads and
wrapped them in beaver skins to mock the French preoccupation
with this article of trade. A search party found the bodies several
days later. The Sioux had disfigured Jean-Baptiste by scoring his
back with knife cuts and driving a stake into his side.[5]

Open warfare was always a threat to the profitability of the fur trade because it reduced the free movement of Indians to the trading posts, and it made exploration dangerous. Small parties of whites and their Indian guides were extremely vulnerable. La Vérendrye talked with the Indians, attempting to persuade them to stop fighting each other. Early in 1737 he was satisfied that the war parties were breaking up and he could get on with his plans to reach the Western Sea. He met and talked with the many Indians gathered at Fort Maurepas where his youngest son, Louis-Joseph, was in charge. When he inquired about the Mandans, the Indians buoyed his spirits by repeating the information that the Mandans's river flowed to the southwest.

At this meeting he heard for the first time about another great river — the Saskatchewan. He was told it rose far in the west, and from the country that was its source a third river flowed south-south westerly into the Western Sea. A Cree brave claimed he had gone down the latter river, which he called the "River of the West," through a land of strange fruit trees to the shores of the sea occupied by white men. It was probably another story told to please la Vérendrye; at this time there were no white settlements on the west coast above Mexico. Still, la Vérendrye must have thought the Saskatchewan could prove to be a road to the Western Sea and filed the information in his memory. If he did not reach his goal by way of the Mandans's river, he would need an alternative route.[6]

The Indians ended the meeting by offering to guide him to the Mandan villages, said to be about 700 km. (450 mi.) distant. Now, suddenly and strangely, he seemed reluctant, saying he had to journey east to consult with the governor before the coming winter.

Back in Quebec la Vérendrye told the governor he had put off the journey to the Mandans because his men were afraid to accompany him. The governor showed scant sympathy for his difficulties, real and imagined, reminding him that he had been ten years in the Northwest, and he threatened to dismiss him if the journey to the Western Sea was not soon undertaken.

La Vérendrye was back in Fort Maurepas in September, 1738. When he announced his intention of traveling west to the country of the Mandans, none of his men showed any fear at the prospect. He ascended the Red River to the site of Winnipeg where he turned up the shallow, meandering Assiniboine River and followed it as far as the portage leading to Lake Manitoba — the site of Portage la Prairie, where he built a post. This was an old crossroads and, he believed, a good location for an advance post for future exploration thrusts into the Northwest. He named it Fort la Reine.

The Mandans

Late in October, 1738, la Vérendrye began the journey south-westward, across country, to find the Mandans and the river that would float him down to the Western Sea. The party included his sons Francois and Louis-Joseph and consisted of twenty-five whites and men of mixed blood, and twenty-seven Indians. At first they followed a trail used by Indians to travel overland from the Missouri River to Lake Winnipeg and the start of the long canoe voyage to York Factory on Hudson Bay. At the site of today's town of Snowflake, Manitoba, their Indian guide swung west, past the north end of Turtle Mountain, across the Souris River and then southward into North Dakota. They crossed the Souris River again, this time a short distance above today's Minot.

Indian runners had arranged for a party of Mandans to come some distance from their villages to greet la Vérendrye. As the time for the rendezvous neared, the Indians heightened the anticipation of the Frenchmen by reminding them that the Mandans were white. When the meet was made, la Vérendrye saw that the Mandans were red men not noticeably different from the Assiniboines with whom he was traveling. At first he was alarmed, fearing he had been led deliberately into a trap deep in Indian country. He could perceive no signs of hostility, however, and concluded that it was simply another of the many inexplicable ways in which the Indians behaved. They had invented the story of a white tribe and when they noticed it excited the Frenchmen, they amplified it, never worrying that eventually they would be faced with the lie.

La Vérendrye's party had grown to almost a thousand people by the time it reached the main Mandan village on December 3,

1738. It had been a leisurely journey, their guide zigzagging through the country to pause at various villages on the way, moving when it suited him and at a pace he chose. It had occupied forty-two days when less than half that number should have sufficed.

The river of the Mandans had come to figure prominently in la Vérendrye's plans to execute the French government's orders to discover the Western Sea. He had been scheming for ten years to reach the river and now, at the Mandan village, he was less than a day's march away. Yet instead of hurrying to see it, he was content to send his son Louis-Joseph, accompanied by Mandan guides, to investigate it for him. Louis-Joseph reached the river — the Missouri — near the site of New Town, North Dakota, at a bend, as luck would have it, where the river flows for a short distance in a south-south westerly direction.[7] High bluffs at this point hid the view downstream and prevented Louis-Joseph from seeing that the river resumes its generally southeasterly course towards the Mississippi below the bend. When he asked the guides about the river's direction downstream, he deduced from their sign language that it swung even more to the west. Satisfied with this answer and his brief glimpse of the river, Louis-Joseph hurried back to his father with the news that this was indeed the "River of the West" and the road down to the Western Sea.

La Vérendrye had planned to spend the winter with the Mandans and to push on in the spring if the river looked to be navigable, but his instruments and the box of presents which he had brought to buy assistance from Indians along the way had been stolen. To make matters worse, his interpreter, smitten with the charms of a young Assiniboine girl, deserted when she refused to live out the winter in the village. La Vérendrye decided to go back to Fort la Reine and return when he was better prepared for the journey to the west. He left two of his men with the Mandans to learn their language and to familiarize themselves with the country.

The start of the trek back to the fort had to be delayed for a few days when la Vérendrye became violently ill. It was the middle of December before the party left the village and began crossing the open, snowswept prairie. They traveled slowly, stopping for days at a time to get some relief from the cold wind that seemed to blow continuously. La Vérendrye suffered — he was far from well — and it was February 10 before they reached the questionable comfort of Fort la Reine where he was able to rest and regain his health.

La Vérendrye learned, in the spring of 1739, that the Assiniboines were building canoes on Lake Manitoba to make the lengthy voyage to Hudson Bay with their furs. They had become discouraged with his inability to guarantee them supplies. His efforts to keep their trade were doomed to fail unless he could keep his posts stocked with an attractive variety of goods. He seemed always to be living on the edge of bankruptcy, encumbered by debts, in danger of having his furs seized by creditors, never sure of next season's supplies. He had to make do without financial support from the government which expected him to finance expeditions of discovery in return for the right to trade with the Indians. It was a circle of despair.

La Vérendrye made the long voyage east in 1740 to talk with his creditors and suppliers. He assured the governor he would undertake the expedition to the Western Sea, and pleaded for understanding of his difficulties and for time to best them. He was met in Montreal with the news that his wife had passed away in the previous year. There was more bad news in Quebec. The governor received him cordially enough but when la Vérendrye left Montreal for the Northwest in June, 1741, he went with a warning. If he came east again before he had made a serious attempt to reach far into the west, he would lose his trading rights and his sons would be recalled. He had a promise of supplies, however, but the transactions had left him deeply in debt.

La Vérendrye reached Fort la Reine in the middle of October to find that the two Frenchmen he had left with the Mandans had returned in September, 1739. They had been told that white men, probably Spanish, lived far to the southwest in brick houses in towns near a "great lake" whose water rose and fell and was not fit to drink. It was said the settlements could be reached in one summer's travel by going overland with horses.[8] Son Pierre had just returned from an attempt to follow up this two-year-old lead.

He had spent two months in a Mandan village waiting in vain for a suitable guide.[9]

Pierre must have visited the Mandans's river at this time and discovered that its course was generally southeast and not southwest as his brother Louis-Joseph had reported in 1738. If the la Vérendryes had come to realize that the river was the Missouri, they did not mention it in a report they sent to Beauharnois. In any case, the river was now discarded as a route to the Western Sea. The new plan was to go overland to investigate the story of the "great lake" near which white people were said to live. It was too late in the year, however, to mount an expedition; it would have to wait for the spring.

La Vérendrye now came to a decision that must have left him bitter with frustration. The Indians were restless again, the Cree and the Assiniboine preparing to attack the Sioux. If the skirmishes developed into war, his posts might be attacked and destroyed. He was more capable of preventing this than any other Frenchman at the frontier; in the eyes of the Indians, he represented the "White Father" and had their respect. It was important to the government to maintain the fur trading posts. As to the discovery of the Western Sea — it was of no consequence who made the journey as long as it was a Frenchman. La Vérendrye's course of action was obvious. He would stay to deal with the Indians and his sons would go and discover the secret of the Western Sea.

Expedition to the Western Sea, 1742-3

The expedition to the Western Sea was pitifully small, consisting of the la Vérendrye brothers, Louis-Joseph and Francois, and two voyageurs. They left Fort la Reine on April 29, 1742, traveling along what was now a familiar route and reaching the Mandan village twenty days later. They settled there to await the arrival of a band of Horse Indians who, the Mandans said, could guide them to their destination. They waited for more that two months. Late in July, the summer half gone, Louis-Joseph hired two Mandans to help him find the Horse Indians. The party of six crossed the Missouri and struck out over the prairie in a southwesterly direction.

125

They changed guides several times as the Indians lost interest in the mission or became apprehensive in country strange to them. They moved at a leisurely pace, as was the native way. In October they caught up with the Horse Indians, only to be told that none of the tribe had ever been to the great lake. They were informed that a band of Bow Indians was rumored to be friendly with tribes that traded with white men at the coast. Not very encouraged, Louis-Joseph continued towards the southwest and in November met up with the Bows. It was not a good time for the meeting as the Bows were preparing an expedition against the Shoshone Indians. Their chief said his warriors would be marching towards "the high mountains"[10] and the Frenchmen could accompany them. Although he spoke knowingly about white men at the coast, he had no direct knowledge of them. All his information was hearsay.

The war party, enlarged to two thousand warriors and their families by volunteers along the way, came in sight of the Big Horn Mountains in what is now Wyoming in January, 1743. The Bows informed Louis-Joseph that the great lake he wished to visit lay beyond these mountains. Later, in a report to Governor Beauharnois, Louis-Joseph wrote that he had "a strong desire to see the sea from the top of the mountains."[11] Little did he know that almost sixteen hundred kilometers (a thousand miles) of mountainous terrain lay between him and the Pacific Ocean which was the "great lake." He never got to the top of the Big Horn; there was a sudden alarm that the Shoshone were circling to the rear with the intent of capturing the baggage. The Bows began to retreat and Louis-Joseph did not dare go on without them.

The expedition now moved east, skirting the Black Hills on the north, intercepting a large river in South Dakota at an Indian village. The Frenchmen were told this was the Missouri River. A party, much reduced in size, took them north, following the river. The suspicion that this was the Mandans's river began to grow in the minds of the la Vérendrye brothers. It was confirmed when they reached the village where they had begun their journey to reach the Western Sea.

The la Vérendryes did not linger at the Missouri. They left the Mandan village in June and took the trail to the Assiniboine

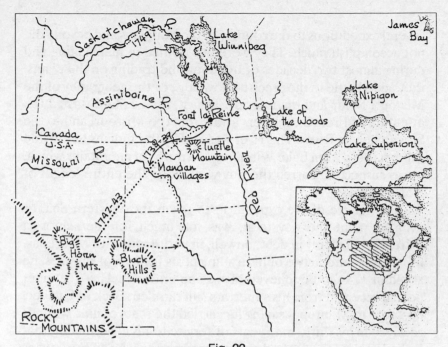

Fig. 22
The French thrust into the heart of North America in the middle of the
eighteenth century in search of the River of the West and the Western Sea;
the la Vérendrye journeys from Fort la Reine on the Assiniboine River.

River, reaching Fort la Reine on July 2, 1743. They had been
traveling fourteen months.

La Vérendrye's last years

The la Vérendryes had failed to reach the Western Sea but it
would be unkind to count this against them. Had Louis-Joseph
and his companions ascended the Missouri River, crossed the
Continental Divide and gained the Pacific — or had they gone
overland and reached the Spanish settlements in Mexico — the
journey would have ranked as a remarkable feat of exploration
and equivalent to the most noteworthy. They did succeed in
penetrating to the very center of the North American continent
and two of the sons were probably the first white Canadians to
see the Rocky Mountains from the interior. Otherwise, the

several expeditions to the country of the Mandans and beyond did not accomplish much. They were not trained in mapmaking and during almost two decades of traveling and trading on the plains, they added little to the precise knowledge of the geography of the Missouri River and the interior. In fact, their failure turned the attention of French explorers away from the Missouri and to the Saskatchewan River. This river was said by the Indians to provide a direct route from Lake Winnipeg to a range of mountains which, it was suspected, barred the way west along the entire length of North America.

The failure of the expedition to reach the Western Sea, or even to point the way to it, was too much for the senior la Vérendrye. Deeply in debt, unwell, in poor favor with Maurepas, forced to abandon two of his trading posts for lack of supplies, he asked in 1744 to be relieved of his appointment. The treatment he had received from his superiors still rankled. Back in Quebec, he wrote to Maurepas saying he carried the scars of nine wounds received in his thirty-nine years of service to his government; that he had pushed the fur trade west to places not seen by Europeans before he came into the Northwest; and that he had done it at no expense to the French government. He said he was poorer now than when he started his explorations and all he wanted for his efforts was to have them appreciated. Beauharnois wrote on his behalf, urging a commendation. Maurepas replied coldly, pointing to la Vérendrye's failures and accusing him of an old charge that he had been too interested in furthering his own causes to put sufficient time and energy into the search for the Western Sea, suggesting that he had not made an honest attempt to reach the sea.

Nicolas-Joseph de Noyelles, the man who succeeded to the post of commander in the Northwest, had no better success in exploring the west. Unless the explorer or one of his own people knew the language, he had to rely on an interpreter to communicate with the guide and the natives. Guides and interpreters were of limited value if the explorer was unable to control their behavior. If the party moved at the whim of the guide, the Indian habit of wandering from village to village soon had the timing, direction and even the purpose of the expedition in a shambles.

It came down to a battle of wills. To be successful, the explorer had to gain the upper hand and keep it; no mean accomplishment — la Vérendrye could not do it and nor could his successor. Noyelles resigned in 1746, two years after taking the commission. Despite his shortcomings, la Vérendrye was still the best qualified man to command the French effort in the Northwest. In 1747, Beauharnois sent him west again, this time with adequate supplies and a virtual monopoly of the French trade with the Indians.

Louis-Joseph continued to serve in the Northwest. In February, 1748, he was sent to discipline the Mohawks with a force of a dozen men, of whom half were Cree. He returned in March with two scalps which was proof of some kind of success. In 1749, he ascended the Saskatchewan River to its forks and there, at a gathering of Cree, he heard for the first time of a large body of salt water beyond the range of mountains in which the Saskatchewan had its source.

The elder la Vérendrye, back in Montreal for the 1749-50 winter, seized on Louis-Joseph's news and began planning an expedition up the Saskatchewan to reach the salt water. His fortunes had changed for the better after the king had dismissed Maurepas. He was accepted by the upper level of society of Montreal and enjoyed the social life he had missed during his years in the Northwest. He was over sixty but not too old to pursue a well-to-do widow, competing for her favors with another suitor. The lady eventually refused him, and his rival, deciding she wanted someone more amusing.

The plan for the expedition evolved into a two-year project — the senior la Vérendrye would ascend the Saskatchewan River to the mountains in 1750, build a fort there for residence through the winter, and in the spring set out in search of the salt water body. He never made the journey. He worked happily throughout the summer of 1749, arranging for supplies and men. Late in the year he was taken ill and he died on December 5. He was buried in Ste. Anne's chapel in the church of Notre Dame.

18

Alexander Mackenzie, First Man to Cross the North American Continent

Alexander Mackenzie

The Treaty of Utrecht, signed in 1713, had left the French with control of the Mississippi River and the adjoining lands. Their strength in this region was based in the scattered settlements, founded by colonists who began moving south from New France after Joliet and La Salle had traced the course of the Mississippi late in the seventeenth century. Inevitably, the lands on the eastern side of the river, adjacent to the English colonies, came into dispute. The English and French, differing in politics, religion, culture and language, could not occupy the same territory indefinitely without serious conflict. The quarrel over ownership erupted into open warfare in 1754, with French troops opposing the Virginian militia under George Washington. The objective was control of the rich Ohio River valley. Two years later, with the initiation of the Seven Years War (1756-63) in Europe, the fighting in North America evolved into a struggle between the French and British for mastery of the New World. If the French had plans to follow up on the la Vérendrye expeditions into the southwestern plains and up the Saskatchewan River in search of the "River of the West" and the Western Sea, they were shelved. There was more serious business at hand.

Wolfe's victory for England over the Frenchman Montcalm on the Plains of Abraham at Quebec in 1759 foreshadowed the final and decisive stages of the war in North America. The formal end of both the European and the colonial phases of the war came with the Treaty of Paris, signed in 1763. The British were heavy

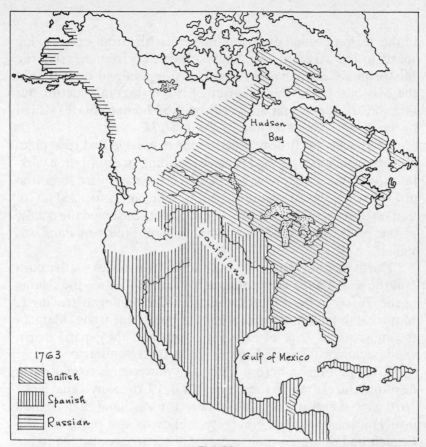

Fig. 23

European spheres of influence in North America following the Treaty of Paris, 1763 (after D. G. G. Kerr: *Historical Atlas of Canada*. Thomas Nelson & Sons (Canada) Ltd., 1975).

winners in North America at the expense of the French, who were forced to withdraw from virtually all of the mainland. The British failed to acquire Louisiana, a huge region loosely defined as the western part of the Mississippi River drainage basin. France had ceded it to Spain by secret treaty in the previous year to keep it out of British hands. The Mississippi River became the boundary between the Anglo-American colonies on the east and Louisiana.

Exploration in Louisiana, which included the Missouri River, was at the discretion of the Spanish. They had no great interest

131

in the region beyond discouraging Canadians from encroaching south to the Missouri and Anglo-Americans from crossing the Mississippi. Canadian and American trappers and traders used the Missouri in the third quarter of the eighteenth century but they did not venture far upriver from the Mandan villages visited by the la Vérendryes between 1738 and 1743.

Any ideas the British government may have had to supplement their victory over the French by sending an exploration party into Louisiana, either from the north or the east, were forgotten in 1775 when the American Revolution began. It focused attention on the east side of the Mississippi and it consumed the energy of the participants until 1783 when a new Treaty of Paris was signed.

North of Louisiana — in the Indian Territories — the push into the west gained momentum after 1763, following the signing of the Treaty of Paris. Merchants from Britain began arriving in Montreal in large numbers, attracted by the fur trade. Many of the newcomers were of Scottish origin and they, particularly, were peculiarly fascinated by the life in Indian country.

Like the French before them, the newcomers from Britain disputed the claim that the Hudson's Bay Company's charter of 1670 gave it exclusive trade rights to the vast land that drained into Hudson Bay. The company, believing the defeat of the French had rendered their monopoly secure, continued to expect the Indians to take their furs to the posts on Hudson Bay. It was an invitation to compete that the "Pedlars from Montreal," as the traders from the lower St. Lawrence River were contemptuously dubbed, could no more resist than had the French. They moved into the Northwest, challenging the old company in the region west of Lake Winnipeg, and established themselves on the main waterways, intent on intercepting furs bound for the Bay.

To counter the competition, the Hudson's Bay Company's Samuel Hearne built a trading post — Cumberland House — on the Saskatchewan River near the present Manitoba-Saskatchewan border in 1774. The next year, however, thirty canoes manned by well over a hundred men arrived from Montreal to trade near the House.

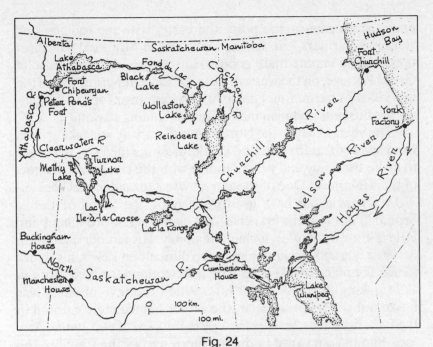

Fig. 24

The "Crosse Road" between Hudson Bay and Lake Athabasca. Note that
Wollaston Lake is drained by the Cochrane River to the east and by the
Fond du Lac River to the west.

In 1776, Joseph and Thomas Frobisher ascended the Stur-
geon-weir River, crossed Frog Portage to the Churchill River and
began intercepting furs bound for Fort Churchill on Hudson Bay.
The old company's stranglehold on trade in the Northwest had
been broken in little more than a decade following the French
withdrawal from the mainland.

The traders from Montreal were originally banded into small
partnerships, competing with one another as well as with the
Hudson's Bay Company. It soon became evident that this resulted
in raising the price of furs. The venture could be more profitable for
everyone (except the natives) if the partnerships worked out an
agreement to pool the costs and divide the trade among themselves.
The first loose arrangement, in 1779, of several independents
evolved within five years into the North West Company headed
by Simon McTavish. He devised an organization of "wintering

133

partners" to manage the posts and barter with the Indians, and "business partners," or agents, stationed in Montreal to export the furs and import trade goods. He set up a clearing house at Grand Portage, on the western shore of Lake Superior, where the two kinds of partner met each July to exchange furs and goods, discuss business and plan tactics for the coming season.[1]

The years in which the North West Company was taking form were heady times for bold and adventuresome men — men eager to make their way and willing to live with the rigors and dangers of the wilderness. One of these men was Alexander Mackenzie.

Mackenzie was born in Stornoway on the island of Lewis, Scotland, in 1764. His branch of the clan was not prominent and little is known about his immediate family. His mother died when he was a boy and because times were difficult on Lewis, his father joined the many Mackenzies who left Scotland for New York in 1774, taking Alexander with him. When the revolutionary war broke out the following year, the father immediately enlisted in the Royalist forces, leaving the boy in the care of two aunts. They took him to Johnstown in the northern part of the state but the continuing hostilities induced them to send Alexander to Montreal in 1778, where he began to attend school. The following year, at the age of fifteen, he left school and began working in the office of the fur trading firm of Finlay & Gregory. It was one of the small partnerships that provided the early competition for the Hudson's Bay Company west of Lake Winnipeg.

Mackenzie was now at the hub of the business activity of the Pedlars from Montreal and his imagination was excited by the rapid expansion of the trade. In 1784, when he was only twenty, he decided to make use of the business experience he had gained and strike out on his own. Staked to a quantity of trade goods by Finlay & Gregory, he headed for Detroit, then the shipping center of the fur trade south of the Great Lakes. It was a poor choice. By the Treaty of Paris, this territory had been awarded to the new United States in the previous year and it soon became evident to British traders that they were not wanted there. When Mackenzie arrived in 1784, they had already begun moving out and into the Northwest, lured by stories of the rich returns to be won west of Lake Winnipeg.

Young Mackenzie had evidently made a good impression on his former employers, for Gregory immediately offered him a share in a new firm — Gregory & McLeod — if he would go into Indian country. Mackenzie was willing and left Detroit for Lake Superior to join his new associates at Grand Portage.

Peter Pond

The push into the unknown territory of the Northwest spawned an outstanding explorer who had a profound effect on Alexander Mackenzie. Peter Pond, born in Connecticut in 1740, had served with the British forces against the French. He was trading with the Indians along the Mississippi River when the American Revolution began. He had had his fill of war and to avoid becoming involved, he moved north and began trading around Cumberland House in the fall of 1775. In 1778 he was induced by his business associates to head an expedition into Athabasca, "a country hitherto unknown from Indian report."[2] He followed the route pioneered by the Frobishers to reach the Churchill River and moved upstream (west) through Lac Ile-à-la-Crosse and Methy Lake. He used the Methy Portage to cross into the Arctic drainage basin and came to the Clearwater River. He followed it downstream to discover the Athabasca River and descended it into Lake Athabasca. His route, from Lake Winnipeg to Athabsca, became known as the Crosse Road. Pond built a fort on the Athabasca River about 65 km. (40 mi.) south of the lake and began trading. He obtained so many furs he had to store half of them for want of enough transportation back to the Saskatchewan valley.

Pond may have been tired of war but he was not above engaging in private battles. He was a belligerent, quarrelsome, quick-tempered man and dangerous as an enemy. He did not take kindly to competition. In the winter of 1781-2, while representing the North West Company in Lac la Ronge, he got into a fight with one Etienne Wadin, trading for another partnership; Wadin was fatally wounded.

The independent firm of Gregory & McLeod, in which Mackenzie had a share, undertook to compete head on with the rising North West Company. In the fall of 1785, Mackenzie, barely twenty-one and with no bush experience, was put in charge at Ile-à-la-Crosse and another shareholder, John Ross, was sent into Athabasca to oppose Peter Pond. The upstart partnership was quite successful and the arrangements were repeated in the winter of 1786-7, but Pond's temper got the better of him and he quarreled with Ross. Ross was shot and died of the wound. The news, carried to Grand Portage in the spring, shocked the various partners. The incident provided more proof that too much competition was not in their best interests. It precipitated a broadening of the North West Company and the surviving members of Gregory & McLeod were taken into the company. Mackenzie, now a Nor'Wester like Pond, was sent into Athabasca to work with the forty-seven-year-old Pond and the two men spent the winter of 1787-8 at Pond's fort.

Bellicose and difficult though he was to deal with, Pond was a tireless and dedicated explorer. He had no knowledge of surveying instruments or methods, but he had an inquiring mind and was skillful at extracting geographical information from the Indians. When Captain James Cook's map of the west coast was published in 1781, he studied it for clues to the courses of large rivers known to exist west of Lake Athabasca. He combined all the information with his own limited and unscientific observations in the Northwest and began constructing maps of the territory between Hudson Bay and the Rockies. The earliest version, made public in 1785, correctly showed Lake Athabasca and Great Slave Lake draining north along a large river to an ocean he called the "Ice Sea" (the Arctic).

Pond produced another version of his map in the summer of 1787 — in the year Mackenzie joined him in Athabasca — this time making a radically different interpretation of the drainage pattern in the Athabasca region. He showed a very large river flowing west out of Great Slave Lake into a blank area of the map (representing unexplored country) which separated it from a river he called Cook's River flowing southwest into the Pacific Ocean in Alaska. His map left the impression that exploration of the blank area would reveal that they were two ends of the same river — that is, that Great Slave Lake drained into the Pacific Ocean by way of his Cook's River. In fact Cook's River — actually Cook Inlet — is an arm of the Pacific Ocean and not the estuary of a great river as Pond chose to portray it.

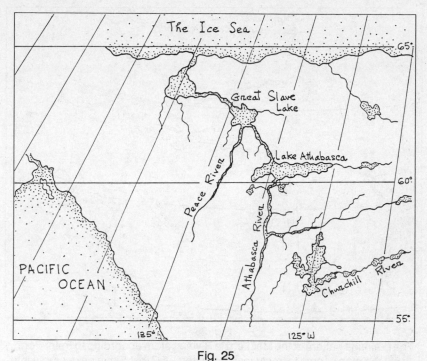

Fig. 25

The Mackenzie River basin correctly shown draining into the Arctic Ocean by Peter Pond, 1785; Lake Athabasca is about 20 degrees of longitude too far to the west (modified; from Henry R. Wagner: *Peter Pond, Fur Trader & Explorer.* Yale University Library, 1955; original map is in the Public Record Office, London).

A major error in all of Pond's maps lay in his positioning of the lakes — he located them too close to the Pacific by about twenty degrees of longitude (about a thousand kilometers or six hundred miles at this latitude). He was certain Lake Athabasca was within six days' travel of the Pacific.

Pond had a marked effect on Mackenzie — the young man undertook his voyages to discover the Western Sea as a direct consequence of his winter with Pond and his maps. He was influenced by the 1787 map to follow the river that flows out of the western end of Great Slave Lake, thinking it was Cook's River and expecting it to take him to the Pacific Ocean.

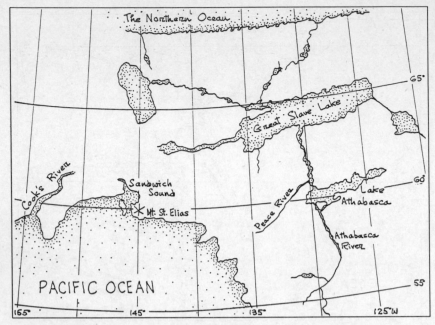

Fig. 26
The drainage pattern of the Mackenzie River system according to Peter Pond, 1787; the map seems to imply that the waters of Great Slave Lake empty into the Pacific Ocean at Cook Inlet (modified; from Henry R. Wagner: *Peter Pond, Fur Trader and Explorer,* Yale University Library, 1955; a copy of Pond's map is in the National Archives of Canada, Ottawa).

The association formed during the 1787-8 winter was shortlived — Pond's value as a fur trader was so diminished by the deaths of Wadin and Ross that he left Athabasca in the spring of 1788 and never returned.

The voyage that started for the Pacific Ocean
but reached the Arctic, 1789

The title of Mackenzie's journal of his voyage to the Arctic included the claim that it was "performed by Order of the N. W. Company"[3] but there is no record of these orders. He was very secretive about his plans. On his way back from visiting his cousin, Roderic Mackenzie, at Ile-à-la-Crosse in January, 1788, he sent a plea to Roderic to "not reveal [my intentions] to any person."[4] Letters

138

he wrote to agents of the company only days before he set out stated he intended "to pass [into Great Slave Lake] on my voyage for a supply of provisions."[5] This mild deception and the secrecy of his preparations suggest that Mackenzie believed it would be a short and routine journey to the Pacific and back.

Mackenzie set out from Fort Chipewyan (a new post on the south shore of Lake Athabasca, 13 km. (8 mi.) east of the mouth of the Athabasca River) on June 3, 1789, with four Canadian voyageurs, a young German and several Indian men and women who were to act as interpreters, hunters, guides and retainers. He carried gifts to ensure a friendly reception but made certain his men were well armed in case they had to defend themselves.

They entered the river shown draining west out of Great Slave Lake in Pond's 1787 map (the Mackenzie River) on June 29 and began its descent. Mackenzie's Indians had no illusions about a quick journey to the sea and back. On July 1 when he cached two bags of pemmican for their return to the fort, they informed him they had no expectations about backtracking there that season. They were already complaining about the pace he set, being used to a more leisurely type of travel. By July 5 they were advising him to turn back, that the journey was too lengthy and the scarcity of game would cause them all to starve. Young Mackenzie, buoyed by his voyageurs who declared themselves ready to go wherever he chose to lead them, would not be deterred. To get him to change his mind, the guides and interpreters professed a complete ignorance of the country. Mackenzie began using local natives as guides, when they declined to continue or deserted, he compelled natives further downstream to take their places.[6]

It is not clear when he first knew he was not bound for the Pacific. After flowing in a generally westerly direction for about 250 km. (150 mi.), the river had turned abruptly northwest and to his chagrin, held that bearing. On July 10, he recorded in his journal that it was "evident these waters emptied themselves into the Hyperborean Sea."[7] The realization must have been a blow.

Early in July, the river a maze of shallow water passages flowing around numerous low islands covered with ice, it was impossible to know which channel was the best route to the sea.

They camped on July 13 beside what seemed to be a large lake. A fog hindered their vision but they thought the water was covered with winter ice which had not yet floated out to sea. From a high point nearby, Mackenzie observed that the way ahead appeared to be blocked by solid ice. He concluded it was time to turn for home. They were in latitude 69°N.

During the night of July 13, Mackenzie and his people had to get up from their beds and move the baggage because the river had risen. They thought it was due to the wind. They began the ascent of the river in the morning. Two nights later the river wet their baggage again and they knew the change in water level was caused by the tide. They felt a sense of disappointment that they had been close to the ocean but unable to quite attain their goal. In fact, they had reached the southeast shore of Garry Island which is well into the Arctic Ocean.

Mackenzie's voyage of almost 5,000 km. (3,000 mi.) to the Arctic Ocean and back to Fort Chipewyan in 102 days ranks as one of the great feats of exploration in the Canadian Northwest. It is all the more remarkable for the fact that he was only twenty-five years old, with barely four years of experience in the interior. Nothing in his background had prepared him for this venture.

His journal gives no cause to think Mackenzie was motivated to make the voyage by a need to satisfy an appetite for excitement or adventure. He made it to promote the fur trade for his company. He already perceived that the economic well-being of the traders from Montreal depended on finding a seaport to service the Northwest; Montreal was too far away and the ports on Hudson Bay were barred to them. When he set out from Fort Chipewyan in June, Mackenzie thought he was on a "River of the West" (although not the fabled one Aguilar had discovered in 1603) and he must have hoped he would discover useful harbors on the coast. We can speculate that he expected to reach the Pacific on the imaginary stream Pond had called Cook's River. It turned out he was on a "River of the North" and although the newly explored country held the potential for trade, he was inclined to regard the voyage as something of a failure.

Mackenzie went down to Grand Portage in July, 1790, for the annual meeting of wintering partners and agents. The news of his trip to the Arctic seemed to cause little stir but a new partnership agreement was drawn up at that meeting and it gave two of the twenty shares of the North West Company to Mackenzie; previously he had held one. Apparently the Nor' Westers recognized the young Scot's potential.

Preparations for a second attempt to find the Pacific Ocean, 1792

Mackenzie charted the course of the river that took him to the Arctic by dead reckoning — that is, he measured changes in direction with a compass and estimated the distance between compass readings. He made numerous determinations of latitude along the way, using them to correct the north-south dimension of his map, but he made no observations for longitude, depending instead on his compass bearings for the east-west dimension.

Mackenzie found latitude by observing the altitude of the sun when his watch registered noon. He corrected his compass readings for magnetic declination by comparing the direction of his shadow at this reading of noon with the direction of north given by the compass. Both procedures depend, for accuracy, on taking the readings at the moment of solar noon which changes continuously as the observer moves east or west. His watch was set for Fort Chipewyan time and he did not adjust the setting to keep it on solar time during the voyage, either from ignorance of the need to make adjustments or an unwillingness to spend the time for the necessary celestial observations.

Despite the crude methods, Mackenzie's map of the river is easily recognizable as the course of the Mackenzie River. On average, the position of any point on the map is within 35 km. (22 mi.) of its true location.

Mackenzie met the Hudson's Bay Company's chief surveyor, Philip Turnor, in 1790 and talked with him about the Arctic voyage. Turnor was left with the impression Mackenzie did not know exactly where he had been but he may have been dissembling to this representative of a rival company. Still, the meeting revealed to him his shortcomings in the field of mapmaking and he knew now that he must acquire knowledge of surveying before making another attempt to find the Pacific Ocean. To improve his competence, he spent the 1791-2 winter in England, buying instruments and taking instruction in their use. Even so, he came back to Canada with fewer and more inferior instruments than were desirable for an expedition of discovery. His kit, when he set out the second time, consisted of a compass apparently not refined enough to permit him to read directions in degrees (he recorded directions as WNW), a sextant whose range of measurement was insufficient to read the altitude of the midday sun in summer, a chronometer and a telescope.

On the way to the Arctic, Mackenzie questioned the natives about the source of rivers flowing in from the west. He learned that they rose in the mountains (the Rocky Mountains) that ranged, as far as his informants knew, in a continuous line from the northwest to the southeast.[8] It confirmed what Father Charlevoix had discovered in 1721 — that a range of mountains barred the way to the Sea. Mackenzie had been forced to conclude that there was no river down which he could float to the Pacific Ocean from Fort Chipewyan. He would have to ascend some river, cross at least one range of mountains and then search for the "River of the West" to carry him down to the Pacific. It would be a longer and more arduous voyage than he and Pond ever visualized when they pored over Pond's maps in the winter of 1787-8.

Mackenzie chose to ascend the Peace River to reach mountains. Nor' Westers from eastern Canada had arrived on the Peace in 1786. Their most westerly post on the river — McLeod's Fort, opened in 1790 — lay about 600 km. (380 mi.) upstream from its confluence with the Snake River. They had explored the river above McLeod's Fort to its junction with the Smoky River and perhaps beyond. The Peace was better known to the Nor' Westers than any of the other rivers flowing east from the Rockies.

Mackenzie had a reasonable idea of the distance to the Pacific coast. Philip Turnor had determined the longitude at Fort Chipewyan to be 110 1/2°W. Captain Cook's map gave the longitude at the coast, in the same latitude as the fort (about 59°N), as 142 1/2°W. The thirty-two degrees difference in longitude represents a distance of about 1,800 km. (1,100 mi.) from Fort Chipewyan to the coast, as the crow flies.

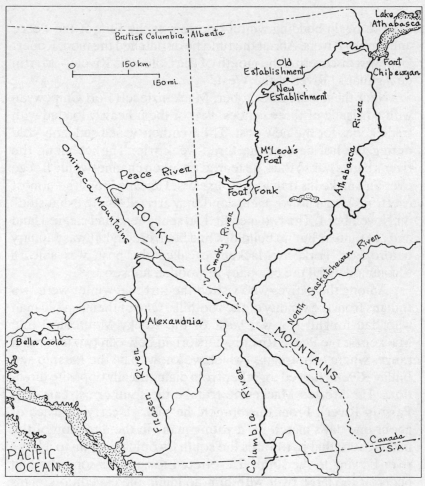

Fig. 27
Alexander Mackenzie's route from Lake Athabasca to the Pacific Ocean, 1793.

Of course, Mackenzie had no illusions about traveling in a straight line. It was only logical to believe he would need to search north and south, after he crossed the mountains, for a passage down to the coast. The journey would be longer than 1,800 km. (1,100 mi.) and to give himself a chance to reach the coast and return in one season, he decided he must winter some distance up the Peace. To this end, he sent two men upriver in the spring of

1792 to begin building winter quarters at the fork of the Peace and Smoky Rivers. About the time he dispatched the men, Robert Gray was discovering the mouth of the Columbia River — Martin de Aguilar's "River of the West."

Near the middle of October, Mackenzie left Fort Chipewyan with a brigade of three canoes, two of them heavily loaded with trade goods for the new post. The weather turned suddenly cold during the last days of the three-week trip. The ice along the river's banks was so thick he feared the open channel would freeze over and make his fragile craft useless. He called for "the utmost exertions" from his voyageurs and they arrived "quite exhausted" on November 1. The two men he had sent ahead had cleared land and cut timbers but no buildings had been erected. It was January before Fort Fork, as Mackenzie called the post, was able to accommodate all the company in wooden houses.

Among the natives who visited the fort that winter were two Indians from the vicinity of the foothills. One of them, an old man who had fought in a war west of the Rocky Mountains, told Mackenzie the Peace River had its origin between two mountain ranges where two streams (which we know to be the Parsnip and Finlay Rivers) flowed together from diametrically opposite directions. He directed Mackenzie to take the southern stream (the Parsnip River). From this branch, he said, "a carrying place of about one day's march for a young man" in the direction of the midday sun (that is, towards the south), would take him to a large river flowing to the south. He offered to send his son, who had been on the large river with him, to guide the expedition.[9] This was the most promising information Mackenzie had gleaned from all his questioning; if the large river flowed towards the south, it might well be the "River of the West."

Mackenzie adjusted his chronometer to Fort Fork solar time and he checked the accuracy of the timepiece by repeating the procedure at various times throughout the winter, finding that it ran slow by twenty-two seconds in twenty-four hours. He made several observations of Jupiter's moons to obtain Greenwich time and he compared the time with Fort Fork solar time to find the longitude of the post. He deduced latitude from the altitude of the sun at local noon. He settled on a value of 56°09'N for the

144

latitude and 117°35'15"W for the longitude.[10] Modern surveys locate the fork of the Peace and Smoky Rivers (8-10 km. or 5-6 mi. east of the fort) at 56°11'N, 117°19'W.

Captain James Cook's map of the west coast showed a longitude of about 139°W at the latitude of Fort Fork. The 21 1/2 degrees difference in longitude between coast and fort represented a distance of about 1,350 km. (about 850 mi.) at this latitude. An entry in Mackenzie's journal suggests that the sudden winter thaws at the fort brought on by chinook winds had convinced him the Cook map was in error. He thought the Pacific Ocean was influencing the weather and therefore the coast was much closer than 1,350 km. (850 mi.).[11] In fact Cook's map was in error by seven or eight degrees of longitude at the latitude of the fort; the distance to the coast was more like 900 km. (550 mi.).

The winter finally broke on March 16 when the wind blew steadily from the southwest. Soon the sight and sound of geese flying north was common and on April 1, hunters shot five. By April 5, all the snow had disappeared and two weeks later, the trees were in bud and many kinds of plants bloomed; and the mosquitoes were out in force.

The early part of April was occupied in bartering with the Indians for their winter's catch of furs. It had been a successful year of trading, requiring fully six canoes to carry the furs east. Mackenzie dispatched them on May 8, soon after the river cleared of ice, with letters and accounts for his partners who would be meeting at Grand Portage in July.

Mackenzie had experienced little difficulty in persuading whites to accompany him in the coming search for the Pacific Ocean and he took seven volunteers for the enterprise. It was a different matter with the Indians. The young man who had been sent by his father to guide the party to the large river that lay towards the midday sun, deserted, easily persuaded to leave by another Indian whom Mackenzie had refused to hire.[12] In general, the Indians had no stomach for the unknown. They readily agreed to go with him but at the least provocation they just as readily changed their minds. Mackenzie remarked in a letter to his cousin Roderic: "none of them like the voyage [and] . . . without Indians I have very little hopes of succeeding."[13] He

145

needed them as interpreters as well as guides, to question the natives they would meet concerning the geography of the country that lay west of the foothills.

On May 9, 1793, all was ready and the canoe was put in the water.

> Her dimensions were twenty-five feet long within, exclusive of the curves of stem and stern, twenty six inches hold, and four feet nine inches beam. At the same time she was so light, that two men could carry her on a good road three or four miles without resting. In this slender vessel, we shipped provisions, goods for presents, arms, ammunition, and baggage, to the weight of three thousand pounds, and an equippage of ten people [and a large dog].[14]

Up the Peace River, May 9 - 31, 1793[15]

Mackenzie had the canoe on the river at 3:15 A.M. on May 9. There was a nip in the air but the weather was clear and the scenery as beautiful as any he had seen. The valley of the river was a broad plain dotted with groves of trees and vast herds of buffalo grazed within sight of the canoe. Away from the river, the land rose to uplands on which numerous elk fed, and beyond them on the horizon, rocky precipices thrust into the sky. The grass was freshening in the spring air and the trees were in bud, displaying "an exuberant verdure" and the men's spirits rose.

They spent the second night on an island where they were visited by numerous natives. Most were Rocky Mountain Indians and Mackenzie questioned them about the country that lay beyond the first range of mountains. They expressed total ignorance but they were certain the strength of the river's current and its rapids would prevent him from getting there by water. Mackenzie asked after the old man who had told him, back at Fort Fork, about the large river towards the midday sun, but the Indians said he had not been seen for "upwards of a moon." It was clear to Mackenzie that he would have to depend on the guides he had engaged at the fort. They were quite uninformed about what lay ahead but at least they could converse with the natives that lived in the mountains. Mackenzie concluded privately that if they deserted, it would be fruitless to go on.

146

On May 15, they came to a point on the river where it cut through a high ridge of land running across their course. It was the first definite sign of the foothills. Next day they passed through another ridge. Yet all about them they could see plains on which great herds of elk and buffalo fed, apparently unmolested by hunters. Mackenzie noted that "the country is so crowded with animals as to have the appearance, in some places, of a stallyard, from the state of the ground, and the quantity of dung which is scattered over it."[16]

In the afternoon of May 17 the Rocky Mountains came into view, their summits covered with snow. Mackenzie and his men were agreeably surprised at the sight for it was only four days since they had left an Indian encampment where they had been told it would take ten days to reach the mountains. Twice on May 18 they ran onto obstructions in the water and tore the bottom of the canoe. Stretches of rapid water became more frequent and in some the current was so swift they could not make headway against it. They found slack water alongside the shore but often it put them in danger from large boulders which, loosened by rain, rolled down the steep banks and into the river.

Soon after they embarked on May 19, they encountered a current so strong Mackenzie took to the shore with several men and the dog to lighten the canoe. They climbed the river bank to reconnoiter but very soon they heard the sound of two shots — the signal to return to the river. Mackenzie found his voyageurs at the foot of a steep rapid leading up to a series of waterfalls. They had been warned to expect a long succession of rapids and falls on the eastern fringe of the mountains and the voyageurs were wary. They did not like the look of the river and wanted to fall back to a trail they had passed thinking, rightly, it was the start of a portage around this stretch of fast water.

Mackenzie had been over many waterways declared impassable by natives and he decided to ignore the warning, lulled perhaps, by the easy going from Fort Fork. The expedition almost foundered on his resolve to defy the river. They had arrived at the lower end of the Peace River Canyon, which has the form of a U-shaped curve about 15 km. (9 mi.) in width at the open end, winding around the south side of Portage Mountain. The waters of the Peace River, fed by melting snow, poured violently through this canyon in a rapid descent from the Rocky Mountains.

At Mackenzie's insistence, the men continued up the river, moving from one side to the other to avoid the most turbulent water. They could make little headway with the paddles and had to resort to towing or poling as the river dictated. Several times they were on the edge of disaster — in danger of losing canoe, equipment and firearms. Late in the afternoon of the second day, with the river above them a white sheet of foam flowing between walls of rock barely 50 m. (160 ft.) apart, Mackenzie called a halt. The men had had enough of the river and were muttering about turning back. Mackenzie refused to consider this but he had the weary men carry the battered canoe up the river bank and they rested there. He occupied them next day with small tasks — patching and gumming the canoe, making new ax handles, carrying up the baggage — and he sent scouts ahead to reconnoiter the river. They reported back that the rapids ended about 15 km. (9 mi.) distant; although wearing, they could cut a trail across the top of the mountain and carry everything to calm water. They had a tot of rum, ate a kettle of rice sweetened with sugar for their supper, and went to bed with their spirits renewed.

It took three days to cut the trail and complete the portage. They came to the river a hundred meters (three hundred feet) above the uppermost rapids of the canyon (at the future site of the W. A. C. Bennett Dam) at 4:00 P.M. on May 24. They stood for a time and gazed downstream, contemplating the river pouring out of the Rocky Mountains, thinking perhaps, the river was misnamed. Mackenzie recorded the sight in his journal:

> the stream rushed with an astonishing but silent velocity, between perpendicular rocks, which are not more than thirty-five yards asunder. [Below this] the channel widens in a kind of zig-zag progression; and it was really awful to behold with what infinite force the water drives against the rocks on one side, and with what impetuous strength it is repelled to the other.[17]

They had spent five days getting past the canyon and the work of doing it had been hard and frustrating. Before they left the river for the portage, men and equipment had been at risk and severely tested. They had come through the experience relatively unmarked and Mackenzie knew he had been fortunate. One wonders, in retrospect, why he did not investigate the trail his voyageurs had seen below the canyon, and attempt to discover how the local Indians dealt with the river. He learned later that the trail was a 20 km. (12.5 mi.) portage used by the natives to get around the north side of the mountain and avoid the canyon. The present highway between the town of Hudson's Hope and the W. A. C. Bennett Dam occupies, roughly, the course of the portage.

The river above the canyon was broad, interrupted by minor rapids and small falls, but they were always able to pass around hazardous parts. At noon on May 31, they came to a fork in the river, one branch coming in from the southeast (the Parsnip), the other (the Finlay) from the northwest — both flowing alongside a range of mountains (the Omineca Mountains). Mackenzie was inclined to take the northwest branch. The Peace River had carried them about four degrees of latitude south of Cook's River which, it appeared from Cook's map, offered the shortest route to the Pacific Ocean. The southeast branch would take them even farther south, as well as east and away from the coast. The old man back at Fort Fork had directed him to take the southeast branch saying it would lead to a portage "not exceeding a day's march" from a large river. Rivers on this side of the mountains should flow to the sea. The old warrior's description of the Peace River had proved to be accurate and Mackenzie felt he had no option but to accept his advice. Accordingly, he directed his steerman to turn up the Parsnip River.

Across the Continental Divide to the Fraser River, May 31 - June 18[18]

The Finlay and Parsnip Rivers flow along the Rocky Mountain Trench, a well-defined valley between the Rocky Mountains and the mountain ranges immediately west of them. The valley runs the full length of British Columbia and is broad and flat in the country through which Mackenzie was now traveling. It was overrun with beaver when he passed that way in 1793. The animals had dammed the river, causing it to flood and create numerous and confusing channelways. The water was high at this time of year and rising. In places the current was too swift for the paddles and the water too deep for the poles. Often the shore was so thickly lined with willows that they could not carry a line to tow the canoe. Then the men were forced to haul themselves and the canoe upstream, hand over hand from one willow branch to the next. When they found an open spot to land for the night, the ground was damp and uncomfortable. It rained frequently and heavily — everything and everyone was continually wet.

The condition of the canoe deteriorated steadily. The frequent patching over patches, and gumming, had made it heavy and unwieldy. The men became discouraged. Mackenzie dealt kindly with them and was sympathetic, and he comforted them at night with a "consolatory dram."

It was difficult to gain a notion of the geography of the region from the river; sometimes they could not even see the Rocky Mountains. Not surprisingly, in the heavily wooded valley, they passed by the entrance to the Pack River on their right without seeing it. The Pack River connects the Crooked River chain of lakes and rivers with the Parsnip. Summit Lake, at the head of the chain, is separated from the Fraser River by a portage of 15 km. (9 mi.) across the Continental Divide. This portage was evidently the "carrying place of about one day's march" the old man had directed Mackenzie to take to reach the large river that flowed to the south. He had neglected to say that the road to it lay up the small Pack River so Mackenzie was not watching for the entrance.

After a week on the Parsnip they were becoming concerned because they had not come to the carrying place and they had seen no native people of whom they could ask guidance. Mackenzie considered undertaking probes of two or three days' march to search for another river but decided in the end to stay on the Parsnip as long as it was navigable. On June 9, ten days after they left the Peace, they finally came upon some natives. First there was the smell of campfires on the heavy mist that blanketed the river that morning following rain in the night. Then they heard the noise of people in a state of great agitation as they fled at sight of the white strangers.

150

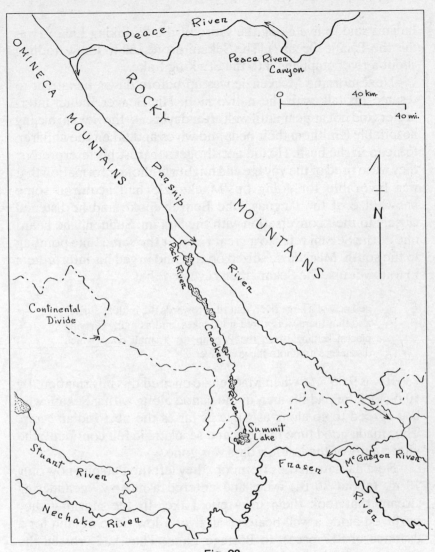

Fig. 28
Alexander Mackenzie's route from the Peace to the Fraser River.

It was late afternoon by the time Mackenzie had coaxed all the Indians — three men, three women and seven or eight children — back to their camp. They were Sekani Indians and they had a few iron tools and vessels, obtained by trade from Carrier Indians who lived to the west and who, in turn, had got them from

Indians said to live along the shore of the "Stinking Lake" (was this the Pacific Ocean?). The Sekani professed to know nothing about a river emptying into the Stinking Lake.

Next morning Mackenzie was up before dawn, impatient to resume his talk with the native men. His Beaver Indian interpreters did not appear until well after daybreak, the Sekani having hospitably lent them their beds and wives and taken the children to sleep in the bush. He did not altogether trust his interpreters; they were tired of the voyage and might withhold information that was favorable for going on. Mackenzie had acquired some knowledge of the language the Beaver spoke and he listened closely to their conversation with the Sekani. Suddenly he heard one of the Sekani refer to a great river, at the same time pointing to the south. Mackenzie seized on this and urged his interpreters to follow it up. The Sekani then revealed that

> he knew of a large river, that runs towards the midday sun . . . and that there were three small lakes, and as many carrying places, leading [from the Parsnip] to a small river, which discharges itself into the great river.[19]

It was 9:00 A.M. when Mackenzie elicited this information. By 10 o'clock he had his men in the canoe along with a Sekani who had agreed to go along as guide as far as the next Indian camp. They made good time that day and Mackenzie felt confident; the uncertainty of the last few days was gone.

Next day late in the afternoon, they left the Parsnip, now only 10 m. (about 30 ft.) wide, and entered a narrow, meandering stream that took them to Arctic Lake. In the morning they portaged along a well-beaten trail over a low ridge of land for a distance of 817 paces, to Portage Lake. They had crossed the Continental Divide between two vast watersheds — from the Mackenzie River system which drains into the Arctic Ocean, to the great Fraser River complex which empties into the Pacific Ocean. A small stream carried them out of Portage Lake to Pacific Lake. They were going with the current for the first time since they had started up the Peace River.

They crossed Pacific Lake and forced their way past its shallow exit, choked with fallen trees, into James Creek. It was

152

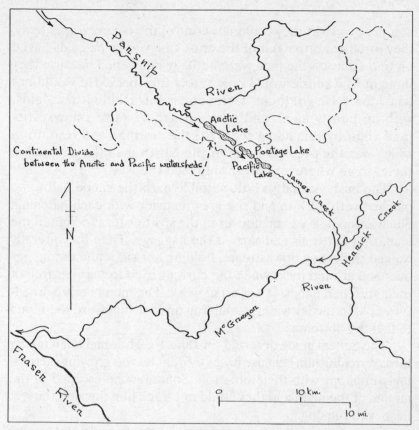

Fig. 29
The route of Alexander Mackenzie's journey from the Parsnip River,
across the Continental Divide, to the Fraser River.

normally a small stream but at this time of year it was fed by
numerous rivulets of melting snow that cascaded down the rugged
sides of its valley. Fallen trees continued to hamper their progress;
often it was necessary to cut a passage through the debris, standing
in icy water to swing the axes. Still, at 5:00 P.M. they entered a
place where the creek widened into a small lake; they had covered
almost 10 km. (6 mi.) of the 15 km. (9 mi.) length of James Creek.

The journey down the remaining 5 km. (3 mi.) proved to be a
nightmare that lasted five days. The creek, narrow and shallow,
its rocky bed littered with fallen trees and boulders, rushed down

153

at a pace so swift they could not control the canoe. Repeatedly, they tore the bottom out of the craft. She was so badly damaged on one occasion the men were actually heartened because they thought Mackenzie would now surely turn back. He would not consider it. He got them "warm and comfortable [that night], with an hearty meal, and rum enough to raise their spirits [and then by reminding them of] the courage and resolution which was the peculiar boast of the North men [he persuaded them] to go wherever [he] should lead the way."[20]

The bush yielded so little suitable bark the canoe had to be patched with oilcloth and she grew heavier with each patching. She was too heavy to maneuver in the swift water. To lighten the load, they cut trails and carried the baggage. Then they literally walked the canoe downstream, holding her sides and easing her over and around rocks while the current tried to tear her free of their stiffened hands. It was cruel work. The men became dreadfully cold in the icy water, stumbling on feet that were too numb to feel the bottom.

The Sekani guide deserted on June 16. They had been taking turns watching him because it was evident he was growing increasingly unhappy with their situation. Somehow he escaped in the middle of the night and they could not track him through the wet bush with the dog.

In the morning they resumed their labors, forced now to move alternately by land and water. At noon they came to a part of the river where it degenerated into numerous small branches, none of which would float the canoe. It was time to leave the river; they began cutting a road across a neck of land — the shortest distance to the large river they knew lay close below them. At 8:00 P.M. they reached the the bank of Herrick Creek. They were finally headed downstream on a large, easily navigable river west of the Rocky Mountains. They had breached the first great barrier to the Pacific Ocean.

On the Fraser River, June 18 - July 4[21]

The mist lay heavy on Herrick Creek when they embarked next morning but they could discern that the river was about 200 m.

154

(about 660 ft.) wide. They passed imperceptibly in the haze into McGregor River and soon they came to its junction with the Fraser River — three-quarters of a kilometer (half a mile) wide here and flowing sluggishly to the northwest. It was so broad it looked like a lake to them. They rounded the "horn" of the river and now it flowed almost directly south. They could see columns of smoke, presumably from cooking fires, rising from many parts of the bush as they eased along.

The canoe was so weak she sagged and broke under her own weight as the men carried her around Fort George Canyon. Back on the river after repairing her, they passed the mouth of the West Road River and came to Cottonwood Canyon where the river narrowed and flowed violently down rapids between steep rock walls. They portaged their goods to the foot of the canyon but the canoe was too heavy; the men preferred to take their chances on the river and run her through the rapids. They got her down without ramming any rocks but she filled with water, half drowning the men. They soon recovered; the canoe, however, took three hours to repair.

The local natives displayed an innate fear and suspicion when Mackenzie tried to approach them. They ran away and when his men got too close, shot arrows at them. Finally, aided by the offer of gifts, curiosity overcame apprehension at one camp and Mackenzie was able to make contact with the Indians. He questioned them about the nature of the river downstream and the route to the sea. They said it was a long river with a uniformly strong current and in three places was made impassable by rapids and falls flanked by vertical rock walls. (It was a reasonably accurate description of the Fraser River Canyon between the towns of Lytton and Yale). They said these stretches were far more dangerous than the canyons they had already passed. They added that the people living along the river were hostile and numerous. Mackenzie tended to discount these stories as being at least partly exaggerated and they did not shake his determination. When two of the Indians readily agreed to accompany him, he must have felt his assessment of the accounts was correct.

Mackenzie's new guides proved their value twice the next day when apprehensive bands of Indians openly threatened the white men with their weapons. They persuaded the natives to put up their arms and offer the strangers their friendship. Once he was admitted into a camp, Mackenzie won the people over, offering his hand to the men and women and a taste of sugar to the children. A native in one of the camps drew a sketch of the country for him on a piece of bark and others willingly talked about the river. Their descriptions were very discouraging. They said it was interrupted every 30 to 35 km. (20 mi.) by rapids and falls of which six were impassable and the portages around them long and over difficult terrain. Also, the valley of the river was inhabited, successively, by three savage tribes who spoke different languages. Furthermore, it was a long way to the sea.

Having delivered themselves of this disheartening news, the natives added, gratuitously, that the distance across country to the sea was quite short. They said they frequently traveled in that direction to trade furs and dressed leather for metals with Indians (the Bella Coolas) who dealt directly with traders on the coast. The meeting place with these Indians was a six-day journey over a well-marked trail that started inland near the mouth of the West Road River about 100 km. (60 mi.) upstream.

The story sounded plausible. Mackenzie could deduce from Cook's map of the Pacific coast a value of 131°W for the longitude at the coast opposite his present location (modern day Alexandria). He had read John Meares's account of his voyages to the Northwest coast and he knew Meares had determined the longitude at Cape Flattery to be 125°W.[22] Admittedly this was far to the south but Cook's outline of the coast looked to be little better than a sketch and seemed quite unreliable. Perhaps an average of the two values, say 128°W, was a reasonable approximation of the longitude at the coast. He had found the longitude of his present location to be 122 1/2°W, giving a difference of about six degrees between river and coast. That worked out to a distance of 400 km. (250 mi.) at this latitude.

Whatever data or deductions Mackenzie used, he made a good guess at the distance to the coast. The longitude of open water opposite Alexandria is 129°W. The 6 1/2 degrees difference in longitude is equivalent to 430 km. (270 mi.).

Mackenzie was convinced that the river he was on flowed into the Pacific, but far to the south.

The more [he] heard of the river, the more [he] was convinced it could not empty itself into the ocean to the north of what is called the River of the West.[23]

Possibly it was the river discerned by Bruno de Hezeta as he cruised along the west coast in latitude 46°N in 1775. If it was that river, the distance to its mouth and the sea seemed too great to attempt with his scanty supply of provisions and ammunition. The return journey up the river, past the many rapids he had been warned about, would be slow — probably too slow to let him reach Fort Fork before freezeup. His people were discontented and thought it madness to even contemplate a voyage down the river. Their reception by the natives on the west side of the Rocky Mountains had not been open and friendly at first meeting. They were alarmed at the prospect of entering the more densely populated parts of the river valley said to be peopled by savage tribes. Mackenzie decided if he was to give himself any chance of reaching the sea and returning this year, it would have to be over the shorter land route.

His men were delighted by the change in plans, and having secured a promise from one of the local Indians to guide them, he turned back upriver on June 23.

The canoe had become so leaky it required the constant bailing of one man to keep her afloat. On June 26 they ran her over a submerged stump and tore a large hole in her bottom. It was suddenly imperative to replace her. Fortunately, early next day, they saw a stand of trees that would provide all the bark needed to build a new canoe and they immediately made camp. They finished the canoe on June 30 and the next day they were back on the river, traveling upstream again towards the West Road River.

Their local guide had slipped away while they were building the canoe but they easily found a well-beaten trail near the mouth of the West Road River — presumably the start of the inland road to the sea. Before they could take it, their errant guide appeared with six of his relatives and the information that they must start at a point 8 or 10 km. (5 or 6 mi.) upriver.

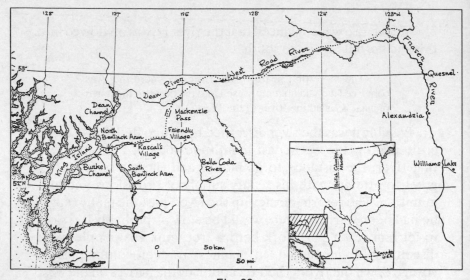

Fig. 30
Mackenzie's overland route from the Fraser River to the Pacific Ocean.

Overland to the Pacific Ocean, July 4 - 22[24]

Early on July 4 Mackenzie had his men secretly cache a quantity of food, gunpowder and various articles of merchandise — supplies he would need for the journey back to Fort Fork. The canoe was secured on an elevated platform, shaded lest the gum bubble in the heat of the sun. Each voyageur carried, in addition to his gun and ammunition, a backpack weighing about 40 kg. (90 lb.), consisting of pemmican and other food, gifts and intruments. Mackenzie's pack weighed about 32 kg. (70 lb.) and he carried his three-foot telescope slung across his shoulders. His Indians were indignant at the prospect of backpacking — such disagreeable tasks were generally assigned to their women — but they agreed to carry small packs. The local guide carried nothing.

The road to the sea was so well marked there was little chance of losing their way. The principal function of their guide was to alert the many travelers on the road of the white men's approach and to assure them that the strangers came in peace. He generally earned them a kindly reception, food, and a place to sleep for the night. Unfortunately, he turned back after a few days and Mac-

158

kenzie had to find a substitute. He soon discovered that the natives would accompany him willingly only as far as the first settlement beyond their own.

The country was almost destitute of game; the natives lived mainly on fish which were plentiful in the rivers. Mackenzie hoarded his precious supplies of pemmican against an emergency and, because he would not take the time to fish, he soon came to rely on the local people for his daily sustenance. They usually generously shared their food but Mackenzie worried about his growing dependence on them.

The road led them to the headwaters of the West Road River on July 12. Looking ahead they could see a range of snow-covered mountains in the distance — an obstacle they would have to cross to reach the Pacific. Here, however, the land rose gently as they left the drainage basin of the Fraser River. They came to the Dean River on July 14. The water in this river flowed west — they felt the end of the journey must be near. The trail turned southwest, climbing towards a pass (later called Mackenzie Pass) in the mountains they had seen from the Dean River. They reached its summit in the morning of July 17; it was the highest point on the long journey from Lake Athabasca. They were in the Coast Range Mountains; before them "appeared a stupendous mountain, whose snow-clad summit was lost in the clouds; between it and [their] immediate course, flowed the river to which [they] were going."[25] It was the Bella Coola River, far below them, the navigable river that would carry them to the sea. It was dark before the tired whites reached the river and entered a settlement. They were received with kindness, thanks to their guide, fed roasted salmon and given a place to sleep. Mackenzie named the settlement Friendly Village.

Mackenzie was already fully dependent on the natives for food and now he had to borrow canoes and the people to guide the unfamiliar craft down the swift waters of the river. As they neared the coast, however, matters took a serious turn. The Indians they met on the Bella Coola River were increasingly hostile and inclined to bully the white men, pilfering their baggage and acting insolently, testing Mackenzie's mettle. He refused to be intimidated no matter how badly his party was outnumbered, acting

159

fearlessly where a lesser man might have quailed. On one occasion, in a settlement Mackenzie later dubbed Rascal's Village, he was about ready to leave when one of his men said an ax was missing. The chief chose not to understand a request for its return until Mackenzie seated himself on a rock, his gun ready, and made it clear he would not leave without the ax. The village broke into an uproar but the ax was soon returned.

They entered the North Bentinck Arm of the sea about 8:00 A.M. on July 20. Technically, Mackenzie had now crossed the continent — the effect of the tides was clearly visible on the rocks, but he wanted to see the open water and he pushed on. They had not obtained any food at Rascal's Village and they were saddened because they had become separated from their dog.

> Our stock was, at this time, reduced to twenty pounds weight of pemmican, fifteen pounds of rice, and six pounds of flour, among ten half-starved men, in a leaky vessel, and on a barbarous coast.[26]

In midafternoon they were forced ashore by high winds and the mood was gloomy.

Next morning, in calmer water, they passed Burke Channel, keeping King Island on their left. Here they were accosted by three canoe loads of Indians who goaded them, insisting on examining everything in the canoe while treating them with disdain, interfering with their progress and persuading Mackenzie's guide to come over to them. One particularly insolent Indian forced his way into Mackenzie's canoe, demanding he be given pieces of clothing and other articles he fancied. They continued in this way for about 10 km. (6 mi.) when they came to Dean Channel where Mackenzie turned towards the sea, steering southwest, still encumbered with his tormentors. When two boys came alongside in a canoe, the Indians sent them off to round up more natives to join in the fun.

Seeing a few sheds on shore and thinking it might be the remains of a fort that would offer a place to defend himself, Mackenzie had the canoe landed nearby, but it was only the ruins of an Indian village. They were joined there by ten canoes filled with warriors who said the white men were expected at their village where they would be fed and entertained. Mackenzie had

160

no intention of accompanying the Indians; if there was to be entertainment at the village, he was sure he and his men were slated to be the subject of it.

Back in the canoe, Mackenzie knew that if a native was hurt in the constant jostling — if he allowed himself to be provoked into a fight — the Indians would fall on him and his men and kill them all. It was imperative to break away. He directed his men to make for a small rocky knoll where there was space for little more than his own party. They gained it and from this position they successfully declined all efforts to entice them into the village and they resisted all attempts to irritate them into a fight. Finally they were left in peace to build a small fire to warm themselves and eat some supper although "there was little of that, for our whole daily allowance did not amount to what was sufficient for a single meal."[27]

In the morning a lone Indian came to them "with about half a pound of boiled seal's flesh, and the head of a small salmon, for which he asked an handkerchief, but afterwards accepted a few beads."[28] Later, two canoe loads of Indians, including their guide, arrived with some pieces of raw seal meat for which they demanded an extravagant price. Hunger compelled Mackenzie's people to pay what they asked.

The guide urged Mackenzie to leave but Mackenzie would not go until he had established the geographical coordinates of this, his most westerly point of progress. He calmly went about making observations for latitude even while more Indians were arriving. The guide, who could understand the Indians' language, said they were plotting to kill the whites. His agitation grew so great he foamed at the mouth. Despite the increasing belligerence of the Indians, the frantic pleas of his guide and the growing panic of his voyageurs, Mackenzie was determined to leave with dignity; he would only consent to have the canoe loaded and made ready. He finished the observations (his value of 52°21'N compares well with the modern value of 52°22'30"N) and then, with a mixture of vermilion and melted grease, he painted the inscription

Alexander Mackenzie, from Canada, by land, the twenty-second of July, one thousand seven hundred and ninety-three[29]

161

on the southeast face of the knoll — the first man to cross North America. Only then did he agree to retreat to a small cove where they could not be attacked except from the water. The cove is less than a day's travel by canoe from the open water Mackenzie longed to see.

The weather was clear enough that night to enable him to observe Jupiter's moons to find longitude. The average of his measurements gave 128°02'W (the true position of the cove is 127°26'W). It was 10:00 P.M. when he finished and immediately they quit the place, retracing the route that had taken them there.

Mackenzie and his people "landed at four in the afternoon [of August 24, 1793], at the place which [they] left on the ninth of May."[30] He had been seventy-four days reaching the Pacific Ocean; it took thirty-three days to return. Again, as in the voyage to the Arctic, he brought his people home without any of them suffering a serious mishap despite, at times, extreme provocation from the Indians at the coast. He even recovered his lost dog in the bush above Rascal's Village and took him home too. Once again he had demonstrated courage, determination and an ability to lead men — men who were probably older than his thirty years and much more experienced in the bush and on the water. He worked them long hours — from 4:00 A.M. and earlier, until dusk — with no time off unless the weather dictated it. He cajoled, sympathized, encouraged and appealed to their pride. He shared a dram with them over the supper fire when the outlook was black, and they always bent to his will.

Mackenzie's Columbian Enterprise

Mackenzie spent the 1793-4 winter at Fort Chipewyan. He had planned to use the solitude of the north country to work on his journals preparatory to writing a book on his voyages of discovery to the Arctic and Pacific Oceans. The sudden quiet and inaction, however, following closely on the stress of the long journey to the Pacific, brought on an inevitable reaction. He suffered from a deep depression and he accomplished little. He resolved, that winter, to give up his explorations and get out of the Northwest. He wrote as much to Roderic Mackenzie on January 13, 1794:

> I am fully bent on going down. I am more anxious now than ever. For I think it unpardonable in any man to remain in this country who can afford to leave it.[31]

He left the Northwest for the last time in the spring of 1794, bound for Montreal. He stopped at Grand Portage for the annual meeting of wintering partners and agents, and again at York (Toronto) early in September to talk with John Graves Simcoe, the Lieutenant-Governor of Upper Canada. It is clear from an account he sent the governor that Mackenzie believed the large river he had been on — the Fraser — was the upper part of the Columbia River or a branch of it:

> from the best information I could procure [I] judged it did not discharge itself to the Northward of the River of the West [the Columbia]; a Branch if not the whole of which I take it to be.[32]

The account left the impression that the "River of the West" had been discovered in the interior and that it remained only to explore its headwaters and follow it down to the ocean to unravel the details of its geography. Curiously, there was no rush on anyone's part to undertake these next steps.

Mackenzie also had an audience with Lord Dorchester, Governor-in-Chief of British North America. The purpose of his visits with British officials was to gain support for a grand strategy he had worked out for conducting the fur trade in the Northwest. It was founded on the conviction that travel and commerce between the deep interior of the continent and the Pacific Ocean was practical over the route he had pioneered. It was based, principally, on three requirements:

1) the development by Britain of a civil and military establishment at Nootka (latitude 50°N) and subordinate stations at 46°N (the mouth of the Columbia River) and 55°N, to assure British control of the coast from Alaska to the California-Oregon border

2) a commercial alliance between the Hudson's Bay Company and the traders from Montreal to eliminate costly competition and to share facilities (mainly the ports on Hudson Bay)[33]

3) the use of the Pacific ports to service traders operating west of Lake Athabasca (Fort Chipewyan was about the most distant post from which furs could be taken east at a profit).

The scheme became known as the Columbian Enterprise from the belief, which persisted for a decade and a half after Mackenzie's voyage, that the Columbia River was the link between the Peace River and the Pacific Ocean.·

19

David Thompson

David Thompson

David Thompson was born in the parish of St. John the Evangelist, Westminister, England on April 30, 1770. His father died two years later, apparently a very poor man for he was buried at the expense of the parish. At the age of seven, young Thompson was enrolled in Grey Coat School, situated near Westminister Abbey, a school dedicated to the education of poor boys "in the principles of piety and virtue."[1] In 1783, the Hudson's Bay Company requested the school to "furnish them with 4 boys against the month of May next, for their settlements in America."[2] The Master had only two boys, including David Thompson, who could be recommended. Apparently the other boy wanted no part of America for he immediately fled the school. Thompson accepted his fate; the sum of £5 was paid by the school to the company and he was bound over as an apprentice for seven years.

Thompson sailed from London in May, 1784, in the company's ship *Prince Rupert*, arriving at Fort Churchill in September. He had lived in the heart of London and now, not yet fifteen, he was at an outpost of civilization. His superior was Samuel Hearne who, fifteen years earlier, had traveled to the mouth of the Coppermine River on the Arctic Ocean. It was the stuff to fire the spirit of adventure in any young boy. He developed a genuine and lasting love for the life in his raw surroundings; it kept him in the Northwest for more than a quarter of a century.

The Northwest could be divided for convenience, at this time, into three areas — the region between Hudson Bay and Lake

Winnipeg (the "Muskrat Country"), Athabasca (the "Northward Country") and the valley of the Saskatchewan River. The Hudson's Bay Company got most of the furs taken in Muskrat Country, carried by Indians the relatively short distance to Fort Churchill, York Factory or Fort Severn on Hudson Bay. The company had no posts in the Northward Country and received few furs from this region. It had built Cumberland House on the Saskatchewan River in 1774, but had to struggle with Nor' Westers and others for a share of the trade along the river. It sought to improve this situation in 1779, by building Hudson House a short distance upstream from the site of Prince Albert, Saskatchewan. Still the competition remained fierce on the river and it induced the company to send a party of men, including Thompson, west in 1786. They built Manchester House on the north branch of the river, 650 km. (400 mi.) above Hudson House. The country beyond this house was virtually unknown to the white man. At the age of sixteen, David Thompson had reached the western extremity of the white man's commercial activity on the Saskatchewan River.

The company was convinced that the key to success in trade lay in gaining the friendship of the local Indians, particularly the warlike Piegans. To promote this, Thompson and six others were ordered out of the newly built fort and onto the plains. They found a large settlement of Piegans on the Bow River near the site of Calgary and Thompson remained here. He passed the winter of 1787-8 in the tent of an old chief named Saukamappee; it was the winter Alexander Mackenzie spent with Peter Pond in Athabasca.

In December, 1788, Thompson fell and broke his leg while hauling a sled loaded with wood into Manchester House. The incident changed his life. The leg was set by the trader, but badly, and Thompson became very sick. In May, 1789, the trader recorded: "David Thompson's leg I am afraid will turn out to be mortification as the joint of his ancle has never lowered on the swelling."[3] It was August before he could get about on crutches. He was sent downriver to Cumberland House and he remained there through the summer and winter of 1789-90. The company's senior surveyor, Philip Turnor, lived that winter at Cumberland House and Thompson, with time on his hands, became interested

166

in Turnor's work. The interest grew rapidly and soon Turnor found he had an apt and serious pupil.

Thompson's seven-year apprenticeship ended in 1791. He was now well grounded in both the fur trade and in surveying. Good reports earned him a new three-year contract at £15 a year, a letter encouraging his interest in mapping and, a year later, a case of instruments including a brass compass and a Fahrenheit thermometer — a gift "as a reward for [his] assiduity."[4]

The governors of the Hudson's Bay Company were determined to get a share of the furs coming out of Athabasca where the Nor' Westers had been trading since 1778. As a start they appointed Malcolm Ross "Master of the Northward" in 1793 with orders to build a post there and begin trading. The following year Thompson was awarded a new three-year contract as Ross's assistant — at £60 a year. Despite these initiatives, Ross and Thompson had not succeeded in establishing a post on Lake Athabasca when summer arrived in 1796. The Hudson's Bay Company's slow progress in the Northward Country was in marked contrast to the exploits of the Nor' Wester, Alexander Mackenzie, who had voyaged from Lake Athabasca to the Arctic Ocean in 1789 and to the Pacific Ocean in 1793. Still, the governors had confidence in Thompson. When Ross, ready to retire after twenty-two years with the company, gave the customary year's notice, they named Thompson to succeed him. He would become Master of the Northward at the age of twenty-seven.

The route between Hudson Bay and Athabasca was a fifteen hundred kilometer (thousand mile) arc of water passages and portages. It was an arduous journey and no doubt contributed to the delay in gaining a foothold in the Northward Country. Thompson was anxious to find a shorter route. In June, 1796, with two young Chipewyan Indians, he went up the Reindeer River from its confluence with the Churchill River, into Reindeer Lake. He turned up a shallow stream flowing into its western side and after traveling over ponds, brooks and portages for a distance of 80 km. (50 mi.), he came to Wollaston Lake. He crossed the lake and found the Fond du lac River and descended it over a number of falls and rapids into the east end of Lake Athabasca. On his return to York Factory in August, Thompson persuaded Ross that he had found a shorter route, practicable for freight canoes, to Athabasca. Reluctantly, Ross agreed to try the route and set off in September with five canoes. The brigade came to a halt between Reindeer and Wollaston Lakes, on a creek too shallow to float even a small canoe with "nothing in it but 3 blankets."[5] Thompson had accepted the word of the Chipewyans that, contrary to the usual circumstances, the shallow waterways between the lakes, fed mainly by swamps, would be deeper in fall than in midsummer. He had not realized that the natives believed it was more important to give a welcome answer than a truthful one.

It was too late in the year to return to the Churchill River and take the Crosse Road to Athabasca. The brigade would have to winter on Reindeer Lake in country not noted for an abundance of game or fish; and trading in the Northward Country would be delayed again. Ross brought his men through the winter but they lived on near-starvation rations. No doubt the men knew Thompson was responsible for their plight and did not spare his feelings throughout the long winter. They were not likely to soon forget this winter and perhaps for this reason, Thompson decided to quit the Hudson's Bay Company. In May, having completed his second three-year contract, he told Ross he was leaving. Two days later he left the camp to join the North West Company — so much for the appointment as Master of the Northward and the usual practice of giving a year's notice.[6]

To get enough people to take charge of their posts the rapidly expanding North West Company was forced to use men only recently out of Britain. Not all of them were suited to the raw surroundings and the style of life they adopted made a strong impression on Philip Turnor:

> The [North West Company] give Men which never saw an Indian One Hundred Pounds Pr. Annum, his Feather Bed carried in the Canoe, his Tent, which is exceeding good, pitched for him, his Bed made and he and his girl carried in and out of the Canoe and when in the Canoe he never touches a Paddle unless for his own Pleasure.[7]

A Hudson's Bay man was expected to take his share of the paddling and at night, like his men, "role him self in a Blanket and lay under a Tree if nigh unto them."[8] He lived with the Indians if that helped his company, and learned to speak their languages.

The Nor' Westers were happy to have Thompson join them. He had twelve years of experience in the Northwest, was as tough as the hardiest Indian or voyageur and willing to learn from the natives:

> I had always admired the tact of the Indian in being able to guide himself through the darkest pine forests to exactly the place he intended to go, his keen, constant attention on every thing; the removal of the smallest stone; the bent or broken twig; a slight mark on the ground, all spoke plain language to him. I was anxious to acquire this knowledge, and often being in company with them, sometimes for several months, I paid attention to what they pointed out to me, and became almost equal to some of them; which became of great use to me.[9]

The Indians and voyageurs, for their part, came to regard Thompson with superstition and perhaps, a touch of amusement:

> Both Canadians and Indians often inquired why I observed the Sun, and sometimes the Moon, in the day time, and passed whole nights with my instruments looking at Moon and Stars. I told them it was to determine the distance and direction from the place I observed to other places; neither the Canadians nor the Indians believed me; for both argued that if what I said was truth, I ought to look to the ground; and over it; and not to the Stars. Their opinions were, that I was looking into futurity and seeing every body, and what they were doing; how to raise the wind. . . . [10]

Thompson's dealings with Indians and voyageurs were governed by a high moral sense and a strict code of personal conduct. Unlike most of his voyageurs, he was not a Catholic. Yet they looked to him for spiritual guidance and listened attentively as he read to them from the Bible in his fractured French, deep in the wilderness. He was a pious man, often ending an entry in his journal with the words "Thank God" or a similar thanksgiving when Providence had been kind to him.

He married Charlotte Small, a fourteen-year old girl of mixed blood, at Ile-à-la-Crosse in 1799. She is thought to have been the

169

daughter of Patrick Small, a native of Glengarry and one of the earliest traders on the Churchill River. It proved to be a long and successful marriage.

Western Indians cross the Continental Divide to trade on the Saskatchewan River, 1798-1800

Duncan McGillivray was a clerk with the North West Company at Grand Portage when Alexander Mackenzie paused there in 1794, on his way to Montreal following his voyage to the Pacific Ocean. McGillivray was stirred when he heard the young trader-explorer expound on his Columbian Enterprise — a simple and logical plan to improve the fortunes of the North West Company.

The distance from a post in the interior to the seaports on Hudson Bay was about the same as the distance to the North West Company depot of Grand Portage on Lake Superior. However, the Nor' Westers' had to travel another 1600 km. (1000 mi.) from Grand Portage to reach their seaport in Montreal. Their goods and furs moved east in 40 kg. (90 lb.) packs carried in fragile canoes over waterways interspersed with rapids and on the backs of men across numerous portages. It took much aggressive trading to discount their rival's superior lines of communication.

The old company's advantage of proximity to the deep interior began to increase. The Indians, spurred by the demand for furs and armed with modern tools, broke the beaver dams and drained the ponds to reach the shelters and kill the animals. In the process they destroyed the beavers' environment and ability to thrive. To maintain the supply of furs to overseas markets, the trade was forced ever deeper into the interior to search for new sources. Then the Hudson's Bay Company's basic advantage — its control of the seaports on Hudson Bay relatively close to the source of furs — began to tell. McGillivray was convinced that Mackenzie's scheme for a merger of rival interests in the Northwest could ensure the economic well-being of the North West Company. A common transportation network over which commerce could move through Hudson Bay or Montreal or a still-to-be discovered port on the Pacific coast, seemed to offer a practical method of organizing the fur trade.[11]

170

The search for new fur-bearing regions had moved west — swiftly in Athabasca country but rather more slowly up the Saskatchewan River; but move it did, and in 1795, the rival companies were established in Fort Augustus (NWC) and Fort Edmonton (HBC). In the spring of 1798, two Kootenay Indians visited these posts from their country at the source of two great rivers (which we know to be the Columbia and Kootenay Rivers) west of the Rockies. They said the region could yield a rich trade but whenever they crossed the mountains they were harassed by the warlike Piegans who lived opposite them east of the Divide. The Piegans saw the growth of trade with the Kootenays as providing the western Indians with better arms and improving their capacity to do battle. They were determined to prevent this and keep the upper hand. Clearly, if trade with the Kootenays was to be initiated, the traders would have to cross the Divide, establish posts there and bring out the furs.

In the spring of 1799, in response to the visit of the Kootenays, the companies each built a trading post — Rocky Mountain House (NWC) and Acton House (HBC) — at the junction of the Clearwater and Saskatchewan Rivers, only 160 km. (100 mi.) from the Continental Divide. It was another step towards the mountains that barred the way to the Pacific Ocean. In 1800, at the annual meeting in Grand Portage, the Nor' Westers agreed to send an exploration party across the Rocky Mountains and down to the Pacific Ocean in 1801. They decided it should cross the mountains from the headwaters of the Saskatchewan River. Alexander Mackenzie, who had been to both the Arctic and Pacific Oceans, would not be a part of it. Discouraged by the lack of support for his Columbian Enterprise, he had quit the company the previous year. Duncan McGillivray, a partner now, would take charge with James Hughes as second in command and David Thompson as "astronomer" (surveyor).

Late in the year, word was received at Rocky Mountain House that a band of Kootenays from west of the mountains, was on its way to trade. Thompson rode out on October 5 with five North West men and two Indian guides, to meet and conduct the Kootenays through hostile Piegan territory. The Nor' Westers

171

rode south to the Red Deer River and then turned upstream, moving now west-southwestwardly, in the direction of Lake Louise. On the ninth day they met two young Piegans who had seen the Kootenays — in fact, they had stolen two mares from them — and knew where they would be crossing "the Heights of the Mountain the Morrow."[12] Thompson found the Kootenays next morning — a chief attended by twenty-six men and seven women, with only eleven horses among them — about 40 km. (25 mi.) northeast of the site of Banff. Presumably, they had come over the Vermilion Pass (on the route of Highway 93). It offered the shortest and easiest road from the valley of the Kootenay River where these Indians lived, to the meeting with Thompson. The other pass in the vicinity — the Kicking Horse Pass (presently used for the mainline of the Canadian Pacific Railway) — was so difficult to cross that it was never used by the natives.

Late next day, Thompson's party reached a Piegan camp and trouble for the Kootenays came immediately. The Piegans tried to bully them into giving up a horse and only desisted when the Kootenays threatened to use their weapons. Despite the brave showing, many of the Kootenays wanted to turn back — exactly what the Piegans wanted — frightened for their lives. Thompson had to be persuasive to keep them. Next day the torment was worse; five of their horses had been stolen in the night and the Piegans succeeded in intimidating the Kootenays into trading their remaining six horses for the six worst animals in the camp.

Thompson got his party started towards the House again, encumbered by the thieving Piegans who tried to force the Kootenays to make camp at midday so that they could continue their potentially deadly sport, even seizing the horses' heads to stop them. By the fourth day, all but two of the horses had been stolen and the band was effectively immobilized. Thompson decided to get help and with one man, rode swiftly to Rocky Mountain House, returning next day with three men and two extra horses. The following morning — October 21 — after "much Trouble and Dispute with the Pikenows [Piegans] even to drawing of Arms, we arrived at the Fort at 3Pm. Thank God."[13]

To lessen tensions at the fort, Thompson gave the persistent Piegans three gallons of rum to share with his guides and he made the Kootenays a present of half a keg of whiskey. In the afternoon he traded with the Kootenays and queried them about crossing the mountains. (The only pass across the Rockies generally known to white men, was the Peace River route far to the north used by Alexander Mackenzie in 1793). He urged them to return in the spring to guide him back to their country and he arranged for two Canadians — La Gasse and Le Blanc — to winter with them. Presumably he expected the two men to gain some knowledge of the country, including passes through the mountains, and assess the prospects for trade.

The Kootenays left the House on October 22, before La Gasse and Le Blanc were ready to travel. Thompson and the men caught up with the Indians at noon the next day. They were easy to trail; according to an entry in Thompson's journal, "the Route the Kootanaes took to cross the Mountains & avoid the [Piegan] Indians, is on this [the north] Side of the [Saskatchewan] River."[14] The Kootenays' situation on the journey to Rocky Mountain House had been desperate. Except for Thompson, the gradual pilfering of their horses would have led to bloodshed or captivity. They had been fortunate; next time the harassment might have more serious consequences. The outnumbered Kootenays would not immediately risk another confrontation and they chose to return by a different route, following the north bank of the Saskatchewan River and thereby skirting the Piegan's country on the north. Reference to a modern map shows that it would take them to the Howse River and the Howse Pass, one of the several passes discovered long ago by Indians living near the Divide. It was used routinely by the western Indians to cross the mountains and hunt buffalo. The Kootenays were taking the route that leads naturally from the headwaters of the Saskatchewan River into the mountains.

McGillivray and Thompson began probing the foothills after the Kootenays left the House, searching for openings in the Rocky Mountains. Unaccountably, they made no attempt to trail the band into the mountains and find where they crossed the Divide. The ten-day old spoor left by this thirty-man party would have been easy to follow for Thompson with his Indian-like ability to track through the bush. Instead, he and McGillivray used what was left of the year to test the source waters of the Athabasca and

173

Bow Rivers (respectively north and south of the Saskatchewan) for passes.

First white men on the upper Columbia and Kootenay Rivers, 1800-01

The Canadians, La Gasse and Le Blanc, returned safely to Rocky Mountain House on May 23, 1801 but the guide, sent with them to conduct McGillivray's Pacific-bound expedition back across the mountains was killed by Piegans, within sight of the House.

The only known account of the 1800-01 winter adventure of the two men is found in the diary of Peter Fidler, a Hudson's Bay Company trader and surveyor. Fidler met Duncan McGillivray at the House a few weeks after the men returned and discussed the experience. The pertinent entry in Fidler's diary records that La Gasse and Le Blanc

> travelled 17 nights until they arrived at the camp on the west side of the mountains where the Kootenays had left their families. They reported the area across the divide from the head of the Saskatchewan to be thickly wooded country while farther south, opposite Devil's Head Mountain [at 51°21'N, 115°16'W, about 20 km. (12.5 mi.) northeast of Banff], the country was more open. They spent most of the winter in an open country west of Chief Mountain [in Montana, near the Alberta border] and on one occasion made a fourteen day trip over the divide to hunt buffalo on the prairies. They reported another range of mountains nearly as high as the Rockies to the west of their camps. . . . They reported passing a river nearly as large as the Saskatchewan that runs south and south-west from a point opposite the Saskatchewan. On their return they travelled twenty-eight nights, crossing the mountains between the sources of the Red Deer and Saskatchewan.[15]

We can deduce from the account that having crossed the Howse Pass from the Saskatchewan River, late in 1800, the Kootenays came to the Columbia and traveled upstream (south). They crossed Canal Flats to the Kootenay River (the river "nearly as large as the Saskatchewan" flowing "south and south-west") and followed it downstream to their winter camp (opposite Chief

174

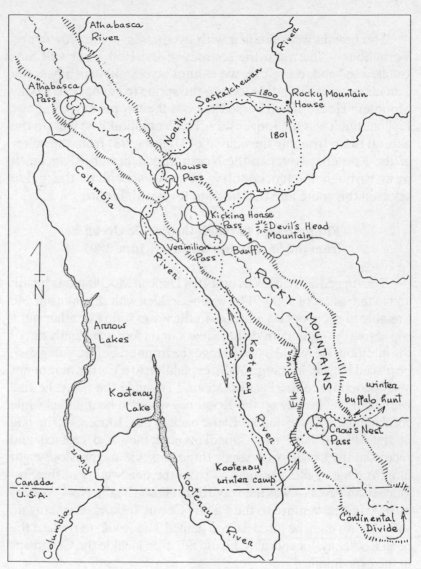

Fig. 31
The probable route of the journeys of La Gasse and Le Blanc, first white men on the upper Columbia and Kootenay Rivers, 1800-01.

Mountain) near the forty-ninth parallel (see Fig. 31). They probably used the Crowsnest Pass, near the camp, when they took the Canadians across the mountains to hunt buffalo on the prairie.

The Indians were familiar with two passes — the Howse and Vermilion — "between the sources of the Red Deer and Saskatchewan" and, therefore, we cannot be certain which pass the Canadians and their guide took in the spring to get back to Rocky Mountain House. The Howse Pass was the safer for avoiding the Piegans but it was the longer way. The Vermilion Pass was on the natural route (roughly the course of Highway 93) from the valley of the Kootenay River to the North Saskatchewan River but it went through Piegan country. We can speculate the guide selected this route and that he paid for it with his life.

First attempt to reach the Pacific Ocean
from the Saskatchewan River, June 1801

The rugged life had taken its toll of Duncan McGillivray's health and in the winter of 1800-01 he was bedridden with rheumatism. He was able to get about on crutches in the warm spring weather but a trip across the mountains on horseback or on foot was clearly out of the question. He would have to leave the frontier. Before going east, he placed Hughes in charge of the expedition to cross the mountains and "penetrate to the Pacific Ocean." To guide the party, he had been counting heavily on the Kootenay who had been killed while conducting La Gasse and Le Blanc back to the House. Still, he had at the House these two Canadians and they had crossed and recrossed the Divide over two or three passes in the previous eight months. One of the crossings — from the headwaters of the Saskatchewan River — was the very route chosen by the Nor' Westers in 1800 for the venture to the Pacific Ocean. Instead of making do with the two men, he hired a Cree named The Rook, to replace the dead Kootenay. Inexplicably, he did not even include the Canadians in the expedition.

The Rook led the party — Hughes, Thompson, nine men, The Rook and his wife, and ten packhorses — on a bizarre journey up the valley of the Ram River, ending at a deep lake bound by steep rock walls. It was impossible to proceed with the horses. When they accused The Rook of deceiving them about the quality of the route for horse travel, he confessed he had forgotten this part. He said they must now leave the baggage and horses and go on foot.

It was unthinkable, of course, to leave the baggage — the goods were needed to get them to the Pacific Ocean. Hughes and Thompson took the packstring northwest to the Saskatchewan River and spent a week building a canoe. When they launched her in the river, swollen now with spring runoff, they could not make headway against the current. They gave up after another week and turned downstream. It took less than six hours to paddle to the House. The mission to reach the Pacific had progressed only 120 km. (75 mi.) from its base before turning back.

"Thus ended the business of 1801" as Thompson put it. It was an ignominious ending and, moreover, Thompson came away from the failure with some naive notions, having learned nothing from observing the Kootenays's method of travel in the mountains:

> However unsuccessfull this Journey has been . . . it has also shewn us plainly, that to employ & depend on Horses, for carrying the Goods, in such Expeditions, it is the most uncertain & most expensive of all the modes of Conveyance.
>
> Whoever wishes to cross the Mountains for the Purposes of Commerce, ought to employ a Canoe, & start early in the Spring, say the beginning of May . . . the Water for that Month being low . . . in this Season they would cross a great Part of the Mountains, without any extraordinary Difficulty [to] the Head of the River; from whence there is said to be a short Road to the Waters which flow on the other Side of the Mountains.[16]

The push to cross the Divide and descend to the Pacific Ocean came to an abrupt halt. Thompson spent the remainder of the summer and the following winter at Rocky Mountain House. In May, 1802, he descended the Saskatchewan River and continued to Lake Superior.

177

20

Lewis And Clark

Thomas Jefferson

The last quarter of the eighteenth century was remarkable for the rapid westward advance of traders and explorers north of the forty-ninth parallel. The most spectacular events had resulted from the drive into Athabasca country. With Fort Chipewyan on Lake Athabasca as base, a young Alexander Mackenzie had explored a mighty river to the Arctic Ocean and four years later, ascended the Peace River, discovered the Fraser River and found a way to the Pacific Ocean. Movement up the broad and more convenient avenue of the North Saskatchewan River had been slower and it had not reached as far west. By 1799, however, rival fur companies had established Rocky Mountain House (NWC) and Acton House (HBC) on opposite sides of the river, only 160 km. (100 mi.) from the Continental Divide.

Circumstances south of the forty-ninth parallel did not favor exploration of the western interior when the last quarter of the century began. In the years between 1775 and 1783 the energies of the American colonists were consumed by the war for independence; the focus of attention was east of the Mississippi River. Interest in the region west of the river — in Louisiana — was subdued but it was not extinguished and men of adventure dreamed of exploring this unknown land adjacent to the new United States.

Thomas Jefferson, for one, grew up with an intense curiosity about Louisiana and what lay between it and the Pacific Ocean. After the war with Britain he became involved in various schemes

178

to satisfy that curiosity. In 1786 he met John Ledyard, an adventuresome countryman and former missionary among the American Indians. He had sailed with Cook on the voyage to the northwest coast and learned that trading in sea otter skins, taken there, could be extremely profitable. He tried to interest Jefferson, then Minister to France, in the trade but Jefferson's priorities lay in exploring the North American continent, and he countered with a challenge for Ledyard. He proposed that Ledyard cross Europe and Asia to Kamchatka, take a Russian ship to Nootka Sound, find the upper Missouri River and descend it to the American settlements along the Mississippi. Ledyard accepted and got well into Asia before the Russians caught up with him; they were having none of it. He was arrested in Irkutsk (north of Mongolia) in 1788, transported back to their western border and unceremoniously dumped into Poland.[1]

In 1793, in his capacity as vice-president of the American Philosophical Society of Philadelphia, Jefferson helped promote an expedition to send the French botanist, Andre Michaux, to

> cross the Mississippi and pass by land to the nearest part of the Missouri above the Spanish settlements, that you may avoid the risk of being stopped; [and then] pursue such of the largest streams of that river as shall lead by the shortest way and the lowest latitudes to the Pacific Ocean.[2]

A young man from Jefferson's home county in Virginia, Meriwether Lewis, eighteen years old and barely out of school, asked Jefferson to help him obtain a place on the expedition. Jefferson refused and it was just as well. Michaux was a French agent with instructions to incite an American attack on New Orleans. He was found out and the expedition was terminated before it could leave Kentucky.

At the turn of the century, Mackenzie's feat of crossing the continent had not been duplicated south of the forty-ninth parallel.

Jefferson became president in February, 1801. The office gave him the authority to organize his own expedition to explore the West; he needed only to persuade Congress to appropriate the funds. It seemed a propitious time for an expedition. Robert

Gray had given the United States a creditable claim on the west coast in 1792 when he rediscovered Hezeta's River (the Columbia) and sailed some distance upstream. Since then Americans had come to dominate the trade along that coast, replacing British mariners forced out by the East India Company's monopoly of the English trade with China and India. The British had not given up on the interior, however. Their traders continued to enter Louisiana from eastern Canada to trade with the Mandans. Jefferson, intensely anti-British, dreamed of taking all the trade in the western part of the continent — in the interior as well as on the coast — away from the British. The Missouri and Mississippi Rivers could be used to ferry goods and furs in the vast region between New Orleans and the eastern slope of the mountains. Never mind that the Missouri flowed through Spanish Louisiana; he would persuade the Spaniards to share the river with him.

Jefferson chose to give no hint of his scheme until details of the expedition had been worked out; then, when the time was right, he would put the proposition to Congress. He needed assistance to plan the expedition but whom could he trust? His thoughts centered on Meriwether Lewis who was serving in the American forces, and he decided to ask him to be his private secretary. Late in February, only a few weeks after he became president, Jefferson wrote to Lewis offering him the position, hinting at the adventure that was the real purpose of the appointment. Lewis may not have understood how his "knoledge of the Western country, of the army and all it's interests & relations"[3] qualified him to be the private secretary of the president but he did not question it. He was on his way to Washington before the end of March.

Meriwether Lewis

Meriwether Lewis was born August 18, 1774, near Charlottesville in Albemarle County, of old and well-to-do Virginia stock. His grandfather, Robert, had emigrated to America in 1635 and had prospered well enough to leave each of his nine children eight hundred hectares (almost two thousand acres) of land and the slaves to work it.

Lewis's father, William, was intensely and actively anti-British and served in the Revolutionary War without pay, even bearing the cost of his expenses. He died of pneumonia during the war after he crossed the Rivanna River in flood and was forced to swim ashore when his horse was swept away. Lewis's mother, Lucy Meriwether, married again — to Captain John Marks, a respected Virginian related by marriage to Thomas Jefferson. Marks decided to migrate to Georgia with his family and when he was detained on his way by business, Lucy took charge and got the family to the new homestead. In Georgia where the family lived while Lewis was a young man, "Indian scares" were part of the normal life of settlers.

His mother was widowed again. She returned to Albemarle County where she became a well-known figure in the countryside, extolled for the quality of her hams (Jefferson secured a few each year for his own use), for the herbs in her garden (for cooking and dosing), and for treating the sick (at the age of seventy she still rode horseback to see her patients).

Lewis began his formal education after the family returned to Virginia. Like most boys of his social standing, he attended various small schools conducted as a part-time business by parsons and, in one instance, a physician. He quit school at the age of eighteen and when he failed to obtain a place on the Michaux expedition, he joined the militia to fight in the Indian Wars that followed the revolution. In the course of these wars, he was assigned to a small company commanded by William Clark who was a veteran at gathering intelligence about the Spanish on the Mississippi River.

After the war with the Indians was concluded, Lewis's unit was sent to quell the Whiskey Rebellion. Pennsylvania farmers of Scottish and Irish extraction objected to a tax on the whiskey they distilled for their own use and for sale from rye grown in excess of their needs for food and the market. They took up arms, vowing rebellion and even secession. The insurrection was easily put down.

Lewis had enjoyed the two adventures so much he joined the Regulars in 1795, at the age of twenty-one. He was promoted to the rank of lieutenant in 1799, and captain in 1800. He performed a variety of army duties, from dealing with Indians to reconnaissance along the frontier. When the president's offer of an appointment reached him in 1801, he was paymaster for the army, traveling regularly between Detroit and Pittsburgh on the Ohio River.

The Louisiana Purchase

Ever since the French had lost sovereignty of the lands east of the Mississippi River in 1763, Americans had been moving west, settling in the valleys of the rivers that feed the Mississippi from the east. In 1795, the Spanish acknowledged that these settlers and other Americans had rights to the Mississippi River and the port of New Orleans. They could use the river to ship goods free of duty to and from the American ports on the Atlantic coast and even store goods awaiting shipment in New Orleans. The new century brought disquieting news to the United States government.

French power under Napoleon Bonaparte was on the rise in the world and in 1800, Napoleon persuaded King Charles of Spain to return Louisiana to France. The move seemed innocuous because the Spanish remained in place as the legal authority. Suddenly, in 1802, the Spaniards revoked the right of Americans to store goods in New Orleans. Was Napoleon responsible for this unfriendly act? Would it be followed by closing the Mississippi to American traffic?

There seemed to be cause for additional concern in the north. For years, British traders had dealt openly and actively with the Mandans on the Missouri River, transporting goods and furs through the Great Lakes. Now, in a book published in 1801, Alexander Mackenzie called on Britain to develop a strategy to control the fur trade in most of North America, from coast to coast. It was rumored the British planned to explore Louisiana from the Mississippi west to California as a first step towards that goal. If Napoleon renewed his warfare with Britain, would the British use it as an excuse to take possession of Louisiana?

The prospect of having France or Britain as a neighbor on the west side of the Mississippi was disturbing to Jefferson. An unfriendly or uncooperative nation at New Orleans could throttle the United States interior and turn the Mississippi into a foreign river. All American commerce west of the Appalachian Mountains moved on the rivers that flowed into the Mississippi and eventually, almost half of it passed through New Orleans.

Jefferson decided the two great powers could not be allowed the leisure to choose to act in a manner that would be detrimental to the United States. He had to be bold and aggressive to keep the Mississippi open for American commerce. He instructed Robert Livingstone, his Minister to Paris, to approach Charles Talleyrand, Napoleon's minister, with an offer to purchase New Orleans; he could bid as high as $2,000,000. Furthermore, he should hint that the United States might exercise another option — that of taking advantage of Napoleon's military preoccupation elsewhere, ally itself with the British and send a force across the Mississippi into undefended Louisiana.

Meanwhile, Meriwether Lewis and Jefferson planned the expedition to the west and finally, in 1803, Jefferson sent a confidential message to Congress requesting an appropriation of $2,500 for the project. He pointed to the value of the trade the British from Canada enjoyed with the Indians along the Missouri, implying that the United States could do even better. The Columbia and Missouri Rivers could be used to develop a trading empire from the Pacific Ocean to the Atlantic, "possibly with a single portage"[4] to get over the Continental Divide. A common belief held that the western mountains resembled the Appalachians in the east, consisting of a single north-south line of peaks that could be crossed in half a day. Jefferson presented an attractive prospect; at that time the route to the northwest coast was around Cape Horn, a long voyage through some of the most dangerous waters on earth. A transcontinental route held the promise of being shorter, safer and cheaper.

Jefferson told the Congress that the expedition would require only an "intelligent officer, with ten or twelve chosen men"[5] from the army — men who had to be paid anyway. Weapons, scientific instruments and presents for Indians would be the only expense. He added: "the nation claiming the territory [Spain still had jurisdiction over Louisiana] regarding this as a literary pursuit ... would not be disposed to view it with jealousy."[6] He did not tell

183

the Congress that he had asked the Spanish ambassador if his government would "take it badly" if the United States sent a geographical expedition up the Missouri. The ambassador had replied that "an expedition of this nature could not fail to give umbrage to our government."[7] Not for a moment did he believe that the main purpose of the expedition was to gather scientific data. Unaware of the rebuff, Congress appropriated the money.

Meanwhile, the negotiations for the purchase of New Orleans dragged on until early in the spring of 1803, when they took an unexpected turn. Talleyrand, apparently driven by Napoleon's military ambitions, the need to finance them, and the fear that Britain would seize Louisiana in the event of war with France, sent for Livingstone. What would the United States be willing to pay for the whole of Louisiana? The prospect of acquiring all this territory, more than doubling the size of the existing United States, staggered Livingstone and James Monroe who had just arrived to assist him. The two men had no authority to purchase Louisiana but they decided to act as if they had complete freedom of action and to strike a deal if they could. To use the tenuous and slow lines of communication of the day, to involve Jefferson in the talks, was to run the risk of having Talleyrand change his mind. They quickly settled on the sum of $15,000,000 for the region and signed an agreement to purchase on April 30, 1803. Jefferson had the news a few weeks later.

In June, confident now that nothing but the elements and the Indians could stop the expedition to the Pacific, Jefferson set out in detail what he expected it to accomplish. The main objective would be

> to explore the Missouri River, & such principal stream of it, as, by it's course and communication with the waters of the Pacific ocean, may offer the most direct & practical water communication across the continent, for the purpose of commerce.[8]

It was, in fact, the route Father Charlevoix had recommended, in 1721, for reaching the Western Sea.

Jefferson had come surely to the conclusion that Lewis should lead the expedition and the two men had worked with this assumption for some time. The program grew. Jefferson wanted the country mapped, the Indians studied, the fauna and flora collected and recorded, and everything written up during the journey and not afterwards when the memory of it had begun to fade.

As early as 1802, Lewis began taking instruction to acquire "a greater familiarity with the technical language of the natural sciences, and readiness in the astronomical observations necessary for the geography of his route."[9] His instructor, a Mr. Ellicot, thought it would require ten or twelve days. It was soon obvious Lewis could not collect all the scientific data and manage the logistics of the venture by himself. Jefferson authorized him to choose a companion — someone who would complement his own abilities.

Lewis considered the men he knew in the armed forces and he remembered William Clark with whom he had served in the Indian Wars and he wrote to Clark in June, 1803. He said he intended to follow the Missouri and Columbia Rivers to the Pacific Ocean and find passage back on one of the ships calling there to trade. If Clark cared to participate, he would be pleased to have him share "it's fatiegues, it's dangers and it's honors."[10] It took Clark only a day to decide he wanted to be a part of the adventure.

William Clark

William Clark was born on a plantation in Caroline County, in the eastern part of Virginia, August 1, 1770. His parents, John and Anne Rogers Clark, were old Virginia stock, the first Clark having arrived in Virginia in 1680. The Clarks were acquainted with Thomas Jefferson (in fact, Jefferson did some legal work for John Clark) and for a time, the Clark and Lewis families lived within 20 km. (12 mi.) of each other.

Almost nothing is known about William's youth. Judging from the quality of writing in his journals, he had little schooling. He grew up in the shadow of his older brother, George Rogers Clark, who rose to the rank of general in the revolution and later campaigned in the Indian Wars.

John Clark left the Caroline County plantation immediately after the revolution, when William was fourteen, to take up land around Louisville, Kentucky. He wintered in Pittsburgh and in the spring after the ice went out, he loaded his family, slaves, livestock and household goods on a flatboat and floated down the Ohio River. The Clarks were one of a thousand families to make the trek. The Indians were upset by the swell of settlers moving westward, fearing they would be outnumbered and lose control of the territory and the river. They began harassing the settlers, raiding the clumsy flatboats in their easily maneuvered canoes, and then disappearing into the woods.

The Indians were determined to drive the settlers off the land and at first they met little resistance. The federal government had allowed the standing army to dwindle to a handful of men following the revolution, and could do little to defend the settlers. Gradually, however, under General Clark, the militia was built up and, in 1786, Clark's patrols began a running warfare with the Indians. When they succeeded in reaching the Indian villages, they burned the huts, the standing crops of grain and the stores of corn, and they scalped the dead. Young William joined this campaign, perhaps as early as 1786 when he was sixteen, fighting the Indians and becoming knowledgeable in their ways, learning to survive in a hostile environment.

Later, when General Anthony Wayne was given command of the campaign, and had built a line of forts through the disputed region, Clark revealed a special talent. The Spanish, always suspicious of Americans who ventured near the Mississippi and worried, perhaps, that Wayne's preparations might be directed at them, had begun behaving in an increasingly hostile manner. For some time Clark had been overseeing the delivery of supplies to the troops, traveling between Wayne's outposts, of which some were near the Mississippi. It earned him the rank of lieutenant in 1792. Wayne now assigned Clark the additional task of gathering intelligence about the Spanish as he moved around the country. He proved to be extraordinarily good at appearing where and when the Spanish did not want him. They knew he was sent to spy on them but they never managed to find the proof of it. Meriwether Lewis, six years younger, served under Clark in these activities and it was probably under these circumstances that they had become acquainted.

Wayne moved against the Indians in July, 1794, in a well-prepared offensive that forced the natives to make peace. Lewis and Clark served in this final phase of the Indian Wars until they ended in 1795.

Clark had begun suffering from an illness in 1793. In April, 1794, he noted in his diary; "I took a puke verry sick" and five days later: "I am verry sick." The illness worsened until finally he had to ask for retirement. He left the army on July 1, 1796, and returned to the Caroline plantation.

To the Mandan villages,
May 14 - October 26, 1804[11]

Lewis had begun laying in supplies from the time Jefferson was certain the expedition would go west. To map the route, he had acquired a sextant fitted with an artificial horizon (necessary in the mountains), a quadrant, a chronometer and a number of compasses. The War Department constructed, to his specifications, the iron frame of a boat in two sections, weighing less than 50 kg. (about a hundred pounds) and, therefore, portable. It was meant to be covered with birchbark and used on the upper Missouri when the river became too shallow to float the large boats in which they would begin the journey.

Lewis left Washington early in July, 1803, going to Pittsburgh to pick up a keelboat that was being built there, and hoping to get the expedition some distance up the Missouri before winter. The boat was not completed until late in August and it was the middle of November before Lewis and Clark reached the Mississippi River. Lewis presented himself to the Spanish governor in St. Louis early in December only to find that Louisiana had not been transferred to the United States. In fact, the governor professed to have no knowledge of the Louisiana Purchase and no authority to permit the expedition to pass up the Missouri. It was late in the year — better to wait for the transfer, which must be imminent, and prepare for an early spring start. To avoid any chance for conflict with the governor, he chose Riviere du Bois, on the east side of the Mississippi for his headquarters. He could look up the Missouri River from this place and contemplate the future while he made his plans to ascend the river.

The two explorers hired a number of key men to form the nucleus of the party they would take upriver — George Drouillard, a French Canadian woodsman and a dead shot who could "sign talk" about simple, basic matters with almost any tribe of Indians — Sergeant John Ordway whom Lewis knew from his army days — Patrick Gass, a short, powerful man who could build anything from a canoe to a fort with ordinary tools — and eight men from Tennessee, one a blacksmith, another with experience in housebuilding and the others with a variety of skills useful in the backwoods.[12]

Clark kept the carpenters busy cutting trees and sawing them into planks to construct two pirogues (boats shaped like flatirons). Others from the growing complement hunted and prepared provisions for the coming voyage. Sergeant Ordway worked at fashioning a military type force out of the recruits. They needed target practice and they had to learn discipline to cope with the dangers and hardships, both known and unsuspected, that lay up the Missouri. It took several courts-martial, a number of lashings, two dismissals and a winter of drilling before Ordway thought the men ready to leave the protection of their civilization and start into the unknown.

Lewis went into St. Louis to witness the formal transfer of Upper Louisiana from France to the United States on March 10, 1804. Now they could travel all the way to the source of the Missouri within the confines of the United States. Beyond that — on the other side of the Continental Divide — the Spanish claimed first rights to the coastline. The claim was suspect because they had never founded a settlement north of California. Americans had reason to feel they had proprietary rights to the lower Columbia River. A countryman, Robert Gray, had sailed into the river twelve years earlier — the first white man of record to set foot on the shores of the river at its mouth.

The two explorers collected every known scrap of information about the Missouri during the 1803-04 winter. They talked to rivermen, trappers and frontiersmen including an aging Daniel

Boone who lived in the vicinity. Jefferson supplied them with translations of notes left by Spanish explorers of the interior. It added up to pitifully little that was exact and dependable. They were not able to unearth any advance knowledge about the latitude, along the length of the Continental Divide, at which the Missouri had its source. They could only hope that when they came to its headwaters and crossed the Divide, they would be conveniently near the valley of the Columbia River.

Lewis and Clark had an advantage, compared to Alexander Mackenzie when he set out for the Pacific Ocean in 1793, although there is no indication in their journals that the two explorers used the advantage. In Mackenzie's time the best map of the Northwest coast was based on James Cook's 1778 voyage. Cook sighted the mainland only at intervals between Nootka Sound and Cook Inlet; his outline of the coast was merely a sketch and its positioning only approximately accurate. Since that time George Vancouver had mapped the lower Columbia River and recorded its latitude and longitude. Thus Lewis and Clark were in a position to know the exact geographical coordinates of their final destination. They could work out how far they were east, and north or south, of their goal at any point on their journey. Mackenzie had had to rely on information from the local Indians.

The expedition got under way on May 14, 1804, but without Lewis; he was in St. Louis on business but also to take leave of a number of girls who had helped him pass the winter. He could catch up in a few days by riding overland. The dozen men Jefferson had visualized now consisted of forty-eight — the two explorers, Clark's negro slave, three interpreters, twenty-five Americans who had enlisted in the army for the duration of the journey, an escort of seven soldiers, and ten local men of French descent. The youngest was nineteen years old; Clark, at thirty-four, was the oldest.

The expedition's fleet consisted of three boats — a ponderous shallow-draft, 17 m. (55 ft.), twenty-two oar keelboat (the men called it a barge) fitted with a square sail and a cannon mounted on the prow — a red-painted pirogue with seven oars and another, painted white, with six oars, each with a blunderbuss mounted on a swivel. The expedition had four horses that the hunters used to

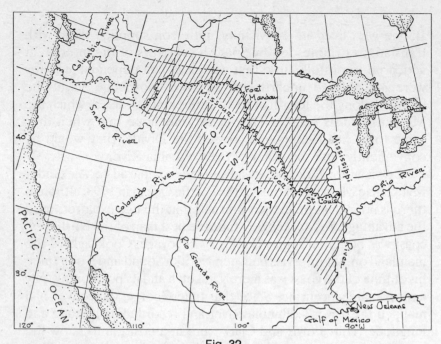

Fig. 32
The route of the Lewis and Clark expedition from St. Louis to the mouth of the Columbia River, 1804-05.

range the prairie for whatever they could shoot; the herd was augmented on the way by a few strays.

The cargo included twenty-one bales of presents to buy good-will, food and services from the Indians — tomahawks, scalping knives, flags, clothing (scarlet coats and leggings, feathered hats, white shirts), quantities of mirrors, beads, earrings, brooches, medals, garters, brass and iron combs, scissors, ribbon, thread, finger and curtain rings and other items of personal adornment. It included clothes, bedding and tents for the men, a portable blacksmith shop, iron, horseshoes, kegs of whiskey and brandy, provisions (corn, flour, biscuit, salt, pork, coffee, beans, peas, sugar, lard, meal, cooking oil) packed in barrels and kegs, candles, candlewick, tools, drugs and medical instruments, and a violin which proved to be one of the most useful items; its owner relieved the monotony and gave the men pleasure, and he astounded the Indians with the sounds he drew from it.[13]

190

Clark had learned something of the art of navigation from Lewis during the winter. He began mapping the course of the Missouri using the methods of previous explorers — fixing its direction with a compass and judging the distance between bends from their speed (as deduced by throwing out a log fastened to a known length of line and measuring the time taken to travel the distance). He planned to correct errors and establish the location of the river, especially where other large rivers joined it, with determinations of latitude and longitude.

Lewis and Clark continued to have disciplinary problems. Men went absent without leave, they misbehaved in the settlements, stole whiskey from the ships' stores and failed to stay awake when on sentry duty. They were approaching the country of the Sioux Indians who had gained a reputation among whites for being untruthful, unpredictable, fierce and barbarous. It was vital that the men learned to remain alert against the possibility of a surprise attack in which they might have to fight for their lives.

Men charged with an offense were judged by a court of enlisted men, usually with Clark presiding. In the beginning the guilty were sentenced to be lashed on the bare back with switches. Curiously, Indians who witnessed floggings were horrified; they did not believe in whipping their people, even their children. When lashing failed to stop the misdemeanors, the courts forced the men to run a gauntlet of their fellows wielding switches — also without effect. Finally, dismissal was added to the sentence. Because a man would probably not survive if he were turned loose, dismissal meant that he remained with the expedition as a common laborer, doing menial work. He was denied the more honorable tasks such as mounting guard and he became ineligible for any commendations and rewards from the federal government. This cured the men of chronic disobedience and they rounded into a happy, efficient force.

They met a few white frontiersmen rafting down the river but this traffic fell off as they penetrated upstream. Indians were not a common sight but there was a sense that the natives were watching the boats. In fact, the Sioux had sent out a call for their wandering bands of warriors to come to the river, presumably to decide how to react to the intrusion of such a formidable force of white men.

Sergeant Charles Floyd had been suffering since late in July from what was diagnosed as a bad cold. By the middle of August he was very sick and by August 20 he could not keep down food or drink. They took him ashore where he died a short time later, probably from a burst appendix. His companions buried him on the top of a high bluff downstream from a small river which today has the name of Floyd River. Nearby is the small Iowa town of Sergeant Bluff, also named in his memory.[14]

Towards the end of August, as the Americans neared the site of today's Sioux City, Iowa, the Sioux began to appear along the shore. Their numbers increased daily and they grew bolder, demanding gifts of ammunition and whiskey. They were suspicious of the expedition. They could tolerate the odd trapper, trader or squawman in their country but this was something else. They did not believe Lewis and Clark when the two white men explained their main purpose was to explore the country. The sheer size of the expedition hinted at a permanence — something that once established, they would not be able to dislodge or dominate.

They grew insolent, goading the whites, often holding the lines of the boats when the Americans tried to cast off. They tried intimidation, ostentatiously stringing their bows and making to pull arrows from their quivers. They stopped short of attacking the intruders, however, uneasy perhaps because they could see they had vastly superior arms. Lewis and Clark held their tempers, making it clear they would not turn back and if they were pushed to it, they would fight.[15] In the face of this disciplined but not arrogant stand, the hostility of the Sioux lessened and in time relations seemed almost amicable.

In October, when the expedition was about 80 km. (50 mi.) below the site of Bismarck, North Dakota, Mandan Indians began to appear along the high mud banks of the river to watch the three boats pass. Their numbers grew, day by day, until the shoreline was often crowded with curious natives. The explorers wanted to winter with the Mandans; to guarantee themselves a welcome, they persuaded two chiefs to come aboard for the remainder of the voyage to the villages. They arrived there on October 26.

The Mandans were used to white men; the la Vérendryes, who had visited them sixty years earlier, had been followed by other traders from Canada. Lewis and Clark found a number of Canadians in the villages, in friendly competition with a few Americans who had ascended the Missouri. The easygoing Mandans seemed quite happy to have the white men in their midst.

The men were in need of rest after the strenuous labor of rowing, poling and lining the boats up the Missouri but first they would have to build solid quarters. They would need protection against the cold prairie winter and a deterrent against attack from the Sioux who were reported to be showing renewed irritation with the white visitors. A fort — they called it Fort Mandan — was finished in November.

Those men who had no knowledge of native life were amazed to discover it was common courtesy among Indian tribes to offer a guest not only food and lodging, but also a female companion for the night. She might be a wife, a sister or a slave. A wife was the property of the husband; he could offer her (or for that matter, his sister) in friendship or sell her services. The Indians did not approve of wifely infidelity. An affair had to have the consent of the husband or, if the girl was not married, of a brother, to be respectable. If a wife engaged in an illicit affair she might be severely punished by the offended warrior. The Americans made much use of these privileges — to such an extent that one of the Indian chiefs remarked that it seemed they had never before seen women.

Among the Indians who visited the fort in January were two squaws. One, little older than a child and eight months pregnant, was named Sacagawea; the other's name is not known. They were Shoshone (Snake) Indians from the mountainous region where the Missouri had its source, captured by Blackfoot Indians living in the foothills and brought east. They had been traded from one warrior to the next until they were acquired by Touissant Charbonneau, a middle-aged French Canadian. Sacagawea was sick and undernourished — an object of pity — and Lewis arranged that she be provided with proper food during the remainder of her pregnancy. On February 11, after a lengthy and painful labor, Sacagawea gave birth to a boy.[16]

Charbonneau was a thoroughly disreputable fellow but he had a valuable commodity — he could converse with the Blackfoot Indians who lived on the plains along the upper Missouri River. Sacagawea, a Shoshone, spoke the language of the Rocky Mountain Indians. Lewis and Clark came to the realization that the pair could be of service to the expedition as guides and interpreters. So they concluded an agreement with Charbonneau — he and Sacagawea and her two-month-old infant would accompany them to the Pacific. The other little "wife" would stay behind.

The explorers talked with all the Indians, trappers and traders who professed to have knowledge about the upper Missouri and the route over the mountains and down to the Pacific. Much of what they were told was legend, some was fabricated, probably little of it was fact. They sifted the stories, Clark gradually compiling a geographical map and Lewis a written account of their conclusions.

They had become convinced the Missouri would lead them past a great waterfall to the Continental Divide, if they always chose the correct branch when the river forked. They had been told that an easy 25 km. (15 mi.) portage would take them from a still-navigable part of the Missouri, over the Divide to a large river in which salmon were plentiful and formed the main diet of the local Indians; surely the Columbia. According to Sacagawea, the Shoshone Indians had any number of horses for packing the baggage over the portage. It looked like a fairly routine operation to the two ex-military explorers.

Fort Mandan to the foothills, April 7 - July 22, 1805[17]

Lewis and Clark had planned to take only ten men across the continent but the hostility of the Sioux had given them reason to think they needed a larger party. They had settled on a complement of thirty-four, including Sacagawea and her infant. The others would go down river, taking a load of Indian curios, animal horns, specimens of plants and a number of live animals in cages. Lewis included a letter to his mother and a long report for Jefferson.

194

They took to the river on April 7, 1805, the St. Louis-bound men in the big barge and the exploration party in the two pirogues and six small dugouts built during the winter. Lewis recorded the start in his diary: "We are now about to penetrate a country of at least two thousand miles in width, on which the foot of civilized man has never trodden."[18] The statement shows that the explorers had not used George Vancouver's measurement of the latitude and longitude at the mouth of the Columbia river to calculate their distance from Fort Mandan. Otherwise Lewis would have known that they were half that distance (about 1,750 km. or 1,100 mi.) almost due east of their objective.

The Sioux, not believing the real purpose of the expedition, expected most of the Americans to go downstream, leaving some to man the fort. A day before the Americans embarked, their old men, women and children began lining the shore below the Mandan village. The cumbersome barge passed by downstream unmolested while the main body of boats went upstream. If the Sioux warriors had intended an attack, they ere disappointed; by the time they realized most of the whites had gone up the river, it was too late for pursuit, either up or down the river.

The character of the river was different above the Mandan villages. It generally flowed faster, sometimes splashing down rapids so swiftly they had to tow the boats. In places the shore was covered with sharp rocks intergrown with prickly plants that tore their deerskin moccasins and left their feet bruised and bleeding. Where the banks were close tot he water's edge, the laboring men could not avoid disturbing the delicate balance of the slopes and loose stones and gravel rolled down on them. Parts of the river were so turbulent they feared the boats would swamp and so the men went over the side and literally carried the boats through the water. Still, they moved west and occasionally they could use the sails and run easily up the river.

They ate well; buffalo and deep and other animals were plentiful and so unafraid it was easy to shoot them. They lived mainly on meat and when they ate their fill each consumed about 5 kg. (about 10 lb.) per day.

195

Almost daily they saw signs of grizzly bear and by the first week in May these had become a common sight. The Mandans had warned them that it took a party of six to ten warriors to kill one and after a series of encounters with the huge, ferocious animals, the white men developed a healthy respect for them.

Curiously, they had not seen one Indian since leaving Fort Mandan, although there was much evidence of their existence in the form of old campsites and discarded clothing.

On June 2, they reached an unexpected fork[19] in the river, one branch flowing in from the northwest (it was Maria's River) and the other from the southwest. The rivers were about equal in size but the southwest branch was clear and swift whereas the other was muddy, much like the part of the Missouri they had been ascending. Which branch would take them into the mountains, opposite the river said to abound in salmon? The nearby hills were not high enough to let them trace the rivers' valleys although they did get a look at a distant range of mountains running counter to their course.

They were inclined, at first, to take the branch that most resembled the Missouri but in the end Lewis chose the southwest river, reasoning that its swift, clear water was characteristic of a mountain stream. The conclusion clashed with the conventional wisdom among whites which held that in Louisiana, no sizable river flowed eastward from the mountains north of latitude 45°N (their present latitude was 47°N).

Before continuing upstream, they concealed in several underground caches, ammunition, lead, a spare ax and other items they could do without. They put up the bigger pirogue on an island, lashing it to trees against the danger of spring floods. The river was narrower and swifter above the fork and too shallow for a vessel of this size.

Lewis had been ill for some days but on June 11 he felt well enough to go ahead of the boats with several men to search for the great falls said by the Mandans to sit astride the Missouri River. The exertion was too much for him and he developed a fever and severe intestinal pains. By evening he was very sick. Remembering his grandmother Lucy's cures, he instructed his men to collect and boil choke cherry twigs. When the water had turned black from the juices, he drank half a liter (two cups) of the bitter stuff and as much again an hour later. By ten o'clock he was free of pain and soon the fever left him. He had a good night and in the morning, fortified by another dose of his medicine, he set off again.

Later that day, Lewis detected the roar of falling water. Hurrying forward, he saw a spray rising above the plain like a column of smoke and as he came nearer, the river falling as a smooth even sheet over a precipice at least 25 m. (80 ft.) high. Now he had the assurance that they were ascending the correct branch of the river. They had arrived at the place which is known today as Great Falls, in Montana.[20]

Clark reached the falls with the boats three days later. He and the men had struggled with the river, slipping and stumbling on cut feet as they dragged the boats up against the increasingly swift current. They were exhausted and suffering from a variety of ailments aggravated by their daily travail. Sacagawea had been ill for weeks and had grown worse in the last few days. Clark bled her twice and dosed her with salts and brews, to no avail. They were afraid she would die and they worried how they would care for her child if this happened.

There was more bad news. A survey indicated it would take a portage of at lest 25 km. (15 mi.) to get around the great falls and four smaller falls and various rapids above them. They would have to make a lengthy halt here to mark out and cut a road and haul the boats and cargo to where they could use the river again. However, for a time they would be free of the demands of the river and for this they were grateful.

Lewis used his grandmother's medical skills on Sacagawea, dosing her with sulphur water from a nearby spring, and medicines brewed from bark. Her delirium and fever vanished within a day and he had her eating buffalo broth. In another two days she was walking about the camp and on the mend.

They built two wagons, using for wheels cross sections sawn from a cottonwood tree more than half a meter (one-and-a-half feet) in diameter at the base — the only tree of that size in the vicinity.[21] They cut up the mast of the remaining pirogue for axles. The wagons were primitive and the axles kept breaking but it was

197

better than backpacking over a portage that was longer (about 30 km. or 18 - 20 mi.) than first estimated. It became easier still when someone thought to hoist sails on the wagons. It took four arduous trips to move their goods around the falls and rapids.

The pirogue was simply too big and heavy to portage and they left it at the foot of the falls. Lewis reckoned the time had come to construct a boat with the iron frame they had transported from St. Louis. No birchbark trees grew in the region and Lewis improvised, covering the frame with elkskins and buffalo hides stitched together with leather thongs. He intended to use pine tar to fill the needle holes and cement the seams but the local pine trees gave no tar. He experimented with other products, finally smearing a mixture of charcoal, beeswax and melted buffalo fat over the openings. When it was put in the water, the boat floated and bobbed like a cork. Lewis was elated and named her the *Experiment*. Alas — as the waterproofing mixture dried, it cracked and flaked off. There was no time for further experimentation; the boat was a failure. Its demise meant they would have to construct additional dugouts and it took a wide-ranging search to find suitably large trees.

On July 15, a month after they reached the falls, they launched the expedition again. They had placed certain excess cargo in a cache against their return and hauled the pirogue out of the river and hidden it near the base of the falls. Their sole means of transport was the dugouts.

The river flowed steadily from the southwest. It was too shallow to use the oars and they had to pole the dugouts upstream. Directly ahead, in the path of the river, loomed the mountains with the threat that not far above them the current would be too swift to navigate. When it seemed they were almost under the brow of the mountains, however, the river abruptly changed direction, flowing from the southeast. The current was faster and the poles slipped on the smooth, flat stones on the river's bottom. They were traveling roughly parallel to the northwest-southeast trend of the Rocky Mountains.

On July 19, the little fleet passed into a canyon; its walls rose from the river as steep cliffs to approximately 350 m. (about 1,200 ft.). Lewis called this canyon entrance the Gates of the Rocky

198

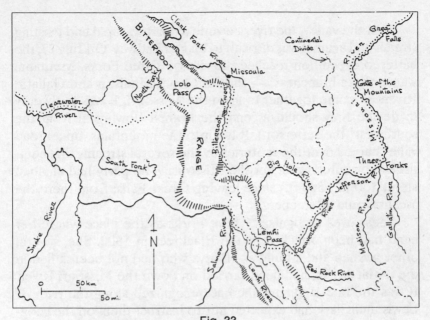

Fig. 33
The Lewis and Clark portage from the Missouri (i.e. Beaverhead) River,
across the Continental Divide, to the Clearwater River.

Mountains. The river ran deep and narrow through the gorge for a distance of 10 km. (6 mi.). It flowed swiftly but they were able to row against the current and in this they were fortunate because there was nowhere to walk had they been forced to tow the boats.

Out of the canyon, the country opened into a wide valley of plains and meadows and the river broadened to a width of 1.5 km. (1 mi.). On their right they could see the mountains soaring into the clouds. It was clear to all that if the Missouri flowed out of those mountains, they would soon have to abandon the heavy, clumsy dugouts and use another method of transportation. There was too much baggage to backpack and besides, the men were bruised, sick and tired. Clark had sprained his ankle and it hurt dreadfully when he put his weight on it. The expedition was going to need horses and to get them they would have to find the Shoshone Indians who lived in the mountains. On July 20, as luck would have it, they was Indian smoke signals ahead, a sure indication the Indians had seen the boats and were spreading the news.[22]

199

Past the valley, the river became a narrow, rapid and twisting stream and again it was difficult to make headway. On July 27, the battered expedition reached the site of Three Forks, Montana, where three branches[23] — the Jefferson, Madison and Gallatin Rivers — come together to form the Missouri. It was fairly easy to decide they should ascend the branch flowing in from the southwest (the Jefferson). It led into the mountains, up a broad valley carved over the centuries by the several streams that comprise the source waters of the Missouri. The party had climbed about 150 m. (500 ft.) since leaving Great Falls; from there the ascent would be steeper.

Sacagawea recognized Three Forks as the place where her band had been attacked by the Blackfeet in 1800. She, several other women and a number of boys who had not been killed in the initial attack, had been carried on down the Missouri River. It was the first landmark she had recognized along the river. If Lewis and Clark had expected her to instruct them on the geography of the region, they must have been disappointed, but she could not be blamed; she had been very young when captured, with only a child's knowledge of her surroundings.

Over the Continental Divide, August 12[24]

The expedition remained at Three Forks for three days while Lewis made some astronomical observations and Clark rested his ankle. Both men needed time to mull over the future. The plan to this point had been simply to ascend the river, choosing the branch when there was a choice, that would lead them towards the Continental Divide. It could be different when they reached the headwaters; they might have to search among several source streams for one that turned into a pass at the summit. It was late in July with little time left before snow could be expected to fall in the high altitudes. Should they abandon the river and backpack what they could carry into the mountains to search for a pass and a route to the Columbia River? Surely this was courting the possibility that they would have to winter in the mountains where shelter, food and firewood was scarce.

200

It was essential to make contact with the Shoshone Indians, to obtain horses and guides from them — but the Shoshone avoided the white men. They were wary of strangers, knowing that when they went down to the plains to hunt buffalo, they were harried and bullied by the Blackfeet, who had superior arms. The Shoshone lived in the mountains because they found a measure of peace and security there. It carried a price — they existed at a bare subsistence level for game was scarce at these elevations. They had seen the men of the Lewis and Clark expedition advancing up the Missouri. Dressed in rough leathers, their faces burned dark by the sun, they looked like Indians. The Shoshone reasoned they were Blackfeet, bent on pursuing and scalping them, for why else would a well-armed force enter the barren mountains? So they made themselves scarce.

The expedition left Three Forks August 1, moving southwest up the Jefferson River. They had barely entered the mountains and already the river was so shallow that often there was not enough water to float the boats. On August 6, while Lewis was scouting ahead, Clark turned up the Big Hole River with the boats, thinking it was the main branch. He struggled against the swift water, clogged with bushes, for 15 km. (9 mi.) before turning back to the Missouri (which is called the Beaverhead River above the Big Hole). On the way down, one of the dugouts sank and another shipped water and wet their medical supplies.

The happenings were not all bad. Above the Big Hole River Sacagawea recognized another landmark in the form of a rock shaped like a beaver's head. She was sure this was Shoshone country and that her people must have a camp nearby. Lewis decided to push ahead and not return to the boats until he found the camp. He recognized the danger in pursuing a band of Indians with only a few companions. If they turned on him he might be killed. Determined to face this prospect, he found a quiet place beside the river and wrote up his reports, trying to put to paper all that might help the expedition if he did not return.

After taking breakfast with the others on August 9, Lewis started up alongside the river with Drouillard and two other men. Almost at once they found abundant evidence that Indians had gone that way. Next day they came to a well-worn trail that led to a fork[25] in the river where one branch (Red Rock River) comes in from the southeast and the other from the west. Looking at the river, Lewis knew the dugouts could not be dragged past this fork. This was as near to the Divide as they could come by water.

They reconnoitered a short distance up each branch on August 11. The horse tracks along the one leading to the west seemed more obvious, but the trail, as well as the tracks, soon grew faint. Lewis gave it up and turned to the main branch (the Red Rock River) and the trail alongside it. This trail, too, with its faint trace of horse tracks, faded into nothing discernible in little more than a kilometer (less than a mile).

Looking about, Lewis saw a depression on the western horizon. Sure that it was part of the route the local Indians used to cross the mountains, Lewis left a message at the river's fork telling Clark to wait there while he investigated. Then, walking abreast to cover a swath of the country, the four men advanced towards the depression. Lewis cautioned the men to move quietly and if one of them sighted a trail, to signal by raising his hat on his rifle. They had walked this way for about 8 km. (5 mi.) when suddenly Lewis saw, about 3 km. (2 mi.) ahead, a horseback rider picking his way through the low growth towards them. He could make out through his telescope that he was dressed in unfamiliar Indian clothes; surely this was a Shoshone.

The Indian detected them soon afterwards and halted his horse, staring suspiciously as, still abreast, four strangers advanced on him. Lewis tried to convey his friendly intentions with signals, holding up gifts and shouting the few Shoshone words of friendship he had learned from Sacagawea. The Indian let them get within two hundred paces before he wheeled his horse and rode off through the brush. It must have appeared to him that Lewis was trying to hold his attention while the others circled around to his rear.

Lewis was bitterly disappointed at this missed opportunity and later he must have blamed himself for not asking Sacagawea to accompany this scouting part and for failing to learn the rudiments of the Shoshone dialect from her.

There was little they could do but try to follow the Indian's tracks and hope that he would not drive the tribe under cover when he reached the Shoshone camp. The tracks led towards the depression and presently the white men came to a well-worn trail.

They camped that night beside a tiny creek less than a man's stride wide. As they drank from its clear cold water they remembered how wide and muddy the Missouri was on the plains. They marveled at the extent of their journey and how the river had changed over its course.

They woke next morning (August 12) with a sense of anticipation, sure that the Continental Divide lay just above them. Indeed, they had climbed only a short time when they topped a rise and saw before them the land fall away to the west. They had reached the Divide and they stood in the Lemhi Pass in the Bitterroot Mountains on the border between Montana and Idaho, at an elevation of 2,247 m. (7,373 ft.). Nothing had prepared them for the sight before their eyes. They had been expecting a single line of peaks and beyond them, a steady descent to the Pacific Ocean — much, in reverse, like their ascent from the plains. Instead, they saw range after immense range of high mountains, their tops covered with snow, fading into the horizon.[26] It would not be an easy journey to the western sea. However, they had reached the top of the principal barrier and were jubilant as they started along a trail leading down its western slope. They had gone only a short distance when they came to a stream; its waters, they knew, would eventually fall into the Pacific Ocean and their spirits rose to new heights.

They saw no more signs of life until midmorning of the next day when they got a distant look at two women and a man who ran off at first sight of the white men. They were certain now that the trail would lead them to the Shoshone camp. Suddenly they came upon three natives — a young woman who immediately ran into the underbrush, and an old woman and a child who cowered in fear as Lewis approached. Lewis bared his arm to show his white skin and assure them he was not a Blackfoot and a traditional enemy, and he offered them gifts from his pack. Soon the young woman came out of hiding and joined them.

Drouillard used his sign language to induce the women to lead them down the trail towards the camp. The whites had a few anxious moments when they came abruptly on a party of sixty warriors, roused, probably, by the Indian they had encountered east of the Divide. The two groups stared at each other for an interval until Lewis broke the tension by making a show of putting up his rifle. Then, carrying a flag, he advanced on the Indians with his men and the Indian women a short distance behind. The chief saw his women were unharmed and unafraid, and when he spoke to them they held up their gifts. In an instant the war party was transformed into a welcoming committee and much to Lewis's disgust, the chief embraced him and rubbed his grease-painted cheeks against the white man's. Drouillard signed to the chief that Lewis wanted to be taken into the Indian camp. The chief was willing and, holding high the flag, he led the way.

Having smoked a pipe of peace in the Shoshone camp, Lewis, with Drouillard's help, explained his mission, telling the chief the main body of the expedition was still on the river. He said he needed help in transporting their baggage over the Divide and he wanted to be guided down to a navigable river. The conference was followed by a meal consisting mainly of berries; it was the only food in camp.

Lewis was taken down to the Lemhi River, flowing northwesterly and parallel to the Divide, a short distance west of the camp. It looked navigable but trees large enough to hollow out for dugouts did not grow at this elevation. The chief told Lewis the Lemhi soon joined another river (he was referring to the Salmon River which flows northwest for a short distance before turning west to join the Snake River). He said the other river could not be navigated and it was not possible to take a packstring of horses down its valley.

Lewis was encouraged by the sight of several hundred horses[27] grazing near the camp and the next day (August 14) he set about persuading the Shoshone to help bring Clark and the rest of the expedition across the Divide. The Indians were reluctant, disinclined to help the white men, not quite trusting them. When Lewis thought to tell them about Clark's negro slave, however, they were wild to see the phenomenon of a black human and they forgot their reservations. The enthusiasm lasted until a warrior spread the rumor that Lewis was plotting an ambush. Lewis countered by challenging their bravery and this got the chief and half a dozen warriors moving towards the Divide. Soon they were joined by more warriors and before they reached the pass, all the men from the camp and a number of women had joined the trek.

Next morning Lewis sent his two men to hunt, hoping the sight of fresh meat would buy him the Indians' support. They shot several deer which the natives literally tore to bits in their frenzy to get a morsel. Lewis thought this had earned the natives' gratitude but next day they began to slip away one by one. He arrived at the Red Rock River with only twenty-eight men and three women. There was no sign of Clark and the Shoshone grew suspicious again. Lewis sent Drouillard to the fork of the river — to bring up Clark or the message he had left for him. Clark was not at the fork but the message, fortunately, was still in place. Lewis showed it to the chief explaining that Clark had sent it ahead by some magic. Suitably impressed, the Indians decided to see what the next day would bring.

The following morning (August 17), Lewis sent Drouillard downriver with instructions to find Clark and bring him back. Lewis was about out of tricks and he doubted he could keep the Indians with him another day. He need not have worried. Drouillard had only just left when a warrior came whooping into camp, shouting that the expedition was a short distance below them. It caused a stampede, each Shoshone eager to see for himself. When the meeting was made, Sacagawea discovered that this was the band from whom she had been taken and the chief was her brother.

The dugouts reached the fork of the river about noon and the men made camp, raising a canopy fashioned from a sail to shade the Indians while they watched the white men work. Later, the explorers joined them there and with the help of Sacagawea and Charbonneau, they talked about the importance of making horses available to the expedition. They said white traders would follow bringing rifles for barter. With modern firearms, the Shoshone could hunt effectively in the mountains. Moreover, they would be able to resist the raiding Blackfeet and even descend in safety to the plains to kill their share of the innumerable buffalo that ranged there. It would be the end of fear and starvation. In the general euphoria that characterized the council, the chief was persuaded to sell three horses and he promised more from the herd at camp.

In answer to their queries about the country to the west, the chief again stressed the difficulties of traveling to the coast. Looking at the towering mountains that barred the way, Clark had to agree.

Nevertheless, the two explorers were optimistic. They decided Clark, accompanied by a few men, should ride to the Salmon River and if it was navigable, build dugouts in readiness for taking the expedition down to the Columbia. Lewis would stay behind to get the baggage across the Divide to the western slope and bargain with the chief for more horses.

Clark started down the Lemhi valley on August 18. He reached the Salmon River and followed it to where it turns abruptly towards the west and begins a descent of 1,800 m. (6,000 ft.) to the Snake River. The Salmon was undoubtedly the shortest way to the coast but it tore down its valley, foaming over and around chunks of rock littering its bed. No crew could survive a passage down this river in a dugout, and the terrain alongside the river was too rough for horses. Clark concluded the Shoshone chief was right — they would have to travel to the sea by a different route.

Lewis, meanwhile, had cached the spare baggage, taking care he was not observed by the Indians. He sank the dugouts in deep water and weighted them with stones to keep them safe from the Shoshone and any fires that might sweep the country. Then, with Sacagawea's help, he began pressing the chief for more horses. The Shoshone readily bartered with the white men for the services of their women but they were extremely reluctant to part with their horses. By August 26, Lewis owned nine horses and a mule but he needed twice as many animals to get down to the Salmon River. He began moving the baggage to the Shoshone camp, with the women carrying what his horses could not.

Lewis received word from Clark on August 29 that the Salmon River was not navigable; they could not rely on water transport to get the expedition down the mountains. It was certain now that he had to have many more horses and he began to bargain in dead earnest with the chief. It netted him twenty-nine animals and the services of a guide they called "Old Toby," his four sons, and another Indian.

Down to the mouth of the Columbia River[29]

Lewis and Clark left the Shoshone camp on August 31 at the head of a packtrain, heading down the valley of the Lemhi River. Old Toby said he would get them to a navigable river in ten days. He led them north alongside the Continental Divide, past the point where the Salmon River turns abruptly to the west, up and over the Bitterroot Mountains and into the valley of the Bitterroot River. By the time they reached this river, early in September, all their Indian helpers except Old Toby and one son had slipped away. They were still high above the Pacific Ocean. It was cold at these altitudes in the fall of the year and they often had to endure sleet and snow as they worked the packtrain through the underbrush.

The Flathead (Salish) Indians who inhabited the Bitterroot valley were perplexed at the sight of the expedition winding through their country. They were wary at first but the strangers did not seem bent on war. The mystery deepened when they discovered that most of them were white. White mariners were known to visit the coast but these men came from the interior of the continent. Curiosity overcame apprehension when the expedition peacefully entered the camp they had abandoned and the chief came out of the bush to greet them.

They moved north again after a few days of rest, continuing down the valley with the jagged Bitterroot Mountains on their left, the packtrain augmented by a number of fresh horses and three colts. On September 9, they made camp near the site of Missoula, Montana, where the Bitterroot River joins the Clark Fork River. They were getting low on provisions and made a meal of berries the first night. The hunters killed a deer and later, two wild horses and a colt, and they ate heartily for a few days.

On September 13, they left the camp and Old Toby led them west. They crossed the Bitterroot range again, using the Lolo Pass[30] (elevation 1,595 m. = 5,233 ft.) to the Lolo Trail. It took them down the western slope of the mountains over rough, broken ground littered with fallen trees. Old Toby twice lost his way and they thrashed up and down and through hollows searching for the trail. Game was scarce; Clark and the hunters ranged widely but all they found to shoot were wolves, pheasants and ducks and they had to augment their meat supply with crayfish. Each day the task of feeding the thirty-four people of the expedition grew more difficult. Finally, they were compelled to kill and eat, one after the other, the three colts. One night they had nothing to eat but a bit of bear oil and a quantity of candles.

The men grew weak and discouraged, but just when they thought they could endure no more, they were in the valley of the Clearwater River amidst groves of tall pine trees. The hunters obtained salmon and bread from the local Indians and there was decent grazing for the horses again. Lewis halted the expedition to let men and animals enjoy the bounty. It was September 22; the ten-day journey Old Toby had promised them had lengthened into three weeks and they were still on the portage. Yet they had crossed the mountains and not a man doubted that the worst of the long trek from St. Louis was behind them. That evening Clark came into camp with the news that he had found a navigable tributary of the Columbia River — only 25 or 30 km. (20 mi.) further on.

Clark guided the straggling expedition to the Clearwater River, reaching it near the site of Orofino, Idaho[31] (elevation 313 m. = 1,027 ft.). The trail from the Lolo Pass had brought them down almost thirteen hundred meters (more than four thousand feet). As the realization dawned that the mountains were behind them and they could look forward to floating down to the sea, the strength that had sustained the men gave way. This was no triumphant parade into the presence of the Nez Perce Indians who lived here. Some of the men fell by the side of the trail and had to be carried to the site Clark had picked for a camp. Others just managed to stay on their feet and stagger along. They journeyed the last few kilometers (miles) strung out in a long, ragged line. Never since they left St. Louis had they been so vulnerable to ambush and attack; but the Nez Perce Indians chose to welcome and succor them.

Once they had recovered their strength, the men began constructing dugouts for the final leg of the voyage. The explorers cached the pack saddles, branded the horses and arranged with the Nez Perce Indians to care for them. All was ready on Octo-

208

ber 6. Thanks to the Indians, they had eaten well at the Clearwater camp and the men were in good spirits. The fare had included dogs which the French Canadians had taught the Americans to enjoy (although Clark always ate the meat under protest).

Old Toby and his son had remained faithful on the long overland portage from the Lemhi Pass, but they decided they wanted no part of the remainder of the voyage to the sea. The two Shoshones quietly disappeared without asking for their pay, heading back to their mountain home.

Navigation on the Snake River was rougher than anticipated. The clumsy dugouts were difficult to guide in the swift water coursing down the crooked channel. They ran them into rocks and upset them on unexpected shoals, often dumping men and goods into the water — losing cargo, including presents for Indians.

They reached the Columbia River[32] on October 16 and signs of traders, and by inference the presence of the coast, became plentiful. They saw Indians wearing articles of men's clothing, woolen blankets, beads and brass items of adornment. The Indians had muskets, pistols, tin powder flasks and the occasional sword, and they used metal tea kettles. No white man had been this far up the river; Lewis surmised the goods had been obtained from other Indians living closer to the sea.

On October 19, they saw Mount Adams (3,751 m. = 12,306 ft.) to the north and next day Mount Hood (3,427 m. = 11,243 ft.) loomed up south of the river.

Two Nez Perce chiefs willingly had accompanied the expedition from their camp on the Clearwater River. In the last few days they had been showing signs of unease, warning the explorers that their lives would be in danger from the Indians on the coast.

By the first week in November they could feel and smell the sea on the wind and each day the river water tasted more salty. The winds were strong enough to whip up waves and the weather was typical of the coast in fall — wet and foggy — altogether too raw for comfort. On November 7, the fog cleared for a time and they were overjoyed to see what they thought was the Pacific Ocean (it was probably the bay at the mouth of the river).[33] They heard the distant roar of the surf and they drove on, unmindful for a while of the weather.

In the afternoon of the next day they found themselves, quite suddenly, in the midst of very high waves that tossed the dugouts unmercifully. Several of the men became seasick and they were forced to land. It was a miserable place to camp. The shoreline was so confined by bluffs there was not sufficient space to stretch out for the night and enjoy what comfort their wet clothes afforded. The river water was too salty to drink and in the night the tide threatened their baggage.

They suffered through another day of heavy rain, and immense waves that drove huge logs into shore; threatening to crush the dugouts. They got away from the site on November 9, but soon had to leave the river again for another uncomfortable day ashore to wait for the storm to spend itself. It was an unpleasant introduction to the western sea, yet the men remained cheerful, anxious to see more of the ocean. Finally, the explorers were able to send out small parties to search in comfort for a better and more permanent campsite.

The Indians they had met since leaving Fort Mandan had been universally friendly if at first wary. Some of the natives they now encountered along the coast were disagreeable, hostile, aggressive and given to stealing, especially the white men's rifles and other arms. If they were detected, they abandoned stealth and subterfuge and tried to have their way by intimidation, threatening the greatly outnumbered visitors with the promise of death. The men of the expedition had experienced thieving with the interior Indians but nothing like this; it had been more of a nuisance than a menace. In the weeks that followed, the coastal Indians had to be watched constantly. Lewis and Clark controlled the thieving finally when they convinced the Indians that they would be shot for the offense.

The explorers chose a campsite with a view of the ocean on the east shore of a bay protected by Cape Disappointment. They built shelters using boards from a nearby abandoned Indian village occupied only by fleas. Fleas were everywhere; they readily deserted a natural habitat to take possession of the men's clothes, forcing a nightly search of bedding before retiring. Once fleas had infested a residence, they could not be dislodged; the owner had to seek new quarters. Hunting was not productive near the mouth

210

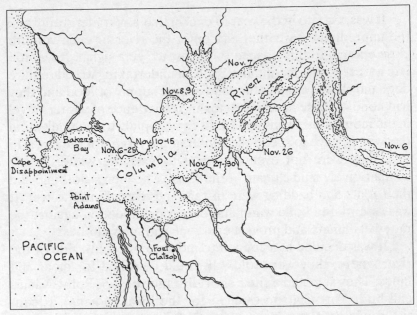

Fig. 34

William Clark's interpretation of the mouth of the Columbia River. Included are the dates and places where the party camped before building Fort Clatsop (modified; from Map 32[111] in the Atlas of *Original Journals of the Lewis and Clark Expedition 1804-06*, ed. by R. G. Thwaites, Dodd, Mead & Co., New York, 1904).

of the Columbia, where the region was well populated, but when the hunters went further afield they had good success and the men ate well in their new camp.

Lewis and Clark, separately, made journeys around Cape Disappointment and up and down the coast. They were amazed at the grandeur of the Pacific Ocean breaking on the limitless beaches and rockstrewn headlands — as are visitors to the coast of Washington and Oregon today. They were awed by pine trees more than 3 m. (10 ft.) in diameter, standing tall and straight. They saw no trading ships along the coast. According to the Indians, a Captain Youens was expected soon and other traders after that. The reports were apparently just Indian stories, made up to please the white men. Captain Youens never came.

It was too late in the year to expect that any trader would risk the unpredictable weather and enter the river or even venture close enough to this treacherous coast to see a signal. It was too late to recross the mountains. Such an undertaking would require dogs and sleds, warm clothes and a large supply of food and they had none of these necessities nor the experience of winter travel in the mountains. Lewis and Clark came rapidly to the realization they would have to spend the winter at the mouth of the river. In fact, they were not even equipped to pass the winter in the comparatively mild climate at the coast. The men's clothing, and their tents and bedding were in rags and everything was wet. It was essential to build warm and dry accommodation against the raw, wet climate and provide everyone with new clothes.

It was decided at a council to move to the south side of the river where, they were told, elk could be killed for meat and hides. They selected a site a short distance east of Point Adams and built Fort Clatsop (named for the local Indians). It consisted of two 41/2 x 15 m. (15 x 50 ft.) cabins, one with three rooms and the other with four, facing each other across a 6 x 15 m. (20 x 50 ft.) parade ground formed by connecting the cabins with a stockade. It was a small fortress when it was finished on December 30.[34] The explorers treated it like a military post, with the men doing regular shifts of sentry duty in groups of four. Indians were admitted but only for the day; with few exceptions they were put out at sundown.

The young Indian women and their male and female mentors were a nuisance. They settled down near the fort and determinedly pestered the men with their advances. One old squaw, supported at times by her husband, was a source of worry to Lewis. The sight of scabs and ulcers made it obvious her nine girls were infected with virulent venereal diseases, the product, probably, of their intimate associations with white sailors. Some were tattooed with Anglo-Saxon names, presumably of previous admirers off the ships.

Clark used the winter to work on his maps. It had become apparent during the portage over the mountains that they had made a large V-shaped detour in traveling from Great Falls to the start of the Lolo Trail. His maps confirmed this and showed how the route to the Columbia River could be shortened by about 400 km. (250 mi.).

Back to St. Louis, 1806

Lewis had the authority to send two men back by ship with the specimens that had been collected or the whole party if he thought it inadvisable to recross the mountains. The first alternative would ease the journey back across the mountains for the main body of men; but two or three men alone in this hostile environment waiting weeks, perhaps months, for a passage would be vulnerable to attack. The explorers apparently never seriously entertained this option, or the second of taking the whole party back by sea. Even if a ship happened along early in the year, the trader would want to use the summer and early fall to acquire furs along the coast. Then late in the year, he would sail to China, sell his harvest and buy a cargo before heading for the United States around Africa or South America. It would be 1807 before they saw the eastern shores of North America again.[35]

In retrospect, it seems that a flaw in the plans for the expedition was the failure to arrange for a ship — naval or merchantman — to wait at the mouth of the Columbia or call there, in the fall of 1805, to take the men back to the United States. We can guess it was prompted by a desire to spend as little money as possible.

So the explorers planned for an overland journey. Among other preparations, they manufactured salt from sea water and put aside more than 50 l. (10 gal.) to make the eating of freshly killed meat more enjoyable. They hoped for the visit of a trading vessel to obtain a supply of trinkets to buy food, horses and various services from the Indians on the homeward journey but in this they were disappointed. They were pushed by circumstances to leave early in the spring. The elk, their chief source of food, had begun migrating back to the mountains before the end of winter. Despite long days of hunting, often there was little more than a day's supply of meat in camp. The explorers were also concerned about their horses. The Nez Perce Indians regularly crossed to the eastern foothills as soon as the mountain passes were open to kill buffalo. They took with them as many horses as were available to pack the meat back to their country. The temptation to include the expedition's horses might be too great to resist. Without horses, Lewis and Clark had little chance of reaching the Missouri and the boats they had cached there, for they had more cargo now than when they left the river.

They abandoned Fort Clatsop March 23, 1806.[36] It is not relevant to this book to describe the return journey except for one incident which had a bearing on the plans of another explorer — David Thompson — who was about to resume probing the Rocky Mountains north of the forty-ninth parallel for a pass across the Divide. The explorers separated after they crossed the Lolo Pass into the Bitterroot valley. Lewis wanted to search for the shorter, more direct route to Great Falls indicated by Clark's charts; Clark would recross the Lemhi Pass and retrieve the boats cached on the upper Missouri. They planned to meet on the Missouri, at its junction with Maria's River, early in August.

The incident occurred on a tributary of Maria's River. Lewis and his men — Drouillard and two brothers, Reuben and Joseph Field — had fallen in with eight Piegan Blackfoot Indians who were scouting for a war party. It was late in the day and Lewis proposed that they spend the night together. After they had eaten, he sent his men to rest while he remained awake and on guard, suspecting an attempt to steal his horses during the night. Near midnight, when all the Indians were asleep, he woke R. Field to take his place, cautioning him to rouse the others if, for any reason, he became suspicious.

The Indians rose at daylight and crowded around the fire where J. Field sat at watch for his comrades, his gun carelessly placed behind him near his brother's weapon. In rapid order, one Indian picked up the two guns and ran off with them, another seized Lewis's weapon while a third reached for Drouillard's. Field took after and caught the first Indian and in the struggle to regain the guns, he drove his knife deep into the man's side. As the knife came out, the Indian turned and broke for the bush. He was already dead; the knife had touched the heart and after a few paces he fell in his tracks.

Fortunately, Drouillard was not asleep and when he saw the Indian take hold of his gun, he shouted "Damn you, let go my gun"

214

and got a hand on it. They fought for it, the Frenchman managing to wrestle it away from the native who, however, retained the pouch.

Lewis, wakened by the shout, jumped up in time to see the Piegan clutching his rifle, turning to make off with it. Lewis caught up his pistol and ran at the Indian, telling him to put down the gun. Meekly, he obeyed. Lewis's men, having regained their weapons, joined him, eager to shoot the prisoner. Lewis would not allow it for it appeared to him the Indians were not intent on killing the white men; they were bent only on stealing.

The other Indians, seeing that the Americans had recovered their arms, were now attempting to drive away the main body of horses. Lewis sent his men to head them off while he ran after two Piegans who were herding the few remaining horses out of the camp. Lewis called to them, threatening to shoot if they did not stop. The horses reached a bluff where they were obliged to stop. One of the natives jumped behind a rock while the other one, now only thirty paces from Lewis, turned, gun in hand. Lewis fired, hitting him in the stomach, causing him to fall to his knees and right elbow and from this position he returned the shot. He missed, but narrowly, for Lewis felt the wind of it. Aware suddenly that he had come away without his shot pouch and could not reload his pistol, Lewis returned to camp.

When the white men took stock of their situation, they found they had come out fairly well. The Indians had stolen some horses but had been forced to leave behind a larger number of their own mounts which looked to be in better condition. They had also abandoned some buffalo meat, a number of shields, bows and arrows, and one of their two rifles. When Lewis went in search of the warrior he had shot, he found him lying dead behind the rock.[37]

The Indians had been beaten but, unquestionably, the six who had escaped would bring the main body of the war party thirsting to avenge the deaths of their two companions. Not wasting any time the four men rode for the Missouri River. They rode all that day and most of the next night and as good fortune would have it, they reached the Missouri just as the dugouts carrying their companions came into view. They were

215

now fifteen strong, well armed and able to withstand any attack the Piegans could throw at them with their inferior weapons. Lewis and his three men had escaped but they were marked for death — the Piegans would not forget the incident.

The whole of the United States had thought the expedition was lost and its members dead from starvation or killed by wild animals or Indians. The report Lewis had sent down the Missouri with the barge from Fort Mandan in the spring of 1805 was the last direct word Jefferson had received. A story told by Indians in January, 1806, that the explorers had crossed the Rockies was not confirmed. In July, 1806, Mandan Indians heard that the expedition had reached the mouth of the Columbia but the explorers were back in the village before this news got to St. Louis.

The expedition landed in St. Louis on September 23, 1806, to be greeted by cheers when the people of the village recognized it. It had been two years and four months completing its task. Lewis immediately sent off a report to Jefferson in which he wrote:

> In obedience to your orders we have penetrated the Continent of North America to the Pacific Ocean and suficiently explored the interior of the country to affirm that we have discovered the most practicable communication which dose exist across the continent by means of the navigable branches of the Missouri and Columbia Rivers.[38]

21

First Trading Posts West of the Rocky Mountains, 1805-07

Alexander Mackenzie's route from Lake Athabasca to the Pacific Ocean at Bella Coola did not find much favor with the North West Company. The western section — the eighteen-day overland journey — could serve for transporting merchandise between the Pacific Ocean and posts on and near the Fraser River. However, the route was too circuitous and arduous to be profitable for moving goods and furs between the eastern foothills of the Rockies and the coast. The Peace River was a satisfactory way into the mountains but from there the Nor' Westers needed a more direct connection with the Pacific Ocean. Indians living near the foothills had discouraged Mackenzie from investigating the Finlay River as a way to the ocean. Despite this advice, some Nor' Westers now favored exploring this river that came in from the northwest and joined the Parsnip to form the Peace. They reasoned that perhaps Peter Pond's "Cook's River" (correponding to Cook Inlet in southern Alaska) could be reached from it. In 1797, they sent James Finlay up the river that now bears his name, to search for a more northerly way to the Pacific. He found no opening in the rugged Coastal Mountains and gave up the quest.

Back at its junction with the Peace, Finlay ascended the Parsnip and discovered the Pack River which is the entrance to the Crooked River water system that Mackenzie had missed in 1793. He went up the Pack only as far as McLeod Lake, however, and did not find the easy way of reaching the Fraser River. As a consequence, Mackenzie's dreadful route up the Parsnip and down James Creek remained for a time as the road to the Fraser. It must have acted as a deterrant because for almost a decade after

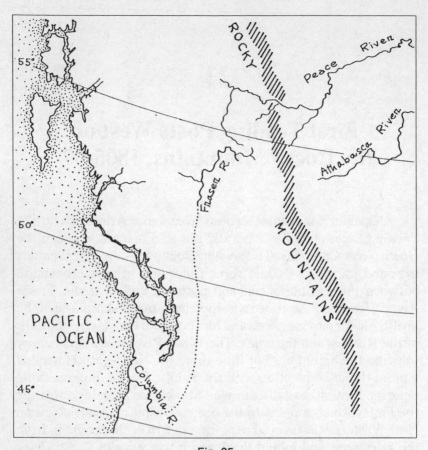

Fig. 35

The course of the Columbia River according to Alexander Mackenzie, joining the known parts of the Fraser and Columbia Rivers (after Alexander Mackenzie: *Voyages from Montreal.* Cadell & Davies, London, 1801).

Finlay's journey, no attempts were made to capitalize on Mackenzie's breach of the Rocky Mountains.

Mackenzie's version of the Columbia River — joining the part of the Fraser he had traversed to the 160 km. (100 mi.) length of the Columbia Lieutenant Broughton had surveyed — was gradually accepted by the Nor' Westers. They concluded that the mystery of the "River of the West" was solved. It remained only to descend the river to its mouth to see if it could be exploited as

218

the long-sought water route between the mountains and the Pacific coast.

It is not known who, in the North West Company, made the decision to send an expedition down the river to test its potential. We can assume it was prompted by the news that the Lewis and Clark expedition had left St. Louis in 1804, bound for the Pacific Ocean. Thomas Jefferson's ambition to funnel all of the trade with the interior Indians to the United States was well known. The Nor' Westers had not taken it seriously enough to mount a concerted push and build on Mackenzie's successes to secure the Pacific Northwest for themselves. News of the expedition turned Jefferson's ambition into a threat; they felt their dominant role in the Northwest challenged and, belatedly, they reacted.

In 1805, Simon Fraser, one of the Nor' Westers trading in Athabasca, received orders to establish trading posts west of the Rocky Mountains. He was instructed to build a depot on the great south-flowing river and use it as a base to explore the river to its mouth. These actions following on Mackenzie's discovery of the river were expected to establish the company's right to trade on the river and use it for transportation to the Western Sea. However, if Fraser's voyage to the Pacific was intended to be a race against Lewis and Clark, it was lost before it began. The two Americans reached the mouth of the Columbia late in 1805, before Fraser began building his first trading post.

Simon Fraser

The choice of Simon Fraser to head the project must have been an obvious one. Although unlettered and quite lacking in polish, he was a fearless and resolute man, tough yet flexible when the situation required it.

Fraser numbered among his ancestors and relatives several Frasers who took part in storied events in history. An earlier Simon Fraser, the fourteenth Lord Lovat, was beheaded with the ax on Tower Hill, London, in 1747 for his part in the Jacobite uprisings. One of his uncles died in the Black Hole of Calcutta in 1756. Two other uncles fought with Wolfe at Quebec and one of

219

them settled in Canada and had a distinguished career which included an appointment as judge in the Montreal courts.

Fraser's father received a good Scottish education and enjoyed a taste for music and poetry. His mother was wellborn — the former Isabella Grant, daughter of the Laird of Daldregan. They emigrated to the American colonies in 1773 (the Mackenzies followed a year later) and settled on a 65 hectare (160 acre) farm in Mapletown, near Bennington, in what is now Vermont. This is where Fraser was born in 1776.

The Frasers were openly loyal to Britain in a community where the sentiment was for rebellion. It brought them active dislike and distrust and when hostilities broke out, harassment. To make matters worse, Fraser's father joined the British forces under General John Burgoyne in 1777, and took part in a battle near Bennington. Burgoyne capitulated at Saratoga in October; Fraser was imprisoned in Albany. The prison conditions were so bad he died after little more than a year.

Fraser's mother was now in desperate trouble; her status in the neighborhood suffered further when it became generally known that her eldest son, and her uncles and brothers, had all joined the British forces. Still, she stayed on the farm until 1784, when she managed to sell it and move to Canada with the proceeds. As United Empire Loyalists, she and her six children each obtained 81 hectare (200 acre) grants of land in Cornwall Township and the family settled there.

Fraser is believed to have attended school in Montreal from the age of fourteen. Two of his uncles were in the fur trade and this may have influenced him to accept an apprenticeship with McTavish, Frobisher & Company in 1792, at the age of sixteen (Mackenzie joined this company in 1794, after his return from the Pacific). Little is known about Fraser's whereabouts and activities in the next ten years. The North West Company's records are scanty and to make his history even more difficult to decipher, at least four Simon Frasers worked for the company in the 1790s. It is known that he became a clerk in the Athabasca department in 1799 and within three years, at the age of twenty-five, he was admitted as a partner. He never rose to be the senior partner in Athabasca.[1]

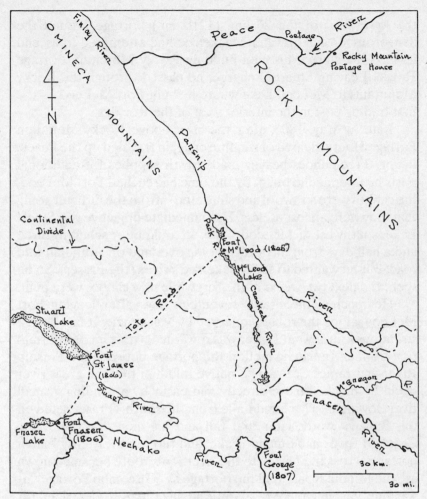

Fig. 36
Simon Fraser's travels between 1805 and 1807.

First trading posts west of the Continental Divide, 1806-07

The activities that won Simon Fraser a place in history began
in the fall of 1805. With two clerks — John Stuart and James
McDougall — he took a brigade of about a dozen voyageurs up
the Peace River to the base of the Peace River Canyon. Here, at

the lower end of the 20 km. (12 1/2 mi.) portage around the dangerous stretch of water Mackenzie had attempted to ascend in 1793, he started his men building Rocky Mountain Portage House. Leaving Stuart in charge, he passed through the Rocky Mountains to McLeod Lake where he built Fort McLeod — the first trading post in the interior west of the Rockies.

Late in May, 1806, after the river above Rocky Mountain Portage House cleared of ice, Fraser again traveled up the Peace, taking three canoes heavily loaded with supplies for additional posts he intended to build. By the time he reached Fort McLeod, the canoes were so "worn and shattered"[2] from the difficult going that they were almost useless. His immediate objective was Stuart Lake, southwest of McLeod Lake. It could be reached in three and a half days from the fort by going overland on an Indian tote road, but he wanted to see Mackenzie's river (the Fraser). So he spent the next two weeks at the fort while new canoes were built.

He reached the Fraser seventeen days after leaving Fort McLeod, along the route pioneered by Mackenzie. It had been a strenuous journey but Fraser was rewarded with a bit of information from an Indian he met on the portage between the Parsnip River and James Creek. The native told him that the great river could be reached more directly and easily by ascending a small river flowing into McLeod Lake from the south.[3] Fraser acted on the Indian's words later that fall and his men discovered the Crooked River and Summit Lake, and the relatively easy Indian portage across the Divide to the river. This route became known as "the Middle Road" and the portage as "Giscombe Portage." It was the "carrying place of about one day's march" described for Alexander Mackenzie by an old Indian at Fort Fork in the winter of 1792-93.

Fraser built Fort St. James on Stuart Lake — the first Nor' Wester post west of the Continental Divide — and Fort Fraser on the Fraser Lake that fall (1806).

Curiously, despite their stated urge to have Fraser explore the river to its mouth, the Nor' Westers were slow to support his initiatives. Early in August he had to write and remind them to send trade goods and men — to supply and manage the new posts and accompany him down the river. He needed provisions; his

222

people and the local Indians were half starved most of the time because the salmon run had failed. His timetable called for a quick trip to the mouth of the river in the fall of 1806, or at the latest in 1807, but there was no response to his request. He grew bitter waiting and increasingly irritated with his people. In September he wrote to John Stuart: "Nothing goes to my likeing. I hate the place and the Indians."[4]

He used 1807 to advantage, improving his three posts and building Fort George on the Fraser at the mouth of the Nechako River, near the site of Prince George. He would begin his descent of the river from this post. Fraser's men and supplies did not arrive until the fall of 1807 — so late in the year that the voyage had to be put off until 1808. He found some consolation in the lonely Northwest. In a letter to John Stuart at Fort St. James in 1807, he remarked he had "once more entered upon the matrimonial state."[5] It was obviously only a casual arrangement with a native woman and not the first. Letters to James McDougall at Fort McLeod that winter suggest there were children of a previous alliance at that post.

Kootanae House — first trading post on the Columbia River, 1807[6]

The attempt by the North West Company to cross the mountains from Rocky Mountain House on the Saskatchewan River had come to a halt with the failure of the Hughes and Thompson expedition of 1801. The Piegan Indians that roamed the foothills in the vicinity of the House still vigilantly discouraged traders from packing goods across the Divide to trade with the western Indians. There was no pressure from Montreal to risk a confrontation with the Piegans. Simon McTavish, the most influential figure in the North West Company, was not interested in Mackenzie's Columbian Enterprise. He was convinced it would diminish the central role of Montreal and, therefore, his dominance of the affairs of the company.

The death of McTavish in 1804, and the news of the Lewis and Clark expedition may have influenced John McDonald, senior partner in the Saskatchewan department, to renew the assault on the Rockies from Rocky Mountain House. He decided in 1806, to defy the Piegans and establish a trading post west of the Divide on the large northwest-flowing river opposite the headwaters of the Saskatchewan River. No one suspected that this was the Columbia River. The Athabasca department of the company had already arranged for Simon Fraser to explore the river generally thought to be the Columbia (the Fraser) to its mouth.

There would be no searching for a way across the mountains this time. In the five years since La Gasse and Le Blanc had crossed the Howse Pass with a band of Kootenay Indians, the pass had become known to whites stationed at both Rocky Mountain House and Acton House. McDonald sent Jaco Finlay, a clerk, to cut out the trail from the pass down alongside the Blaeberry River to the northwest-flowing river. Finlay was instructed, also, to build canoes and store them at the mouth of the Blaeberry.

McDonald then cast about for someone to undertake the perilous task of moving trade goods past the Piegans. He chose David Thompson, newly promoted from clerk to partner, well known to the Piegans and on good terms with them. Thompson learned of the assignment when he put into Grand Portage late in 1806. He returned to Rocky Mountain House in October and remained there throughout the winter, trading with the Indians and preparing for his expedition.

Early in the spring of 1807, Thompson began packing trade goods and baggage, working unobtrusively to avoid detection by the Piegans. Fortunately for him, the killing of two Piegans in the previous year, during an attempt to rob Meriwether Lewis of the Lewis and Clark expedition, still angered the Piegan nation. They withdrew their fighting men from the vicinity of Rocky Mountain House and set off for the Missouri River. Thompson took the opportunity to get his expedition moving towards the mountains.

The trade goods and most of the baggage were loaded into a freight canoe manned by Finan McDonald — a clerk — and five voyageurs. It started up the Saskatchewan River on May 10. Thompson, his wife and family, and three men set off overland on horseback on the north side of the river carrying the balance of the baggage. He planned to meet the canoe party at Kootenay Plain; a flat meadow area in the foothills and the most distant place along the river with enough pasture to maintain the horses for an extended time.

The men in the canoe had a very difficult time. Thompson had decided, in 1801, that the best way to transport cargo across the mountains was to rely heavily on the canoe. He reasoned that if he started early in the spring before the snow had a chance to melt and swell the river, he should have little difficulty in reaching its headwaters. He expected a short portage would take him over the Divide and down to the river on the western side. The plan did not work well in practice for the water shoaled rapidly as they advanced up the river. Within a few days' travel they encountered sections so shallow that the men had to go over the sides to lighten the canoe and keep her from dragging on the bottom. Soon they came to long stretches in which the water was not deep enough for the paddles and they had to tow the canoe to move her upstream. They struggled alongside the river stumbling into pools of icy water while the frigid winds blowing off the snowtopped mountains numbed them to the bone. Often the lines broke, endangering the cargo and the men left in the canoe to steer her. They arrived at Kootenay Plain on May 25, exhausted.

Thompson gave the men time to recover while he assembled and sorted the cargo. On June 5 he sent the canoe upstream again with six men to paddle her but with half the previous load. In the lightened canoe, it took less than a day to reach the forks where the Mistaya River from the southeast and the Howse River from the southwest join the Saskatchewan. The men started up the Howse River but within a few kilometers (a couple of miles) it was obvious the river was too shallow to support a freight canoe. The cargo would have to move beyond the forks on the backs of men and horses.

By June 10 all their goods and the horses had been brought up to a temporary camp above the forks and Thompson turned to the horses to get the cargo over the mountains. Again his strategy of setting out early in the spring worked against him. The way up to the pass was choked with snow and the heavily laden animals sank to their bellies. He would have to wait for the snow to melt. There was more snow than Thompson and his men had ever seen and, to add to their awe, avalanches sweeping "down the Sides of

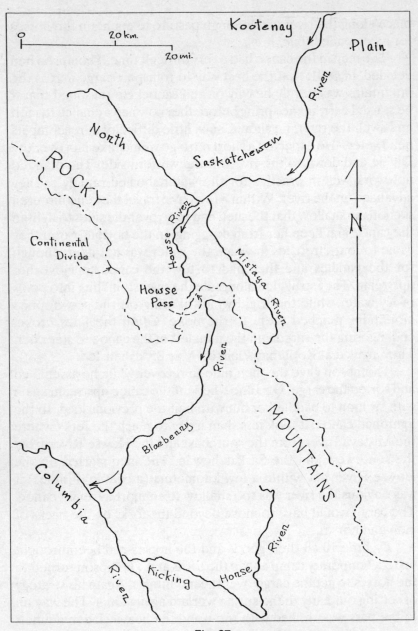

Fig. 37
David Thompson's route from the Saskatchewan River, over the Howse
Pass and down to the Columbia River in 1807.

the Mountains equalled the Thunder in Sound, overturning everything less than solid Rock . . . leaving not a Vestige behind."[7] His supply of pemmican was down to 100 kg. (220 lb.) and he had nine men, himself and his family to feed. There was little prospect of shooting game high in the mountains.

The snow disappeared from the pass in another two weeks but it was not the end of Thompson's troubles. Having seriously underestimated the role of horses, he had only ten animals to move the expedition across the mountain portage and he needed twice that number. On June 25 he loaded as much freight as the ten horses could carry and leaving Finan McDonald to safeguard the remainder of the cargo, he started the packtrain up alongside the Howse River. They attained the summit shortly past noon and made camp to enable Thompson to find the latitude of the pass. It had taken forty-six days to reach this point from Rocky Mountain House.

Next day they began the descent of the western slope, moving down the valley of the Blaeberry River (Thompson called it the Portage Stream). A mere brook near the pass, the melting snow turned the Blaeberry into a raging torrent further down the slope. The forest-choked valley forced the packtrain to cross and recross the river with the men clinging to the horses' tails and manes to avoid being swept away and drowned. There was little trace of the packtrail Jaco Finlay had been sent to cut. Thompson wrote bitterly in his journal about its condition: "Jaco Finlay, with the Men engaged last Summer to clear the Portage Road, had done a mere nothing — the Road was no where cleared any more than just to permit Jaco @ his Family, to squeeze thro' it with their light Baggage."[8]

That night Thompson "gave the Men a large Dog for Supper for want of better."[9]

The party came to the Columbia River (Thompson called it the Kootanie River) on June 30, five days after leaving the Howse River, and made camp. They found the two canoes Jaco Finlay had built but the larger was so badly broken it could not be used; the other was capable of carrying only two men and a small amount of baggage. Thompson immediately dispatched two men in this canoe to locate the camp of the Kootenay Indians and bring

227

a few men back to hunt for food. There was less than 3 kg. (61/2 lb.) of pemmican in the larder. He sent four men back to the Howse River with the horses to bring up the rest of the freight. He kept with him two men, one of whom was very sick. Thompson and the healthy man began searching for birchbark to build a replacement for the broken canoe.

Within a fortnight, Thompson's fortunes began to improve — his men returned with three Kootenays and the meat of a small deer, the canoe was completed and Finan McDonald arrived with the freight. Also, the sick man was better. He had swallowed the quill of a porcupine and it had perforated his intestines. When it made its appearance under the man's ribs, Thompson was able to extract it and recovery was rapid.

On July 12, they packed their goods into the canoes and paddled upstream, reaching Windermere Lake — the lower of the two lakes that are the headwaters of the Columbia River — on July 18, sixty-nine days after leaving Rocky Mountain House. Thompson began building his trading post at the south end of the lake; but he decided the site was not suitable. On July 29, he moved back to the river and built Kootanae House on the west bank of the Columbia. He determined its latitude as 50°31'15"N, which places it about 1.5 km. (1 mi.) north of the lake.

Thompson's first crossing of the mountains had been long and arduous. His difficulties began with the assumption, made in 1801, that the canoe was the proper conveyance for transporting freight across the Rocky Mountains. He may have been overly influenced by Alexander Mackenzie's experience of encountering only a 20 km. (121/2 mi.) portage in voyaging through the Rockies on the Peace River in 1793. Although he had worked a number of years in the foothills and had associated frequently with Indians who regularly crossed the Divide, he was badly informed about conditions of travel in the mountains. If he consulted with Nor' Westers who had been over the Howse Pass — La Gasse and Le Blanc in 1800, Jaco Finlay and his men in 1806, and no doubt others in the interval — it had no worthwhile affect on the logistics he planned for the expedition. It is clear from his account of the crossing that he seriously underestimated the height and breadth of the mountains. He had literally no foreknowledge of the terrain on the portage, the nature of the streams that fall east and west from the Howse Pass or the climate in the mountains.

After 1807 the Howse Pass became, for a few years, a well-traveled traffic artery of the fur trade. It was named for Joseph Howse, a clerk with the Hudson's Bay Company, who first used it two or three years after Thompson's crossing. Traders came up the Saskatchewan River in the fall, transferred their trade goods from canoe to packtrain a couple of days' trek below Kootenay Plain (that being about as far as they could move the heavily burdened freight canoes upstream) and crossed the mountains. Late in the spring they transported the winter's purchase of furs to the west end of the "mountain portage" (at the mouth of the Blaeberry River) and put up their canoes. The furs were carried by packtrain to Kootenay Plain and transferred to canoes for the voyage down the Saskatchewan. When the horses were not packing across the mountains, they were pastured at Kootenay Plain with men stationed there to care for them. By traveling at these selected times of the year, the journey between the Saskatchewan and Columbia Rivers was rapid. It took Thompson seventeen days to travel by horse from Kootanae House to Kootenay Plain in 1808.

22

Simon Fraser's Journey to the Pacific Ocean, 1808

First days on the Fraser River[1]

Simon Fraser started down the river David Thompson later named for him from Fort George on May 28, 1808, thinking he was on the Columbia River. He had a crew of twenty-three — two Indians, nineteen "men" (Canadian voyageurs) and two "gentlemen" (John Stuart and Jules Quesnel). They traveled in four canoes loaded with dried salmon and gifts to buy services and goodwill from the natives on the way. Fraser was thirty-two; his steady right hand, John Stuart, was twenty-nine.

The expedition reached its first formidable obstacle three days later — the rapids at Chimney Creek, below the site of the town of Williams Lake. The noise and turbulence of the river as it flows for two or three kilometers (one or two miles) through a channel that is restricted in places to a width of less than 50 m. (150 ft.) was intimidating. The local chief said his people never challenged this part of the river. Fraser had no way of knowing he had already traversed almost one-third of the distance to the coast but progress had been good and he was filled with optimism. In this mood he decided to run the rapids and avoid the toilsome task of portaging the canoes along the uneven shoreline. The chief encouraged him by saying he knew the whites were superior men and he had so much confidence in Fraser he would accompany him anywhere as guide and interpreter.

Word of Fraser's intention spread quickly along the river and next morning the natives were gathered in numbers to witness the

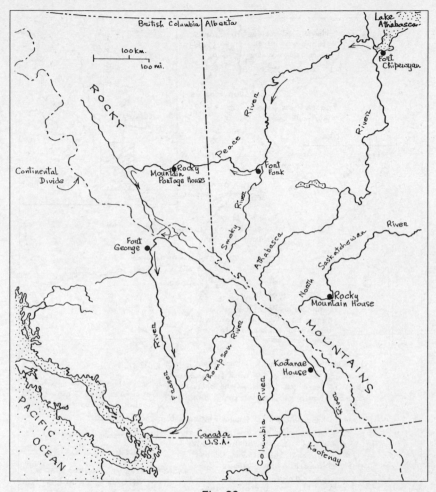

Fig. 38
Simon Fraser's route from Lake Athabasca to the Pacific Ocean.

antics of the white strangers. Fraser started five of his most capable voyageurs down the channel in a lightly loaded canoe. The river was not long in asserting itself. The men lost control at the foot of the first fall of water when the canoe was caught in an eddy and whirled about for a seemingly endless time. The men struggled frantically to keep her from being sucked under and by degrees they got her back into the current. It carried them along, flinging them from one near disaster to the next until they became

231

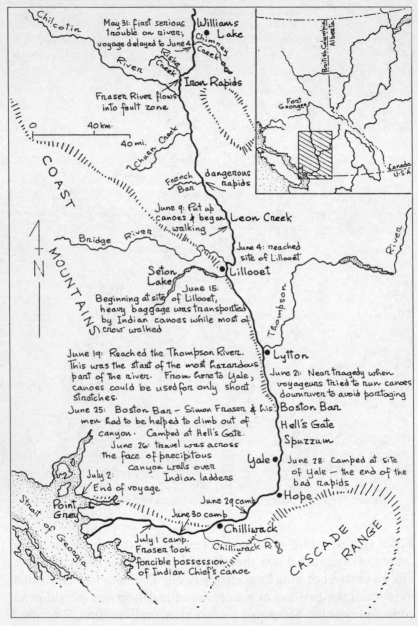

Fig. 39
Simon Fraser's voyage of discovery down the Fraser River to the Pacific
Ocean, May 28 to July 2, 1808.

wedged against a rock projecting into the river above another waterfall. They were able to climb onto the rock and, holding the canoe by a line attached to her bow, they made their way to shore. There was no thought of going on — the most dangerous part of the rapids lay below them.

The Indians informed Fraser he would find parts of the river further south equally perilous. They said a good packroad ran alongside the river to its junction with another large river that came in from the northeast (presumably the Thompson), bypassing all the difficult passages. Thereafter it was "smooth water all the way to the sea"[2] (they were wrong; the most violent part of the river — around Hell's Gate — waited below its confluence with the Thompson). They urged him to store his canoes with them and take the road. They said the journey to the Thompson River could be made with horses in four or five days and they would provide the horses. When Fraser expressed interest and tried to arrange for horses, they encouraged him to use the river. When he persisted, they brought him four horses — not nearly enough for the job.

In one of several meetings, the Indians said that white men had been seen on the other large river (the Thompson). Fraser thought at the time they might be referring to the Lewis and Clark expedition or perhaps to Nor' Westers from the company's Saskatchewan department. There is no record of white men penetrating to the Thompson River in these years. The reference probably applied to David Thompson who had crossed the Rockies from the Saskatchewan River in the previous year (1807) and built Kootanae House on the Columbia. The Thompson and Columbia Rivers flow within 50 km. (30 mi.) of each other and could have been confused by the Indians in passing the news of Thompson's expedition from band to band.

Fraser learned of Thompson's successful 1807 crossing only after he returned to Athabasca. Then, influenced by the Indian stories of seeing white men on the river flowing into the Fraser from the northeast, he assumed that Kootanae House had been built on it and he named it Thomsen's River (modified later to Thompson River) for his fellow Nor' Wester.

It took two days to carry canoes and baggage past the Chimney Creek rapids but "late" in the morning (it was 6:00 A.M.) on June 4, they were on the river again with three canoes. The chief had agreed to accompany them even though Fraser had shown himself to be fallible; he would be their goodwill ambassador. All too soon they came to other rapids. The terrain alongside the river was so rough they could not bear the thought of portaging the canoes the 3 km. (2 mi.) around the obstruction. They could abandon them or take them down empty and carry the baggage. Fraser decided to challenge the river again, with five men in each canoe; he was successful but the struggle and tension exhausted the men.

In its south-southeasterly course from Prince George, the Fraser River crosses a relatively flat region of British Columbia known as the Interior Plateau, and reaches the Coast Mountains at Lillooet. They were still on the Plateau when they camped that night above Iron Rapids. Their location afforded Fraser a long view and looking downstream he could see the mountains rising and barring his way to the sea.

Between Iron Rapids and the town of Hope the river flows in a steeply dipping fault zone and this accounts for its relatively straight course across the Plateau and through the Coast Mountains. It is an old channel that has carried water from the interior to the sea for tens of thousands of years. As the land mass of British Columbia rose and built the Coast Mountains and the Rockies, the Fraser continued to flow, cutting its channel ever deeper, creating a canyon.

The river pours into the fault zone at Iron Rapids through a cut less than 30 m. (100 ft.) wide. According to Fraser, it was "turbulent, noisy, and awful to behold."[3] They had to portage more than a kilometer (about a mile) around this dangerous place. Soon they came to another violent stretch of water. Here they lightened the canoes and ran them down with near tragic results. As Fraser described it, "one of the canoes was sucked into a whirlpool whose force twisted off the stern; but this happening near the bank and the end of the rapid, the men were saved."[4]

June 9 was the worst of a succession of difficult and dangerous days. Fraser noted in his journal:

> this afternoon the rapids were very bad; two in particular were
> worse, if possible, than any we had hitherto met with, being a
> continual series of cascades, mixt with rocky fragments and
> bound by precipices and mountains, that seemed at times to
> have no end . . . while I am writing this, whatever way I turn,
> mountains upon mountains, whose summits are covered with
> eternal snows.[5]

They were camped at Leon Creek, 30 km. (20 mi.) above
Lillooet, the Coast Mountains looming before them, when
Fraser made this observation. For several days they had been
traveling on the river against the advice of the old chief. The
men were showing the strain of living constantly under the
threat of danger, even death. It was time to pause and take
stock of their situation.

Fraser puts up his canoes[6]

Fraser surveyed the river for a considerable distance below
Leon Creek and when this showed that it was not navigable except
for short stretches, he decided to take the chief's advice and
continue on foot. He put up his canoes and cached some food and
all the supplies and baggage they could do without. At 5:00 A.M.
on June 11, each man shouldered a pack of about 35 kg. (75 lb.)
and they started along a trail above the river.

Three days later Fraser woke to find the chief missing. He
had said more than once he feared the natives on the lower
Fraser River. The chief had been a valuable ally, defusing the
hostility of natives when suddenly faced by the white strangers
and assuring them a good reception in the villages. He had
earned them many substantial meals of dried salmon, berries,
wild onions and other vegetables with the Indians. Fraser noted
the loss in his journal:

> Here we are, in a strange Country, surrounded with
> dangers, and difficulties, among numberless tribes of savages,
> who never saw the face of a white man. Our situation is critical
> and highly unpleasant; however . . . what cannot be cured,
> must be endured.[7]

Fraser was told in one village of a large river some distance to the east which, like the river he was exploring, flowed south to the sea. His informants must have been referring to the Columbia River but if Fraser had begun to suspect he was not on the Columbia, he did not mention it in his journal.[8]

They reached the mouth of the Thompson on June 19, to find villages on both sides of the Fraser River; all their occupants seemed bent on shaking the explorer's hand. The local chief made a long address to the people, pointing to the sun, the four quarters of the earth, and finally to Fraser and his men. Meanwhile, the chief's old blind father sat near Fraser and with much show of emotion, frequently touched him. The white men did not understand the address but it was obvious the natives perceived them as more than ordinary beings. Fraser, ever suspicious, observed in his journal that the respect they were accorded might derive from a belief that the white men were superior and invincible. He thought it wise not to become too familiar with them, fearing they would come to see their visitors for what they were — mere mortals hopelessly outnumbered in an alien world.

The chief warned Fraser the going on the river was "very bad and difficult" below the Thompson. Still, next day he provided him with canoes and guides to take the party a short distance downstream. Fraser got the chief's meaning the next day (June 20) at the first portage. The current was so strong at the landing that one of the canoes overturned and sank. The shore was dotted with graves and Fraser learned the reason soon after they started climbing the portage road that led up the wall of the canyon. The road was steep and offered only a precarious footing over loose stones that were easily dislodged. The graves held the remains of people who had lost their footing or been struck by rolling stones and fallen to their deaths.

The expedition had come to the most dangerous part of the river. Between Lytton and Yale, it flows through the most awesome section of the canyon and is virtually one long rapids. The few stretches that were navigable with craft of the kind they were using are separated by long and wearisome portages. The voyageurs had no experience with a river as continuously violent as this one. Some of them failed to grasp that once they were on the river the walls of the canyon prevented them from landing if they sighted trouble. Their inexperience almost brought disaster. On the morning of the second day of the portage, several voyageurs, having found the portaging unbearable, chose to run the canoes down the river to save carrying them. Fraser, called to the scene by the agitated guides, found the men downriver, exhausted. They had gone through a harrowing experience — thrown from the canoes and tossed about like corks, battered against rocks and nearly drowned. One of the canoes was split in two and another was too waterlogged to be of any further use. All hands had survived and they were thankful but the incident left a mark on the voyageurs. Now they openly preferred walking to going by water. They blamed the clumsy wooden canoes which were much less maneuverable than their own birchbark canoes.

Fraser was unwilling to totally abandon travel by water. The river was the route to the sea and back to the safety of Fort George. Every strategy he had learned for survival in hostile country depended on being near the river — for sustenance, escape and defense. In the bush he was vulnerable. He and his party could be surrounded, immobilized and cut to pieces at the enemy's leisure. So he clung to the river and persuaded the natives to ferry his packs if not his men over the navigable parts. When he and his people walked, it was near the river. It made life adventuresome: to stay close to the river below the Thompson, they had to clamber up and down the walls of the canyon and across the face of them.

On June 25, in the vicinity of Boston Bar, scrambling up the precipitous rock faces of the canyon became too difficult and dangerous for the whites to manage on their own. They had to trust their lives, finally, to one of the nimble local natives. He scaled the walls, lowered a pole and drew them up to where they could stand, one after the other.

The next day they reached Hell's Gate and it was worse. Fraser observed:

We have to pass where no human being should venture.
Yet in those places there is a regular footpath impressed.[9]

237

The way led across the face of cliffs, hundreds of feet above the raging river. In places the cliff fell away in a sheer drop to the river and for a space there was no trail. The natives had bridged these gaps with a contraption of poles suspended from above. If the traveler did not maintain an upright stance but leaned at too much of an angle to the face of the cliff, the pole he was treading would swing out and topple him into space. The local men were expert and unafraid, having the advantage of experience, but it was another matter for Fraser and his men; they had nothing but their courage to sustain them.

They rested that night at an encampment below Hell's Gate and Fraser was able to persuade the friendly Indians to lend him canoes for the next stretch of navigable water. The canoes were kept above Hell's Gate. Since no person in his right mind would paddle them down and it was impossible to carry them through the canyon, it was decided to float them down unmanned. "They were turned adrift and left to the mercy of the current."[10] They were found next morning (June 27) after their unguided passage, one smashed and the other badly damaged. The men repaired them and before nightfall the party reached the site of Spuzzum and a camp of sixty Indians who gave them a meal of salmon, berries, oil and onions.

Late in the afternoon of the next day (June 28), they arrived at the site of Yale and the end of the bad rapids. From this place, they were told, the river was navigable to the sea.

End of journey[11]

Fraser was anxious to be free of his dependence on the Indians. They had been uniformly friendly and helpful but he was subject to their whims and it irked him. Recently he had become aware that they were more reluctant than ever to travel any distance downriver, claiming the Indians who lived on the coast and nearby islands were warlike and dangerous. He wanted to travel when and how it pleased him. Having reached the lower Fraser River with the ocean only a few days' run away, he had no need for guides and he tried to buy canoes. The Indians would not deal with him. They were willing to carry him to the next village and they gladly shared their meals with him but they would not barter away their canoes or any quantity of food.

On June 29, the expedition was taken down the last of the rapids, past the site of Hope and put off at a village of about a hundred and seventy people above the site of Chilliwack. Their new hosts promised to provide transportation, but not until next day; they wanted Fraser to stay overnight. As usual, Fraser was uneasy, untrusting of their motives, but next morning (June 30) they ferried him about 40 km. (about 25 mi.) downriver to a village of four hundred people. Fraser found these people dirty and odorous and they were disagreeable, not having been warned that the white strangers were coming. Still, early next morning (July 1) they were on the river again. They could have reached the Pacific that day but much to Fraser's chagrin, his unpleasant hosts put him off at the next village; it was barely 8:00 A.M.

The white men were well received and fed on fish, berries and dried oysters but the chief flatly refused to sell or lend Fraser canoes; and he would not take him downriver, repeating the warning about the coastal Indians. Fraser persisted and finally, in exasperation, the chief agreed to lend him his large canoe and accompany him — but not until the next day.

In the morning (July 2) Fraser reminded the chief of his promise but the chief paid him no attention. Fraser responded by having the canoe carried down to the water. The chief had it carried back. Fraser's men took hold of it again. The Indians resisted while the chief declared he was the greatest man of his nation and that his power was equal to that of the sun. Fraser would not be put off and suddenly, the chief gave in. Attended by several members of his band, he got into the canoe and they were paddled down to the next village. The chief insisted on pausing here and once ashore, he enlisted the aid of the villagers to get his canoe back — by force if necessary. Fraser kept his nerve, even when he and his men were ringed by warriors and some of them "laid violent hands upon the canoe."[12] He maintained that the canoe had been promised to him and he would fight for it. In the face of this firm stand, the natives were unwilling to test his resolve and they let him go. This time no local Indians accompanied the expedition.

Within 3 km. (2 mi.), they reached the site of New Westminster where the Fraser divides before it empties into the Strait of Georgia. By this time they had been detected from shore and as they turned into the North Arm of the river, several canoes closed in. The occupants were armed with bows and arrows, clubs and spears which they brandished while chanting a war song and beating time against the sides of their canoes. Fraser was confident his superiority in arms would let him prevail and he directed his men to continue towards the sea. The Indians, apparently perplexed by their inability to panic the white men and not ready to initiate a fight, fell back.

Finally, they came to the mouth of the river. Fraser turned northwest and traveled alongside the shore to Musqueam village where they landed — the first white men to step ashore at the mouth of the Fraser River. They found only a few old people, the others having fled into the bush. Fraser spent some time examining the village and when he returned to the canoe, the tide had ebbed and left her a considerable distance from the water. The natives watching from the bush, began to gather when they sensed the strangers were in some trouble. Soon they ringed the white men and, howling like wolves, they flourished their weapons at the white men struggling to drag the canoe to the water. The canoe was launched finally, but it was immediately surrounded by natives waiting in their canoes. Fraser's men kept them off but only by leveling their guns and threatening to fire.

Fraser continued up the shoreline to somewhere near Point Grey before turning about. He had no food and no prospect of obtaining any here at the coast where he had not seen one friendly face. He decided to go back upriver and try to obtain provisions, and then return for a more extended exploration of the coastline. As they came abreast of the village, they were again assailed and this time the Indians closed in so tightly Fraser's men had to fend them off with the muzzles of their guns. They broke free and paddled upstream, closely followed by their tormentors though not for long as they soon tired of the fast pace Fraser set. He was anxious to put some considerable distance between himself and the coastal Indians and he kept his men at the paddles until 11 o'clock that night.

They arrived early next morning at the village of the chief whose canoe they were using. Fraser tried to obtain provisions for going back down to the sea. The chief refused to give him any and, moreover, demanded the immediate return of his canoe. Fraser was not ready to give it up and when he made this clear, the men of the village seized it and began pilfering the baggage. Fraser reacted by pretending to fly into a violent rage, gesticulating and shouting, acting as the natives were in the habit of behaving. It stopped the mischief; order was restored and for a time he had control of the unruly crowd. It had been another close call; next time they might be overwhelmed. Fraser decided then and there to continue up the Fraser and make for Fort George. He got away from the village in the chief's canoe but he was hotly pursued and harassed for another three days — until July 7 — when he reached the more friendly villages above Hope.

It was frustrating not to have seen the open ocean but Fraser had established that the mouth of the river was in latitude 49°N — this was not the Columbia River. Reflecting on his adventures, he concluded that had he known from the beginning this was not the Columbia, he would have turned back at Leon Creek where he had stored his canoes.

The expedition arrived at Fort George on August 6 — they had taken thirty-five days to traverse each leg of the voyage. Not one man had been lost and none had suffered any permanent injury. Fraser had avoided shedding any native blood although the provocation had been considerable. It had been a remarkable feat of courage and dedication in the face of almost constant danger, both on the violent river and, when that abated, on the placid delta below Hope. However, it was with a sense of disappointment that Fraser left Fort George to report to his superiors at Fort Chipewyan that the river was not the Columbia River — the fabled "River of the West." The keenest disappointment was the realization that the voyage was of little commercial value to the North West Company. The river could not serve as a water route and make Mackenzie's Columbian Enterprise a reality.

23

John Jacob Astor

During the first winter (1807-08) that David Thompson spent at Kootanae House, his partners in Montreal began to suspect they would face competition for furs taken in the far west from a new source. It was becoming apparent that the American businessman, John Jacob Astor, was determined to challenge the dominance of the North West Company and other, smaller Canadian fur trading companies.

Astor, the son of a butcher in the village of Walldorf, Germany, had landed in Baltimore in 1784, at the age of twenty. He arrived with five guineas in his pocket, seven flutes wrapped in his good suit (he intended to sell musical instruments) and a single-minded, driving ambition to build a fortune. His ship carried a number of Hudson's Bay Company men and during the four-month voyage, in the close quarters of the small vessel, he heard much talk about the fur trade. He became acquainted with an American of German descent who bought and sold furs and he learned from him of the huge profits to be made in the trade. What really stirred his interest was the information that very little capital was needed to get into the business. With an armful of trinkets or items of food, one could barter along the New York waterfront with Indians, farmers and boatmen who had one or two pelts. Astor plied his countryman with questions, learning the art of buying and selling, and the technical details of treating, cleaning and packing furs.

Soon after he landed in the United States, Astor got work hawking baked goods on the streets of New York and he placed his flutes for sale in a shop. Flutes were scarce in the city and when they sold well he ordered more from Germany. Whatever spare time he could manage he spent at the waterfront, exchanging a toy, an adornment or a fancy pastry for a fur pelt. He found a job with an elderly fur dealer and learned still more about the business. His stock of furs grew rapidly. By late fall of his first year in New York, he had enough to warrant a voyage to England — to sell his furs directly and eliminate middleman profits. While in London he bought trade goods and established a contact with a reputable firm for his fur business; and he arranged to represent an English musical-instrument manufacturer in New York.

In 1785, after only a year in the United States, Astor went into Iroquois country to trade at the source of furs — first for a New York buyer but, two years later, for himself. He traveled widely, acquiring an intimate knowledge of the geography, people and resources of his adopted country. He began journeying annually to Montreal, cultivating Canadian traders, drawing on their extensive experience in the far west. In 1788, he accompanied a Canadian brigade of canoes to Lake Superior. It was unlawful for Americans to enter the Canadian interior but he risked it for he wanted to learn how the trade operated in the Northwest.

Astor's wealth, power and influence grew steadily. By 1798, he had added smuggled English firearms and gunpowder, and imported China tea, to the list of merchandise he bought and sold. By 1800, he was worth a quarter of a million dollars. In 1804, he began building ships to carry his goods back and forth across the oceans of the world.

In 1808, in the spring following David Thompson's first winter in Kootanae House, Astor felt ready to initiate an ambitious scheme he had been fashioning for some years. His objective was to gain control over virtually all trade in Louisiana and in the region west of the Rockies drained by the Columbia River system. The Lewis and Clark expedition had made American interest in the Missouri River abundantly clear but Canadians were still trading in the region of the Mandan villages (as they had more or less continually since la Vérendrye's time). Astor approached Governor DeWitt Clinton of New York state, alleging that Canadians were operating illegally on the Missouri; it was United States territory. He warned that they were expanding towards the

Pacific Ocean to establish themselves on the lower Columbia — the river Robert Gray, and Lewis and Clark, had turned into American waters. He said he wanted to thwart the Canadians by building a line of trading posts along the Lewis and Clark route to the coast. He needed a charter from the New York legislature to give his scheme an official status.

Astor got his charter — "An Act to Incorporate the American Fur Company" was passed by the New York legislature early in April, 1808 — and Thomas Jefferson's blessing came a week later. Then he went to Montreal, professing to want an alliance with the Canadians but dallying; trying to lull them into inaction and the belief there was no need for them to race to the Pacific.

Back in New York, Astor continued to scheme for control of trade in the far west. His charter gave him a considerable advantage over other Americans in the drainage basins of the Missouri and lower Columbia Rivers but this did not satisfy him. The lucrative trade in sea otter skins, up and down the Pacific coast, beckoned; it would be more lucrative for him if he had the coastal trade all to himself. The problem lay in forcing out the traders who were already operating there. He decided that a governmental-approved reason for his presence on the coast and permission to build a fort at the mouth of the Columbia River would help him accomplish that objective.

Much of the fur trade on the west coast originated in Russian (Alaskan) waters — an environment that seemed to have an inexhaustible abundance of sea otter and seal. The Chinese ports were closed to the Russians at this time; American traders carried the skins for the Russians and sold them in China as their own. Not content with being only agents, Americans began trading with the natives in Russian waters, bartering firearms for furs. The Russians were unhappy about this development but there was no recourse. They had come to rely on these same American traders for their very existence because they could not depend on their own supply ships. It was difficult in these circumstances, to protect their trade in Alaska and enforce a policy of withholding firearms from the natives.

The Russian Consul-General in the United States complained to the State Department in 1809, citing the illicit trade with the natives and the commerce in firearms. The American government could not control its nationals on the distant west coast; but when Astor heard the complaint, he told the Consul-General that whereas the government might be powerless, he was not. If the Russians would agree to deal exclusively with him, he would establish a supply depot at the mouth of the Columbia and provide the Alaskan settlements with all their necessities. His ships would carry their furs to China. He would guarantee to not trade near the Russian settlements. He would fortify the depot and help them keep their waters clear of intruder-traders. The Consul-General was delighted with the proposal, asking only that he be allowed to present it to his government as his own idea. He urged Astor to dispatch a supply ship to Alaska with a letter to the governor, explaining the proposed agreement.

Astor bought the ship *Enterprise* (291 tons), loaded her with merchandise and sent her out of New York in November, 1809, bound for the Pacific Northwest. Her primary purpose was to carry Russian furs to China; the material for building the depot on the Columbia would follow on another ship. Then Astor journeyed to Montreal. The rumor of his negotiations with the Russians had preceded him and his Nor' Wester acquaintances were apprehensive. When he began interviewing veteran North West Company traders to work for him on the west coast, they became thoroughly alarmed at the scope of his ambitions.

Astor next created the Pacific Fur Company as the western branch of his American Fur Company. Early in 1810, he began organizing two expeditions to the northwest coast — one to go overland from St. Louis, following the Lewis and Clark route, and the other by sea from New York around Cape Horn. His ship, the *Tonquin* (300 tons), armed with twelve guns and manned by a crew of twenty-one, sailed for the Columbia River in September, 1810. She carried material and military hardware for establishing the projected fort, living necessities, vegetable seeds for planting a garden, trade goods, and the frame of a schooner for sailing the coastal waters. On board were four experienced Canadian traders, eleven clerks, thirteen Canadian voyageurs and five mechanics. The overland expedition left St. Louis late in October, intending to take up winter quarters on the Missouri River.

24

The Mystery of
the Columbia River is Solved

**David Thompson comes within 40 km. (25 mi.)
of the lower Columbia River, 1808-10**

In the fall of David Thompson's first year (1807) at Kootanae
House, he was visited by a band of Flatbow Indians from the
vicinity of Kootenay Lake. He questioned them closely about
their country and the way to reach the Pacific Ocean:

> I collected every information possible from them, 2 of
> them were very old Men, they spoke much to the purpose of
> all questions I asked, @ after drawing a Chart of their Country
> @ from thence to the Sea, @ describing the Nations along the
> River, they assured me that from this House to the Sea @
> back again was only the Voyage of a Summer Moon.[1]

Late in April, 1808, Thompson left Kootanae House by
canoe, going south up the Columbia. He crossed the Windermere
and Columbia Lakes and portaged over the 3 km. (2 mi.) Canal
Flats area to the Kootenay River. He thought this might be the
Columbia River; however, he named it McGillivray's River for a
senior partner in the company. He descended the Kootenay
through Montana to an Indian camp near Bonner's Ferry in Idaho
and paused there for a time. Having extracted a promise from the
Indians to trade with him, he moved on, descending the Kootenay
which flows north there, into Kootenay Lake in British Columbia.
He was now close to the river the Flatbow Indians had described
as their road to the sea — the river we know to be the Columbia
River. He could have reached it from Kootenay Lake by descend-

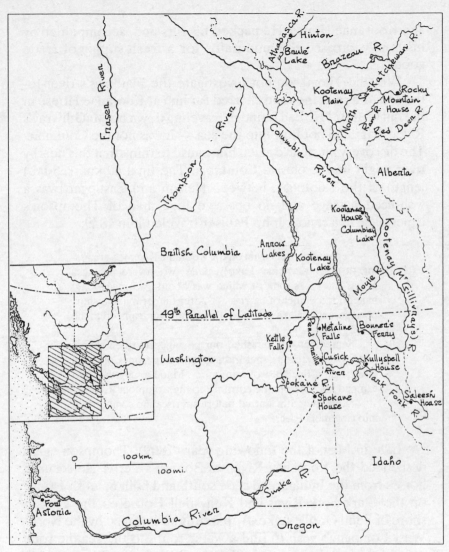

Fig. 40
David Thompson's travels between 1807 and 1811.

ing the final 40 km. (25 mi.) stretch of the Kootenay River (from
Nelson to Castlegar). However, he turned about and went back
upstream to Bonner's Ferry where he obtained horses. He rode
northeast up the valley of the Moyie River to the Kootenay River

247

and Kootanae House. He packed his furs and, accompanied by his family, crossed the mountains for a fresh supply of trade goods.

Why did Thompson not investigate the Flatbows's river-to-the-sea — a river they had charted for him at Kootanae House in the fall of 1807? He had found in traveling down his McGillivray's River that it did not flow into the sea — it was not the Columbia. The discovery must have given him cause to think that this nearby river might be the elusive Columbia. The final 40 km. (25 mi.) length of the Kootenay, between Nelson and Castlegar, was a well-used passage and no obstacle to a man of Thompson's experience in a canoe. John Palliser traveled it in 1859:

> September 3rd: Again on the Kootanie River [after passing through Kootenay Lake]; made two severe portages across the rocks, one of which was about two miles long; halted for a dinner of berries . . . After dinner made a short portage, and made a few miles down the river; camped in the wood . . .
>
> September 4th: Finished our portage, reloaded canoe, and travelled steadily; met Indians returning from Columbia River; had a fine feast of salmon . . . Made a long day, and camped not far from the entrance to the Columbia River.
>
> September 5th: started before sunrise, and soon turned into Columbia River.[2]

Late in May of the following year (1809), Thompson again descended the Kootenay River to Bonner's Ferry. He secured horses from the Indians and rode south and built Saleesh House on the Clark Fork River and Kullyspell House on the eastern shore of Pend Oreille Lake. Apparently still nagged by the North West Company's wish to find a water route to the sea, he rode around the north end of the lake and down the Pend Oreille River. This river flows west into Montana and then north into British Columbia, turning southwest after several kilometers (a few miles) to join the Columbia at the forty-ninth parallel. Near Metaline Falls, Thompson concluded that the last miles of the Pend Oreille River made it impractical as a route to the sea and turned back — again falling 40 km. (25 mi.) short of reaching the Columbia.

Simon Fraser had demonstrated in the summer of 1808, that Mackenzie's great river (the Fraser) was not the Columbia and that it was too turbulent over much of its length to act as a water route to the Pacific. The fabled Columbia River, the river that might yet provide the desired water passage, remained to be found somewhere in the interior. Thompson learned the details of Fraser's voyage in July, 1809, at the company's annual meeting on Lake Superior. Fraser's voyage had forced a rethinking of the drainage pattern west of the Divide and it made exploration of the Flatbows's river-to-the-sea, joined en route by the Kootenay and Pend Oreille Rivers, doubly important. Fraser's voyage was probably responsible for Thompson's decision, in the spring of 1810, to have another look at the Pend Oreille River. He used a canoe this time, descending the river to Metaline Falls again. He decided, as in the previous year, that the last 40 km. (25 mi.) could not be used as a water route. He did not try to reach the nearby river by an overland route and returned to Kootanae House.

Thompson's failure to respond to the challenge of reaching the Flatbows's river may have been dictated by a perceived urgency to build posts in the drainage basins of the Kootenay and Pend Oreille Rivers. Perhaps he felt threatened by Astor's activities and saw it necessary to cement trade relations with the Indians in these regions, presumably in a race with Americans. The North West Company's resolve to secure a claim for itself on the lower Columbia River had a lesser priority for him.

Three times Thompson was within a short voyage of the Pacific coast and never was the explorer in him fired by the prospect of forging the last link in an intercontinental route between the Atlantic and Pacific Oceans. His furs traveled 4,000 km. (2,500 mi.) across the Continental Divide and over numerous waterways and portages to the Atlantic Ocean; his trade goods came west over the same tortuous route. Curiously, the long journey seems to have given Thompson, the trader, no urge to take advantage of his proximity to the Pacific Ocean. He could have altered this pattern and pointed the fur trade west of the mountains towards a more profitable basis by founding a port on the coast to serve the rich market in the Orient.

David Thompson pioneers the use of a new pass, 1811[3]

The agents of the North West Company had begun making written submissions to the British government as early as September, 1809. They warned that Astor's Pacific Fur Company was preparing an expedition to establish a presence on the lower Columbia River. They urged Britain to make a show of its rights on the Pacific coast to counter American claims which rested on Robert Gray's achievement and the explorations of Lewis and Clark. Britain was deeply occupied with Napoleon and by the middle of 1810, when Thompson and his family arrived at Grand Portage with his furs, it was plain they could expect no help from that source. They decided to act on their own to dispute the priority-of-possession claim of the United States. Thompson, now the head of the newly formed Columbia department, was eligible for a year's furlough, which he planned to take in eastern Canada in 1810. The partners called on him to forego his furlough. They wanted him to descend the Columbia River to its mouth, build a fort there and have it flying the Union Jack when Astor's expedition arrived. The instructions suggest it was now generally assumed from Broughton's fixing of the geographical position of the lower Columbia River in 1792, that the river which Thompson had come within 40 km. (25 mi.) of reaching from Kootenay Lake in 1808, and from the Pend Oreille River in 1809 and 1810, was the Columbia River.

Thompson started west with a brigade of four canoes in September, 1810, intending to cross the Rockies over the Howse Pass as he had in the past. Early in this same month Astor's ship *Tonquin* sailed out of New York harbor bound, like Thompson, for the mouth of the Columbia.

Brigades on the Saskatchewan River were normally supplied with meat by hunters on horseback who ranged the country alongside the river. The hunting party would bring its kill to a prearranged rendezvous where the next meeting place would be selected for three or four days hence. Thompson had assumed charge of the hunt on this trip.

Returning to the river after a foray late in September, Thompson did not find the brigade at the appointed place and he

250

settled down to wait, thinking a damaged canoe had caused a delay. One of his Indians had a "bad dream" that night and predicting that the meat would never be eaten, he rode off in the morning. The incident disturbed Thompson.

In the previous year (1809), he had sent a clerk, Finan McDonald, and two voyageurs across the mountains with a party of western Indians to bring buffalo meat back to Kootanae House. They were attacked by a band of Piegans but this time the western Indians were armed with modern guns and iron-tipped arrows and, aided by Thompson's men, they drove off the Piegans. McDonald actually killed one of the attackers. The Piegans were furious at this turn of fortune, blaming it on the founding of Kootanae House and Thompson in particular for supplying the western Indians with modern arms. Except for the intervention of an elderly war chief, they would have attacked Rocky Mountain House. He persuaded them, instead, to blockade the Saskatchewan River above the House, stopping the flow of trade goods and furs over the Divide and throttling the western trade.

Thompson sent his clerk, William Henry, and a young Indian to search for the brigade, cautioning them to move quietly as their lives might depend on it. The two men found the blockading Piegans and, below their camp, signs suggesting a recent struggle. Thinking the voyageurs might be concealed nearby, they foolishly fired a shot and, when that got no response, rode back to Thompson leaving a clear trail in the newfallen snow. Thoroughly shaken by the possibility that the Piegans had engaged his brigade, and sure that the sound of the shot would bring them to his camp, Thompson declared they must ride for their lives.

They started at dawn, fleeing north to the Brazeau River and then down to its confluence with the Saskatchewan River about 65 km. (40 mi.) below Rocky Mountain House (see Fig. 40, p. 247). Thompson chose to quarter there; he sent men to fetch the horses pastured at Kootenay Plain and dispatched William Henry to Rocky Mountain House for news of his brigade.

Henry brought good news from Rocky Mountain House — the brigade had not fought with the Piegans. Finding the way upriver blockaded, the voyageurs had fallen back to the House, where he'd found them waiting.

251

Thompson had felt himself in danger from the time he built Kootanae House in 1807, and he had queried Indians, hunters and trappers about other passes. He became convinced there was a good pass at the headwaters of the Athabasca River and although its use "would be attended with great inconvenience, fatigue, suffering and privation,"[4] it would be free of the Piegan menace. While waiting for Henry to return, he had decided to abandon use of the Howse Pass and search for a new one.

Late in October, Thompson was ready to move out with twenty-four horses and as many men, and an Iroquois named Thomas to show the way. They followed an old hunting trail, bearing slightly north of west. Much of the country had been burned over and the trail was covered with deadfall which had to be cut out for the horses to pass. It was slow going and a month passed before they intercepted the Athabasca River near the site of Hinton (see Fig. 40, p. 247). They traveled upriver to Brulé Lake where they found good pasture for the horses. They spent December there and built sleds and snowshoes, and stored meat for the trip across the mountains.

Thompson set out on December 29, with dogs and sleds and four horses, going up the valley of the Athabasca River. It was cold — on January 5, (1811) Thompson's thermometer registered -32°C (-26°F). He left the horses at the junction of the Miette and Athabasca Rivers — the site of Jasper, Alberta — where there was a patch of marsh land and small ponds. The footing for the animals, through snow and over ice, had grown steadily worse and, looking ahead and up through the stunted pine, aspen and willow, it was clear this was the last pasture where the horses could winter. He pushed on up the Athabasca with eight Canadians and his Iroquois guide.

On January 8, they left the Athabasca and turned southwest up the Whirlpool River. Mount Edith Cavell loomed on their right and the Hooker Ice Fields rose before them. The snow was deep and soft and the dogs had heavy going with the sleds. In a fit of temper one of the men beat a dog to death. Thompson reflected ruefully that this was no time to kill dogs; he would need them all to get up and over the summit and down to wooded country where they might shoot deer or moose for food.

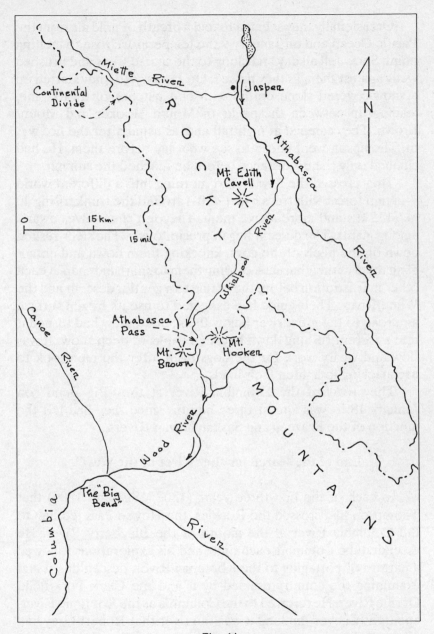

Fig. 41
David Thompson's route from the Athabasca River, over the Athabasca Pass, to the Columbia River, 1810-11.

Occasionally they seemed to feel a breath of mild air from the Pacific Ocean and on January 9 the temperature rose to melting point. Snow fell all day and clung to the sparse trees and brushed wetly against them as they passed. On January 10, they started up a snow-covered slope dotted with odd patches of dwarf pine, leading up between the peaks of Mount Hooker and Mount Brown. They camped at nightfall and, as usual after the fire was lit, Thompson went ahead to see what lay before them. He had climbed only a short distance before he reached the summit.

They crossed the Divide next morning into a different world — a rain forest with trees 6 m. (20 ft.) around the trunk, rising 40 m. (135 ft.) and more above them. They felt themselves dwarfs among giants. The descent began precipitously. The sleds rushed down on the heels of the dogs, knocking them down and entangling them in their harness, causing them to snarl and snap at each other in frustration before they came to a gentler descent and the Wood River. Their guide had expected to use its frozen surface as a road to the great river below them, but a thaw had turned it into a torrent rushing down between banks of deep snow. It was slow and weary work for the dogs even after the men took to backpacking to lighten their loads.

They reached the Columbia River at the "Big Bend" on January 18. It was almost three months since they had left the junction of the Brazeau and Saskatchewan Rivers.

End of the search for the "River of the West"

In each of the first three years (1807, 1808 and 1809) that Thompson had crossed the Rockies, the Howse Pass led him to the Columbia River at the mouth of the Blaeberry River. He ascended the Columbia each time; and his explorations followed a pattern of portaging to the Kootenay River, descending it and examining the country drained by it and the Clark Fork/Pend Oreille River. He referred to the Columbia as the Kootanie River, apparently never thinking it was the river that Robert Gray had discovered at the coast in 1792. Thompson explored the river as far north as the Big Bend during his first winter west of the Divide, observing that it turned there and began flowing south. If, how-

254

ever, he or his men *did* follow the river down below that point, he did not think it worthwhile to record the fact.

Thompson's opinion that his time could be better spent elsewhere may have been hardened after hearing the details of Simon Fraser's voyage to the Pacific in 1808. Fraser named a river for him, thinking it was the river on which Thompson had built Kootanae House — a river found to join the Fraser River above Hell's Gate and other fearsome barriers to the sea. Thus if Fraser's "Thomsen's River" and Thompson's "Kootanie River" were two ends of the same stream, Thompson knew it could not serve as a route to the Pacific Ocean and he would have placed it low on a list of exploration targets. Still, it is curious that this large river, deep in the interior, failed to excite the trader if not the explorer in him.

The company's instructions to Thompson stipulated that his "voyage to the Sea was to proceed down the River."[5] Although the river is not specifically identified in the records, various references to the proposed voyage suggest that the company intended Thompson to round the Big Bend and descend his Kootanie River. It seems the partners had formed a consensus by 1810 that this river did not join the violent Fraser River; but as he came down the valley of the Wood River in January of 1811, Thompson turned upstream, as in previous years, aiming for Kootanae House.

The men had been traveling since September and their discontent with conditions and the shortage of food had been growing steadily since they left Brulé Lake late in December. Suddenly, after four days of struggling through the deep snow alongside the Columbia and traveling only 20 km. (12 mi.) in the process, their frustration boiled over and they refused to go on. Thompson was unable to dissuade them and he was forced to return to the junction of the Wood and Columbia Rivers, arriving there on January 26. Five of the men had reached the limit of their patience and announced an intention of recrossing the mountains; they agreed to carry Thompson's request for supplies. He was left with three men, one of whom was ill.

It is not difficult to find a bond of sympathy with the departing men. They had been traveling for three months between the

Saskatchewan and Columbia Rivers — normally a trip of less than ten days by way of the Howse Pass — in the dead of winter and they could see no end to their travail. Some of them may have felt the long and difficult detour over the Athabasca Pass could have been avoided had Thompson acted coolly and with patience to outwit the Piegans who blockaded his brigade on the Saskatchewan River. They had lost confidence in him and wanted no more of him and his venture to the Pacific Ocean.

Thompson and the remaining men lived out the winter in a hole dug in the snow — a meter (three feet) deep and three meters (ten feet) square — lined and roofed with cedar boards hewn from nearby trees. It kept them warm enough and they fared quite well for food, shooting moose and deer with ease in the deep snow of the valley.

The birchbark in the vicinity was not suitable for building canoes and so they split cedar logs into thin boards, bending them into suitable shapes and sewing them together with thin pine roots. It produced a good, strong boat but it took a long time to build.

The "voyage to the Sea" began on April 17, 1811. Thompson had no idea what Fate and Nature might put in his way if he rounded the Big Bend and traveled downstream as instructed. He concluded that "having only three men . . . we were too weak to make our way through the numerous Indians we had to pass."[6] He chose to start the journey by going upstream through familiar country, avoiding the risks of an unknown river, planning to augment his small party by hiring "free white hunters" south of the forty-ninth parallel.

Thompson's first objective was Kootanae House where he spent several weeks. Then, on May 14, he portaged to the Kootenay River and descended to its southern extremity in Montana. He stored the canoe, obtained horses and rode south to Saleesh House on the Clark Fork River where he hired two Canadian trappers to accompany him to the Pacific (see Fig. 40).

The men built another cedar boat at Saleesh House and, having killed and butchered a horse for meat, the party embarked on June 5. They traveled in a northwesterly direction down the Clark Fork River, through Pend Oreille Lake in Idaho, and down the river of the same name to the "Long Carrying Place" (near the site of Cusick, Washington). This was the start of a trail leading 65 km. (40 mi.) south to Spokane House (built by Finan McDonald in the previous year) on the Spokane River. Thompson sent word to McDonald asking for horses to carry him over this trail. From Spokane House another trail led 100 km. (60 mi.) northwest to Kettle Falls on the Columbia River. McDonald got Thompson there on June 19 after a time-consuming trip during which they had to build several bridges to cross creeks the horses could not ford.

Thompson had become convinced, finally, that the river on which he had spent the winter — the river he called the Kootanie — was the Columbia River. He learned at Kettle Falls that only a few Kootenays lived upstream and they did not constitute a danger to him. He instructed McDonald to reconnoiter the river above the falls; and he sent word across the Divide that he wanted his trade goods for the coming winter taken over the Athabasca Pass and held for him at the Big Bend. If McDonald reported that the Columbia was navigable, he intended to use it for his goods.

On July 3, having constructed a third boat after an extensive search for suitable cedar, Thompson was afloat again on the Columbia. He had with him five voyageurs and two Indians; his provisions included "half a horse for our support." Two and a half months had passed since leaving the Big Bend.

On July 15 Thompson came to a cluster of four low log huts, flying the Stars and Stripes, on the south shore of the Columbia about 11 km. (7 mi.) from the coast. It was Fort Astoria, John Jacob Astor's newly built trading post and fort. The North West Company had lost the race. Astor's ship *Tonquin*, had rounded Cape Horn on Christmas Day, 1810, and reached Hawaii in February where thirty Islanders were hired. The expedition sighted Cape Disappointment at the mouth of the Columbia on March 22, 1811, a month before Thompson started for the Pacific from his winter hut on the Big Bend.

Thompson left Fort Astoria on July 22, after only a week at the coast. The worst rapids he had encountered on the Columbia were a short distance below Kettle Falls. To avoid this stretch, he went up the river to its junction with the Snake and ascended that

257

river to the start of a road leading north to Spokane House. With horses purchased from the local Indians, he rode north to Spokane House where he learned that Finan McDonald had gone a considerable distance up the Columbia without difficulty. There was news also that the packtrain from the east would arrive at the Big Bend about the middle of September. Thompson rode on, traveling to Kettle Falls over the road he had used in June, planning to ascend the Columbia and receive his supplies. First, however, another boat would have to be built.

All was ready on September 2, and Thompson started up the last section of the Columbia he had not traversed, escorted by eight canoes filled with Indians. They parted with him at the mouth of the Kootenay River (near Castlegar) four days later. He reached Devil's Canyon, a fierce stretch of water about 3 km. (2 mi.) above the site of Revelstoke on September 11. This was as far as Finan McDonald had scouted the river for him. They had a wearing time next day, being forced to tow the boat up and over rapids. Three days later it was worse; it took most of the day to tow and portage past rapids and a waterfall. Above this fast water they were able to paddle against the current again.

They came to Thompson's winter hut, at the mouth of the Wood River, about noon on September 18. This finally confirmed that Thompson's Kootanie River was the Columbia and it unraveled the last knot in the complex geography of the Columbia/Kootenay River system. Thompson had now traversed all of its tortuous course — the mystery of the "River of the West" was solved.

Thompson did not have enough packhorses to carry the goods required to supply his many trading posts west of the Divide. He sent the supplies he had received to Finan McDonald at Kettle Falls for distribution to the posts on the Kootenay, Clark Fork/Pend Oreille and Spokane Rivers. Then he crossed the mountains with the horses to transport the rest of his shipment. He started down the Columbia by canoe with the second lot late in October. It was snowing heavily when he passed through the slack water of the Arrow Lakes (between Revelstoke and Castlegar). It accumulated to such a thickness on the water that in places they could not force their way through, even by poling, and they had to carry canoe and goods. Despite this, they traversed the 500 km. (300 mi.) to Kettle Falls in nine days.

The shipment of trade goods down the Columbia in 1811 was an historic event, adding the final link in the first practical transcontinental route in northern North America. Alexander Mackenzie's belief in the existence of a major, navigable river west of the Divide had been proven correct. However, it had taken surprisingly long to find and identify the upper Columbia after Robert Gray sailed into its mouth in 1792.

The Athabasca Pass became the principal and, in fact, almost the only pass used to cross the mountains in Canada — the main portage in the canoe route that joined the country west of the Rockies with eastern Canada. The way over the Howse Pass was shorter and easier, but the traders who used it continued to be molested by the Piegans and it fell into disuse and was forgotten. The Athabasca Pass was a tiresome detour to the north from the Saskatchewan River but it was safe from the Piegans. It was a difficult route for horses; nevertheless, packtrains carried trade goods and furs, provisions and mail over the pass for the next fifty years — first for the Nor' Westers and then for the brigades of the Hudson's Bay Company after the companies were joined in 1821. It was still in use in 1858 when James Hector and other members of the Palliser expedition came searching for passes over which roads and railways could be built.

Part IV

After the Voyages

With the discovery and exploration of its two major rivers — the Columbia and the Fraser — and their tributaries, the physical character of the southern part of the Pacific Northwest was relatively well known. Exploration took the form of improving the routes in the interior; fur traders searched out ways to bypass difficult sections of the rivers and they developed a transportation network over which goods moved by canoe and horse.

Canadians, principally the Nor' Westers, and Astor's Pacific Fur Company had won the Pacific Northwest south of the territory claimed by the Russians. It remained for the politicians to dispose of it.

25

Disposition of the Pacific Northwest

David Thompson's slow pace to the Pacific Ocean was the final chapter in the sequence of events that led to the failure of the North West Company to win the race to the mouth of the Columbia River. Thompson suffered the bad luck of having his Columbian brigade threatened by Piegan Indians on the Saskatchewan River in the fall of 1810. Instead of trying to outwit or outwait the Indians, he took that critical time in his company's affairs to search for a new pass. It cost him three months. When he reached the Columbia early in 1811, there was still time to beat Astor to the mouth of the river. Although it was January, the Columbia was navigable. Thompson's journal records that "from the mildness of the climate [we] ... found ... the River open and only a chance bridge of ice and snow across it"[1] and "about two hundred yards in width running clear."[2] There was plenty of game to feed the men had he chosen to build canoes and make for the coast as he had been directed; and he might have cheered them with the expectation that the climate would be even milder there. Thompson decided, however, to slog through the snow and wait out the winter at Kootanae House. His men rebelled and some of them deserted; and he spent the winter at the Big Bend.

What Thompson did not accomplish for the North West Company at the mouth of the Columbia River in 1811, the War of 1812 between Britain and the United States did, for a time, two years later. News of the war reached the Astorians in 1813 and when their supply ship failed to arrive as scheduled, they concluded the British had an effective blockade in operation. They decided to abandon the fort and go overland to St. Louis. While they were preparing for the journey, a brigade of Nor' Westers arrived and made camp, settling down to wait for their own supply ship, confidently expecting it to be armed and under orders to take the fort. The Astorians, most of whom were former Nor' Westers and still British subjects, quickly assessed the situation. They offered to sell the fort, the posts in the interior and the furs they had acquired to the Nor' Westers. They had already been selling them food and now, to hurry the bargaining, they threatened to withhold supplies. A deal was struck, the Nor' Westers even agreeing to pay any wages due to the Astorians.

The Union Jack did not fly long over Fort Astoria. By the terms of the Treaty of Ghent, signed in 1814, each side restored to the other any territory won in the war and although the North West Company could claim it had bought Fort Astoria, the Stars and Stripes replaced the Union Jack.

The Treaty of Ghent had other consequences for the Pacific Northwest for it was agreed to negotiate the sovereignty of the region. The British claimed that the voyages of Drake, Cook and Vancouver, the inland journeys of Mackenzie and Fraser, and the establishment of trading posts on the Kootenay, Clark Fork/Pend Oreille, Spokane and Columbia Rivers by Thompson and others, gave Britain title to all the territory between the Russian (Alaska) and Spanish (California) claims. This vast region bounded by 54°40'N on the north, 42°N on the south, the Pacific coast on the west, and the Continental Divide on the east became known as the Oregon Territory.

The Americans countered with Gray's rediscovery of the mouth of the Columbia, the Lewis and Clark expedition and the founding of Fort Astoria.

The British negotiators, confronted by aggressive opposition from their American counterparts, gave way and agreed by the Convention of 1818 that any part of the Territory of Oregon claimed by both countries would be "free and open" for a term of ten years to both countries. The Americans immediately claimed the whole of the Territory — a good point from which to begin future negotiations. The British found they had agreed to share British Columbia, Washington, northern Idaho and northwestern Montana which had been discovered and opened for trade by

262

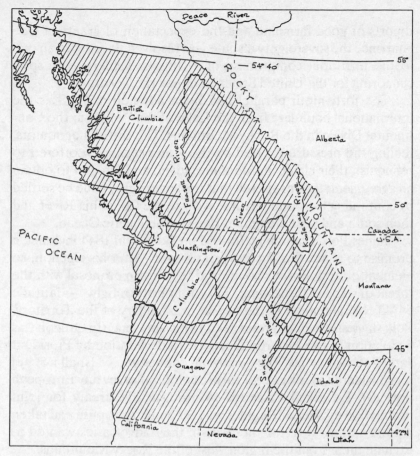

Fig. 42
The Territory of Oregon. It ranged from the Pacific Ocean east to the Rocky Mountains, and from latitude 54°40'N (the supposed southern extent of Russian possessions) south to 42° N (considered to be the northern reach of Spanish claims along the Pacific coast).

Mackenzie, Fraser and Thompson. It was a part of the Pacific Northwest that few if any Americans had ever seen. The agreement, however, allowed the British negotiators to put off for another day the need to take a stand on the sovereignty issue.

Inevitably, joint occupation of the Territory was extended past the ten-year limit. American settlers began streaming into the region along the Oregon Trail in the early 1840s, attracted by

263

reports of good farmland and the expectation of grants of free land once the sovereignty dispute was resolved. It brought an end to the territorial compromise of 1818; the settlers were soon clamoring for the United States to annex the Territory.

The forty-ninth parallel had been adopted in 1818 as the international boundary from the Lake of the Woods to the Continental Divide in the Rocky Mountains. The British negotiators, feeling the pressure exerted by the Americans, now offered to relinquish their claims in Montana, Idaho and Oregon to obtain an agreement; they proposed that the sovereignty issue be settled by continuing the boundary line west to the Columbia River and then south and west along that river to the Pacific Ocean.

James Polk's campaign for the presidency in 1844 included a promise to annex the Territory of Oregon. After his election, an element of his followers countered the British proposal with the threat of war and the slogan: "Fifty-four forty or fight" — latitude 54°40'N being taken as the northern boundary of the Territory. Polk suggested to Congress that a British presence in Oregon was a violation of the Monroe Doctrine (a declaration by President James Monroe, that "the American continents . . . [shall not be] . . . considered as subject for future colonization by any European power"). He asked Congress to abrogate the treaty for joint occupation of Oregon. Suddenly, the boundary dispute had taken a more serious turn for the British; their adversaries wanted to exclude them from the region west of the Rocky Mountains.

Lord Aberdeen, foreign secretary in Sir Robert Peel's administration, had charge of the boundary dispute for Britain between 1841 and 1846. The accomplishments of British mariners and trader-explorers who had won a large part of Pacific Northwest for Britain meant little to him. He persuaded the Prime Minister that no significance should be attached to a piece of land so far away; Oregon was not worth the risk of war with the United States. In the spring of 1846 Peel proposed a compromise — the dispute would be settled by extending the international boundary west from the Divide along the forty-ninth parallel to the Pacific Ocean. The line was bent to carry through the Strait of Juan de Fuca, to avoid the partition of Vancouver Island. Polk found this proposal agreeable and the Senate gave its approval in June.

26

"By the work one knows the workman."
— La Fontaine

Alexander Mackenzie

Alexander Mackenzie received an opportunity to exercise his interest in the business end of the fur trade soon after he arrived in Montreal in 1794, the year following his voyage to the Pacific. McTavish, Frobisher & Company appointed him an agent to represent the firm at the summer meeting in Grand Portage. A year later he was made a partner. Mackenzie continued to advocate his Columbian Enterprise, a policy which would diminish the stature of eastern interests in the fur trade, and a coolness developed between him and Simon McTavish. Meanwhile, exploration and expansion of trade beyond the Divide, boldly begun by Mackenzie, languished.

Mackenzie's agreement with the firm expired in 1799 and was not renewed. We can only guess at the reasons. It has been suggested he attempted a coup to oust McTavish and get on with the expansion of trade and when it failed he was himself ousted. It is said he was self-important and unreasonable in his dealings with the firm. If these charges are true, it is easy to believe his actions were fueled by the intensity of his ambitions for the Columbian Enterprise and the stubborn resistance of Simon Mc-Tavish. Mackenzie had demonstrated a capacity to lead and finding himself in a subordinate position with a curb on his entrepreneurial bent, he grew impatient and bitter towards his old associates and became ineffective when working with them. He joined a rival company in 1800. The death of McTavish in 1804 seemed a time to heal old wounds but Mackenzie was not invited to rejoin the firm; it was feared he would generate too much friction. He had to be content with a minor share in an enlarged North West Company. Thereafter he spent most of his time in Britain.

Mackenzie published an account of his travels — *Voyages from Montreal* — in December, 1801. The book was an instant success. Several new editions followed, including translations into French and German. It helped earn him a knighthood in 1802.

Although Mackenzie exhibited little love for the rugged life of fur trader and explorer, he served the North West Company well in the rough uncharted Northwest, and he did it boldly and brilliantly. It is unfortunate that he chose the Peace River for his venture to the Pacific in 1793. The trail he followed from the Fraser River to Bella Coola has not become the road of commerce he expected. Had he elected to ascend the Athabasca River (also shown on Peter Pond's maps), or selected it for a third attempt, the route over the Athabasca Pass and down the Columbia River could have been in use twenty years before Thompson pioneered it. It might have resulted in a markedly different division of the Pacific Northwest.

Mackenzie's interests lay in grand business strategies that could be directed from the board rooms of Montreal. Had he been as persuasive in dealing with his business associates as he was in bending voyageurs to his will, he might well have come to control the destiny of the North West Company after Simon McTavish's death.

He married Geddes Mackenzie in 1812 when he was about forty-eight, and settled down on an estate in Moray Firth, Scotland. His three children were born there. He did not live to see the union of the Hudson's Bay Company and the North West Company in 1821, something he began advocating in 1794; he died unexpectedly in 1820. His house was destroyed by fire in 1883, resulting in the loss of most of his personal papers.

Lewis and Clark

The achievements of Lewis and Clark became generally known soon after they returned to the United States and an admiring nation sought to honor and reward them. In 1807, in the year the expedition landed in St. Louis, the two explorers received commissions as generals. Lewis was made Governor of the Territory of Louisiana and Clark was appointed Brigadier-General of the Louisiana Militia and its Superintendent of Indian Affairs. In January 1808, Clark married Judy Hancock, a girl he had known for years; Lewis never married.

Lewis arrived in St. Louis in March, 1808, to take up the office of governor. He found nothing but trouble — between American settlers and French residents, between whites and Indians, and with the British who fomented discord where they could. The peevish, quarrelsome and ambitious Secretary of the Interior, Fredrick Bates, opposed him at every opportunity and their relationship was soon reduced to open hostility.

His troubles multiplied when he made extensive purchases of land near St. Louis, binding himself to payments several times the amount his salary brought him. By the fall of 1808, he was so short of cash he had to borrow $49 from Clark to pay his doctor for treating his servant.

Lewis did not feel comfortable as a politician and administrator. As his difficulties increased, his popularity declined and with it his health. The bureaucrats in Washington became overzealous in scrutinizing his official expenditures and even refused to pay some debts he had contracted in the service of the Territory, thereby forcing him to use his own money to pay the bills. Faced with financial ruin, Lewis prepared to journey to Washingon to plead his case.

He left St. Louis in September, 1809, traveling on horseback with one companion and two servants, and carrying with him the records of the expedition which he expected to organize, finally, into a publishable form. The little party stopped one night on its way to Nashville in an unsettled part of Tennessee, on the premises of a squatter who earned a living providing food, liquor and shelter to travelers. There, in the night of October 10, Lewis died slowly, painfully and alone — mysteriously shot in the side and head and refused assistance by the wife of the squatter who was too frightened to open her door when he pleaded for water and attention to his wounds. It has been speculated that he committed suicide or that he was killed for the little money he carried; in fact, his death remains a mystery.

Clark, as the surviving head of the expedition, inherited the task of bringing the explorers' journals to publication. He enlisted the services of a young Nicholas Biddle, a graduate of Princeton University, to edit the material. Biddle finished the writing in July, 1811, but for a time Clark could not find a publisher and the first edition, of two thousand copies, was delayed until 1814.

Clark was appointed Governor of Louisiana (it became known as Missouri Territory in 1812) in 1813, somewhat against his will because he had applied for active service in the War of 1812. He held that position until 1820 when Missouri became a state. He was popular with the Indians; most of them learned to trust and admire him. After 1820, he became Superintendent of Indian Affairs, first for the state of Missouri and then for Indian lands beyond the state. He had not forgotten Sacagawea whom he had learned to like and admire on the way to the Pacific and when Baptiste, the infant who accompanied the expedition, had grown into a boy, Clark took him to St. Louis and arranged for his education.

Clark became reasonably prosperous in later life. He enjoyed his many friends and developed a reputation as a host. He stood out in his community as an agreeable, well-dressed and fine-looking man. His circle of acquaintances grew and, in his later years, foreigners as well as many of the best-known Americans in the land came to see him and many became his friends.

His wife, Judy, and her daughter died in 1820 leaving him with three sons. A year later he married the widowed, childhood friend of Judy and she bore him two more sons. His second wife died in 1831. Clark lived on until 1838, when he was sixty-eight.

David Thompson[1]

David Thompson left the Northwest for the last time in 1812, the year after he completed the circuit of the Columbia River, and settled in Terrebone, Quebec.

The main interest in Thompson's life lay in mapping the country in which he traveled. He worked at it faithfully for more than twenty years from the time he met Philip Turnor, from whom he learned the rudiments of surveying in 1790, until his retirement, using what time he could spare from his duties as a fur trader. Where others were content to record isolated routes of travel, Thompson seems to have had the goal of compiling a comprehensive map of the Northwest; each map prepared became a part of that whole. He worked at it patiently, methodically and carefully using the methods practiced by the qualified mapmakers of his time, fixing the geographical coordinates of prominent physical features and places with astronomical observations and sketching in the intervening geography. He traveled more than 80,000 km. (50,000 mi.), ranging from Lake Athabasca to the headwaters of the Missouri, Red and Mississippi Rivers, from Sault Ste. Marie to the Pacific Ocean. He traveled by canoe, on horseback and on foot, often backpacking or dragging a sled to transport his instruments, provisions and baggage.

When we consider his role in the discovery and exploration of the Pacific Northwest, Thompson presents a perplexing figure. Fate thrust a place in history at him, not once but repeatedly — a place more eminent than the one he holds. The explorer in him seems to have taken the challenge reluctantly, almost fearfully, acting out his part cautiously, never with verve, seldom with daring. Still, in the course of reaching the Pacific Ocean, he pioneered use of the Howse and Athabasca Passes; one may add, perhaps unkindly, he accomplished this more through the forces of circumstance than from his own initiative — the unknown held no great lure for him.

In the first two years after retirement, Thompson worked steadily at completing the details of his map of the Northwest. It was finished in 1814 and it showed, for the first time on any map, that the Fraser and Columbia were two separate rivers. This feature was accepted and copied by cartographers. The map earned him the distinction, years later, of being called Canada's foremost geographer.

To provide for his large family — in time it numbered seven sons and six daughters — Thompson turned to using his extensive experience in surveying, the only qualification he had after giving up the life of a fur trader. He was certified as a land surveyor in

269

1814, and between 1816 and 1826, he worked at the task of surveying the boundary between Canada and the United States.

He moved to Williamstown, Glengarry County, Ontario, where he lived comfortably for a time, but he suffered hard times as a result of being too generous with his money. It began when he invested in a mortgage on the local Presbyterian church. When the congregation professed an inability to pay, he gave them the property. He set his sons up in business but they all failed and he spent the last of his financial reserves to pay their debts.

He moved again, to Longueuil on the St. Lawrence River, opposite Montreal, and earned a decent living until his eyesight failed; and then he became very poor. He sold his instruments and pawned his overcoat for food. He tried to sell his maps of Lake Superior and a number of sketches of the Rocky Mountains but he succeeded only in getting a loan of $5. His sons and several sons-in-law seem to have given him little help.

At the age of seventy-four, in 1844, he began writing a book on his experience of twenty-five years in the Northwest, hoping to duplicate Alexander Mackenzie's success. He tried to organize a company of subscribers that would pay him a total of $1 per day while he was writing, for living expenses, in return for a share of the profits. He could not raise the money. Despite this, he worked at the book until about 1850, without finding a publisher.

Thompson died at the age of eighty-seven on February 10, 1857; his wife, Charlotte, lived another three months. They are buried in Mount Royal Cemetery, in Montreal.

After Thompson's death, one of his sons sold most of the manuscripts of the proposed book to a collector who eventually sold them to the Canadian geologist, J. B. Tyrrell. With the help of others, Tyrrell edited the material and drew on his own experience in the Northwest to illuminate the text with copious footnotes and an itinerary of Thompson's travels. It was published, finally, in 1916 under the title: *David Thompson's Narrative, 1784-1812*.

Simon Fraser

Simon Fraser remained in the Northwest after his strenuous and dangerous voyage, in 1808, down the river that bears his name today. Curiously, he did not rise to be the senior partner in the Athabasca department of the North West Company. In 1815, tired of the lonely and spartan life, he applied for retirement but he was persuaded to stay for a few more years. The company was losing an alarming number of its experienced men and could ill afford to give up one with Fraser's qualifications.

In 1816, Fraser and a number of his fellow Nor' Westers were arrested by Lord Selkirk at Fort William while attending the annual meeting of partners and agents. The charge was suspicion of having an indirect part in the Seven Oaks Massacre in which Robert Semple, Governor of the Red River Colony, and nineteen of his men were killed near the site of Winnipeg. The North West Company may have had a hand in inciting the Métis, but Fraser claimed he was merely passing through the region on his way from Athabasca to Grand Portage on Lake Superior.

Fraser left the Northwest in 1817, at the age of forty-one, and settled in the township of Cornwall in Stormount County, Lower Canada. The next year he had to journey to York (Toronto) to defend himself against Selkirk's charges of treason, conspiracy and accessory to murder. He was acquitted.

He married Catherine Macdonell, aged twenty-nine, in 1820, and took her to Cornwall where the couple lived for forty years, farming and operating a sawmill. They raised five sons and three daughters.

Fraser was sixty-one in 1837 when the Canadian rebellions broke out. He volunteered for the militia and served in 1837-8. He suffered a fall in the fighting and permanently injured his right knee. He petitioned the government of Upper Canada for compensation and was granted £20 per year. He also applied to the British government but he was refused aid. Apparently the injury prevented him from looking after his farm and mill for he lived in poverty during his last years.

He was an unlettered man when he first went into Athabasca country. His journals and letters for the period of his years of exploration and trading are badly composed (of course, poor spelling was common even among educated people). Fraser recognized his shortcomings and sought help from John Stuart: "With this I send you over my Journal since the 5th April except

271

from the time we arrived at Nakazleh until the 20th August which I expect you will be able to bring up. It is exceeding ill wrote worse worded & not well spelt. But there I know you can make a good Journal of it."[2]

Letters written thirty years later show he had greatly improved his education and he was now well-informed on current matters.

He had hopes of getting his journals published but he was unable to arrange this. It is believed he lent a manuscript to Roderic Mackenzie (cousin of Alexander) for possible inclusion in a projected history of the fur trade. The history was never written and Fraser's narrative was not published until 1889, twenty-seven years after his death.

Several retired Nor' Westers, including David Thompson, lived near Fraser. Eventually only he and one John McDonald were left alive. When the two men met in 1859, they drafted a memorandum, knowing not much time was left to them:

> We are the last of the N W Partners. We have known each other for many years. . . . We are both aged, we have lived in mutual esteem and fellowship, we have done our duty in the stations allotted to us without fear, or repriach. We have braved many dangers, we have run many risks. . . . We have both crossed this continent, we have explored many new points, we have met many new tribes, we have run our Race, & as this is probably the last time we meet on earth, we part as we have lived in sincere friendship & mutual good will.[3]

McDonald passed away the next year. Fraser and his wife died in 1862, within a day of each other, and were buried in a single grave at St. Andrews, Quebec.

Notes

Preface
  1. *Encyc. Brit.*, vol. 22, p. 609

Part 1, Chapter 1
  1. *The History of Herodotus*, p. 216.
  2. see also J. N. Wilford: *The Mapmakers*, pp. 56-9.
  3. J. A. Williamson: *Maritime Enterprise,* p. 127.
  4. *Encyc. Brit.*, vol. 22, p. 88.

Chapter 2
  1. J. N. Wilford: *The Mapmakers*, p.113.
  2. see also P. S. Paige: *The Voyage of Magellan.*
  3. *Ibid.*, p. 88.
  4. R. Greenhow: *The History of Oregon and California*, p. 67.

Chapter 3
  1. M. Komroff: *The Travels of Marco Polo*, p. 269.
  2. G. Nunn: *Origin of the Strait of Anian concept.*
  3. S. E. Morison: *The Great Explorers*, p. 675.
  4. Francis Drake: *The World Encompassed.*
  5. *Ibid.*, p. 114.
  6. *Ibid.*, p. 115.
  7. S. E. Morison: *The Great Explorers*, p. 703.

Chapter 4
  1. R. Greenhow: *Memoir, Historical and Political,* p. 42, 207; J. T. Walbran: *British Columbia Coast Names*, p. 274.
  2. R. Greenhow: *Memoir, Historical and Political,* p. 40, 205.
  3. R. Greenhow: *The History of Oregon and California*, p. 91.

4. *Ibid.*, p. 91.
5. *Ibid.*, p. 93.
6. *Ibid.*, p. 94.

Chapter 5
1. R. H. Fisher: *Bering's Voyages*, p. 47.

Chapter 6
1. R. H. Fisher: *Bering's Voyages*, p. 38.
2. *Ibid.*, p. 10.
3. *Ibid.*, p. 23.
4. P. Lauridsen: *Vitus Bering*, p. 20.
5. R. H. Fisher: *Bering's Voyages*, pp. 81-4; F. A. Golder: *Russian Expansion*, pp. 140-9; P. Lauridsen: *Vitus Bering*, pp. 29-34.

Chapter 7
1. F. A. Golder: *Russian Expansion, pp. 151-63; P. Lauridsen: Vitus Bering*, pp. 166-8.

Chapter 8
1. P. Lauridsen: *Vitus Bering*, p. 53.
2. *Ibid.*, p. 64.
3. *Ibid.*, p. 66.
4. *Ibid.*, p. 132.
5. *Ibid.*, pp. 135-87.

Part 2, Chapter 9
1. M. de la Campa: *A Journal of Explorations*, p. 52.
2. *Ibid.*, p. 54.
3. R. Greenhow: *The History of Oregon and California*, p. 432.
4. *Ibid.*, p. 433.

Chapter 10
1. F. Knight: *A Guide to Ocean Navigation*, p. 84.
2. P. Collinder: *A History of Marine Navigation*, p. 138; R. Hough: *The Murder of Captain James Cook*, p. 260.
3. B. Hill: *The remarkable world of Frances Barkley*, p. 24.
4. Ibid., pp. 23-4. See also D. Pope: *Life in Nelson's Navy*, pp. 137-45.
5. J. C. Beaglehole: *The Life of Captain James Cook*, p. 135.
6. *Ibid.*, p. 170.
7. *A Voyage to the Pacific*, vol. 3, p. 48.

8. J. C. Beaglehole: *The Life of Captain James Cook*, p. 705.
9. *Ibid.*, p. 170.
10. F. Knight: *A Guide to Ocean Navigation*, p. 97.
11. see also J. C. Beaglehole: *The Life of Captain James Cook*, pp. 170-1, 703-06.
12. *A Voyage to the Pacific*, vol. 1, p. xxxiii.
13. *Ibid.*, vol. 1, p. xxxiii.
14. *Ibid.*, vol, 2, p. 258.
15. S. Muller: *Voyages from Asia to America*.
16. *A Voyage to the Pacific*, vol. 2, p. 261.
17. *Ibid.*, vol. 2, p. 263.
18. *Ibid.*, vol. 2, p. 401.
19. *Ibid.*, vol. 2, p. 422.
20. see also Beaglehole: *The Life of Captain James Cook*, pp. 591-636.

Chapter 11

1. J. Meares: *Voyages*, p. xxi.
2. J. T. Walbran: *British Columbia Coast Names*, p. 33.
3. B. Hill: *The remarkable world of Frances Barkley*, p. 40.
4. J. Meares: *Voyages*, p. 152.
5. *Ibid.*, p. 153.
6. *Ibid.*, p. 157.
7. *Ibid.*, p. 167.
8. *Ibid.*, p. 168.

Chapter 12

1. H. R. Wagner: *Spanish Explorations*, p. 151.

Chapter 13

1. F. W. Howay: *Voyages of the "Columbia,"* p. 388.
2. *Ibid.*, p. 388.
3. *Ibid.*, p. 389.
4. *Ibid.*, p. 390.
5. *Ibid.*, p. xiv.
6. *Ibid.*, p. xiv.
7. *Ibid.*, p. xiv.
8. J. Hoskins: *The narrative of a Voyage*, p. 9.

Chapter 14

1. J. Meares: *Voyages*.
2. *Ibid.*, p. lvi.

3. G. Vancouver: *A Voyage of Discovery,* vol. 1, p. xx.
4. *Ibid.,* vol. 1, p. 209.
5. J. Meares: *Voyages,* p. 168.
6. *Ibid.,* p. lvi.
7. G. Vancouver: *A Voyage of Discovery,* vol. 1, p. 205.
8. *Ibid.,* vol. 1, p. 205.
9. *Ibid.,* vol. 1, p. 224.
10. H. R. Wagner: *Spanish Explorations,* p. 252.
11. G. Vancouver: *A Voyage of Discovery,* vol. 1, p. 300.
12. *Ibid.,* vol. 1, p. 314.

Chapter 15
1. F. W. Howay: *Voyages of the "Columbia,"* p. 435.
2. *Ibid.,* p. 395.
3. *Ibid.,* p. 436.
4. *Ibid.,* p. 436.
5. G. Simpson: *Narrative of a Journey,* p. 258.
6. *Ibid.,* p. 259.
7. *Ibid.,* p. 259.
8. *Ibid.,* p. 258.

Chapter 16
1. G. Vancouver: *A Voyage of Discovery,* vol. 1, p. 415.
2. *Ibid.,* vol. 1, p. 415.

Part 3
1. M. W. Campbell: *The Saskatchewan,* p. 72.
2. *Ibid.,* p. 41.
3. Earl of Southesk: *Saskatchewan and the Rocky Mountains,* p. 301.

Chapter 17
1. N. M. Crouse: *La Vérendrye: Fur Trader and Explorer,* pp. 4-13; G. H. Smith: *The explorations of the la Vérendryes,* pp. 3-6.
2. N. M. Crouse: *La Vérendrye: Fur Trader and Explorer,* pp. 15-6.
3. *Ibid.,* pp. 29-33.
4. *Ibid.,* p. 97.
5. *Ibid.,* p. 107.
6. *Ibid.,* p. 121.
7. G. H. Smith: *The explorations of the La Vérendryes,* p. 60.
8. *Ibid.,* p. 98.
9. N. M. Crouse: *La Vérendrye: Fur Trader and Explorer,* p. 173.

10. *Ibid.*, p. 181.
11. G. H. Smith: *The explorations of the La Vérendryes,* p. 109.

Chapter 18
1. *The Letters and Journals of Simon Fraser,* pp. 9-11.
2. A. Mackenzie: *Voyages from Montreal,* p. xii.
3. *The Journals and Letters of Sir Alexander Mackenzie,* p. 163.
4. *Ibid.*, p. 432.
5. *Ibid.*, p. 438.
6. A. Mackenzie: *Voyages from Montreal,* pp. 34, 46.
7. *Ibid.*, p. 54.
8. *Ibid.*, pp. 54, 60.
9. *Ibid.*, pp. 140, 158.
10. *Ibid.*, p. 151.
11. *Ibid.*, p. 139.
12. *Ibid.*, p. 159.
13. *The Journals and Letters of Sir Alexander Mackenzie,* p. 450.
14. A. Mackenzie: *Voyages from Montreal,* p. 151.
15. *Ibid.*, pp. 153-86.
16. *Ibid.*, p. 164.
17. *Ibid.*, p. 180.
18. *Ibid.*, pp. 187-228.
19. *Ibid.*, p. 203.
20. *Ibid.*, p. 220.
21. *Ibid.*, pp. 229-82.
22. J. Meares: *Voyages,* p. 158.
23. A. Mackenzie: *Voyages fromMontreal,* p. 256.
24. *Ibid.*, pp. 283-397.
25. *Ibid.*, p. 316.
26. *Ibid.*, p. 343.
27. *Ibid.*, p. 347.
28. *Ibid.*, p. 347.
29. *Ibid.*, p. 349.
30. *Ibid.*, p. 397.
31. *The Journals and Letters of Sir Alexander Mackenzie,* p. 453.
32. *Ibid.*, p. 455.
33. *Ibid.*, p. 504.

Chapter 19
1. *David Thompson's Narrative . . . 1784-1812,* ed. J. B. Tyrrell, p. xxiv.
2. *Ibid.*, p. xxiv.

3. *David Thompson's Narrative, 1784-1812*, ed. R. Glover, p. xxiii.
4. *Ibid.*, p. xxiv.
5. *Ibid.*, p. xxxiv.
6. *Ibid.*, pp. xxxii-xxxv, xl-xli.
7. *Ibid.*, p. xliii.
8. *Ibid.*, p. xliii.
9. *David Thomspn's Narrative . . . 1784-1812*, ed. J. B. Tyrell, p. 105.
10. *Ibid.*, p. 104.
11. *The Letters and Journals of Simon Fraser*, p. 11.
12. H. A. Dempsey: *Thompson's Journey*, p. 4.
13. *Ibid.*, p. 8.
14. *Ibid.*, p. 8.
15. H. A. Dempsey: *David Thompson under scrutiny*, p. 25.
16. F. W. Howay: *David Thompson's Account*, vol. 40, of the Queen's Quarterly, p. 356.

Chapter 20

1. *Original Journals of Lewis and Clark*, vol. 1, p. xx.
2. *Ibid.*, p. xxi.
3. *Letters of Lewis and Clark*, vol. 1, p. 2.
4. *Original Journals . . . Clark Expedition 1804-1806*, vol. 7, p. 208.
5. *Ibid.*, vol. 7, p. 208.
6. *Ibid.*, vol. 7, p. 208.
7. *Letters of the Lewis and Clark . . . 1783-1854*, vol. 1, p. 4.
8. *Original Journals . . . Clark Expedition 1804-1806*, vol. 7, p. 248.
9. *Ibid.*, vol. 1, p. xxxvi.
10. *Ibid.*, vol. 7, p. 230.
11. *Ibid.*, vol. 1, p. 3-276.
12. *Ibid.*, vol. 1, pp. 11-14.
13. *Ibid.*, vol. 1, p. 15.
14. *Ibid.*, vol. 1, p. 114.
15. *Ibid.*, vol. 1, p. 164.
16. *Ibid.*, vol. 1, p. 257.
17. *Ibid.*, vol. 1, p. 277 − vol. 2, p. 280.
18. *Ibid.*, vol. 1, p. 284.
19. *Ibid.*, vol. 2, p. 112, 117, 130, 132.
20. *Ibid.*, vol. 2, p. 147, 159.
21. *Ibid.*, vol. 2, p. 166.
22. *Ibid.*, vol. 2, p. 252.
23. *Ibid.*, vol. 2, p. 276.
24. *Ibid.*, vol. 2, p. 281 − vol. 3, p. 44.

25. *Ibid.*, vol. 2, p. 325.
26. *Ibid.*, vol. 2, p. 335.
27. *Ibid.*, vol. 2, p. 347.
28. *Ibid.*, vol. 2, p. 361.
29. *Ibid.*, vol. 3, pp. 45-298.
30. *Ibid.*, vol. 3, p. 64.
31. *Ibid.*, vol. 3, p. 84.
32. *Ibid.*, vol. 3, p. 119.
33. *Ibid.*, vol. 3, p. 210.
34. *Ibid.*, vol. 3, p. 297.
35. *Ibid.*, vol. 4, pp. 181-3.
36. *Ibid.*, vol. 4, p. 197.
37. *Ibid.*, vol. 5, p. 223.
38. *Ibid.*, vol. 7, p. 334.

Chapter 21
1. *The Letters and Journals of Simon Fraser,* p. 2.
2. *Ibid.*, p. 198, 230.
3. *Ibid.*, p. 211, 230.
4. *Ibid.*, p. 241.
5. *Ibid.*, p. 250.
6. T. C. Elliott: *The discovery . . . Columbia River,* pp. 28-49; *David Thompson's Narrative,* ed. R. Glover, pp. 273-9.
7. T. C. Elliott: *The discovery . . . Columbia River,* p. 29.
8. *Ibid.*, p. 34.
9. *Ibid.*, p. 31.

Chapter 22
1. *The Letters and Journals of Simon Fraser,* pp. 61-77, 131-61.
2. *Ibid.*, p. 69.
3. *Ibid.*, p. 73.
4. *Ibid.*, p. 73.
5. *Ibid.*, p. 76.
6. *Ibid.*, pp. 77-100.
7. *Ibid.*, p. 81.
8. *Ibid.*, p. 82.
9. *Ibid.*, p. 96.
10. *Ibid.*, p. 97.
11. *Ibid.*, pp. 100-28.
12. *Ibid.*, p. 105.

Chapter 24

1. T. C. Elliott: *The discovery . . . Columbia River*, p. 47.
2. J. Palliser: *Papers relative . . . Rocky Mountains*, p. 478.
3. *David Thompson's Narrative, 1784-1812*, ed. R. Glover, pp. 315-23.
4. *Ibid.*, p. 317.
5. *David Thompson's Narrative . . . 1784-1812*, ed. J. B. Tyrrell, p. 455.
6. *Ibid.*, p. 455.

Chapter 25

1. *David Thompson's Narrative . . . 1784-1812*, ed. J. B. Tyrrell, p. 453.
2. *Ibid.*, p. 455.

Chapter 26

1. *David Thompson's Narrative . . . 1784-1812*, ed. J. B. Tyrrell, pp. liii-lvi.
2. *The Letters and Journals of Simon Fraser*, p. 252.
3. *Ibid.*, p. 271.

References

Beaglehole, J. C.: *The Life of Captain James Cook.* Adam & Charles Black, London, 1974.

Campa, Miguel de la: *A Journal of Explorations northward along the coast from Monterey in the year 1775*, ed. John Galvin. John Howell, San Francisco, 1964.

Campbell, Marjorie Wilkins: *The Saskatchewan.* Clarke, Irwin & Co. Ltd., Toronto, 1950.

Collinder, Per: *A History of Marine Navigation.* B. T. Batsford Ltd., London, 1954.

A Voyage to the Pacific Ocean performed under the direction of Captains Cook, Clerke and Gore in His Majesty's ships the Resolution and Discovery in the years 1776 to 1780. Printed by W. and A. Strahan for G. Nicol and T. Cadell, 1784.

Journal of Captain Cook's Last Voyage to the Pacific Ocean on Discovery, 1776-1779. E. Newberry, London, 1781 (Fig. 15, p. 81.)

Crouse, Nellie M.: *La Vérendrye: Fur Trader and Explorer.* Cornell University Press, Ithaca, N.Y., 1956.

Dempsey, Hugh A.: *Thompson's journey to the Red Deer River.* Alberta Historical Review, vol. 13, no. 1, p. 1, 1965.

——*David Thompson under scrutiny.* Alberta Historical Review, vol. 12, no. 1, p. 22, 1964.

Drake, Francis: *The World Encompassed.* Printed for Nicholas Bovrne, London, 1628. Reprinted by Burt Franklin, New York for the Hukluyt Society.

Elliott, T. C.: *The discovery of the source of the Columbia River.* Oregon Historical Review, Quarterly, vol. 26, p. 23, 1925.

——*The Log of H.M.S. "Chatham."* Oregon Hist. Soc., Quarterly, vol. 18, p. 231, 1917. (Fig. 17, p. 106.)

Encyclopaedia Britannica, 1969. William Bench, Publisher.

Fisher, Raymond H.: *Bering's Voyages, Whither and Why.* University of Washington Press, Seattle, 1977.

The Letters and Journals of Simon Fraser, 1806-1808, edited with an introduction by W. Kaye Lamb. Macmillan of Canada, 1960.

Golder, F. A.: *Russian Expansion in the Pacific 1641-1850.* Paragon Book Reprint Corp., New York, 1971.

——*Bering's Voyages.* In two volumes, vol. 1, Amer. Geog. Soc., 1922. (Fig.10, p. 57.)

Greenhow, Robert: *Memoir, Historical and Political, on the Northwest Coast of North America and the adjacent Territories.* Wiley and Putnam, New York, 1840.

——*The History of Oregon and California.* John Murray, London, 1844.

The History of Herodotus, trans. George Rawlinson, ed. M. Komroff. Tudor Publishing Co., New York, 1928.

Hill, Beth: *The remarkable world of Frances Barkley: 1769-1845.* Gray's Publishing Ltd., Sidney, B. C., 1978.

Hoskins, John: *The narrative of a voyage to the north west coast of America and China on trade and discoveries performed in the ship Columbia Rediviva, 1790, 1791, 1792 & 1793.* Unpublished manuscript in the library of the Massachusetts Historical Society.

Hough, Richard: *The Murder of Captain James Cook.* Macmillan, London, 1979.

Howay, Frederick William: *David Thompson's account of his first attempt to cross the Rockies.* Queen's Quarterly, vol. 40, p. 333, 1933.

——*Voyages of the "Columbia" to the Northwest coast, 1787-1790 and 1790-1793.* Massachusetts Historical Society Collections, vol. 79. Printed by the Merrymount Press, Boston, 1941.

Kerr, D. G. G.: *Historical Atlas of Canada.* Thomas Nelson & Sons (Canada) Ltd., 1975. (Fig. 23, p. 131.)

Knight, Frank: *A Guide to Ocean Navigation.* Macmillan & Co. Ltd., London, 1959.

Lauridsen, Peter: *Vitus Bering: The Discoverer of Bering Strait*, trans. Julius E. Olson. S.C. Griggs, Chicago, 1889. Reprinted by Books for Libraries Press, Freeport, N. Y., 1969.

Original Journals of the Lewis and Clark Expedition 1804-1806, ed. R. G. Thwaites. Dodd, Mead & Co., New York, 1904.

Letters of the Lewis and Clark Expedition with related documents 1783-1854, 2nd ed., ed. Donald Jackson. University of Illinois Press, Urbana, 1978.

Mackenzie, Alexander: *Voyages from Montreal on the river St. Laurence, through the continent of North America, to the frozen and Pacific Oceans; in the years 1789 and 1793. With a preliminary account of the rise, progress and present state of the fur trade of the country.* Cadell & Davies, London, 1801.

The Journals and Letters of Sir Alexander Mackenzie, ed. W. Kaye Lamb. Hakluyt Society, Extra Series No. 41. Cambridge University Press, Cambridge.

The Voyage of Magellan – The Journal of Antonio Pagafetta, trans. Paula Spurlin Paige. Prentice-Hall, Inc., Englewood Cliffs, N. J., 1969.

The Travels of Marco Polo (The Venetian), revised from Marsden's translation; edited with introduction by Manuel Komroff. Liveright Publishing Corp., New York, 1926.

Meares, John: *Voyages made in the years 1788 and 1789 from China to the North West coast of America.* Logographic Press, London, 1790.

Morison, Samuel Eliot: *The Great Explorers.* Oxford University Press, New York, 1978.

Muller, S.: *History of Russia,* 1754. Published in English as *Voyages from Asia to America*, Thomas Jefferys, London, 1761.

Nunn, George E.: *Origin of the Strait of Anian Concept.* Privately printed, Philadelphia, 1929.

Palliser, John: *Papers relative to the exploration by Captain Palliser of that portion of British North America which lies between the northern branch of the River Saskatchewan and the frontier of the United States; and between the Red River and Rocky Mountains.* Report to Her Majesty, June 1859.

Pope, Dudley: *Life in Nelson's Navy.* Naval Institute Press, Annapolis, Maryland, 1981.

Simpson, George: *Narrative of a Journey around the World during the years 1841 and 1842.* Henry Colburn, London, 1847.

Smith, G. Hubert: *The explorations of the la Verendryes in the Northern Plains, 1738-43.* University of Nebraska Press, Lincoln, Nebraska, 1980.

Southesk, The Earl of: *Saskatchewan and the Rocky Mountains. A diary and narrative of travel, sport, and adventure, during a journey through the Hudson's Bay Company's territories, in 1859 and 1860.* London, 1875 (reprinted by M. G. Hurtig, Edmonton, 1969).

David Thompson's Narrative of his explorations in Western America 1784-1812, ed. J. B. Tyrrell. The Champlain Society, Toronto, 1916.

David Thompson's Narrative, 1784-1812, ed. Richard Glover. The Champlain Society, Toronto, 1962.

Vancouver, George: *A Voyage of Discovery to the North Pacific Ocean, and Round the World, 1790-05.* G. G. & J. Robinson, London, 1798.

Wagner, Henry R.: *Spanish Explorations in the Strait of Juan de Fuca.* Fine Arts Press, Santa Ana, California, 1933.

Wagner, R.: *Peter Pond, Fur Trader & Explorer.* Yale University Library, 1955. (Fig 25-6, p. 137-8.)

Walbran, John T.: *British Columbia Coast Names 1592-1906; their origin and history.* J. J. Douglas Ltd., Vancouver, 1971.

Wilford, John Noble: *The Mapmakers.* Alfred A. Knopf, New York, 1981.

Williamson, James A.: *The First Circumnavigation in the Great Age of Discovery*, ed. A. P. Newton, London, 1932.

——*Maritime Enterprise, 1485 - 1558.* Octagon Books, New York, 1972.

Index

A

Aberdeen, Lord: 264.
Acton House: 171, 178, 224.
Adventure: 89-90, 102-3.
Alaska: 62.
Alaska Panhandle: 57, 67.
Alaska Peninsula: 57, 77.
Aleutian Islands: 57-8, 77.
Alexandria: 156, 158.
American Fur Company: 244- 5.
Antarctica: 68.
Argonaut: 86.
Arnarson, Ingolfur: 13.
Arrow Lakes: 175, 247, 258.
Arctic Lake: 152-3.
Assiniboine Indians: 123-5.
Assiniboine River: 122, 126, 231.
Astor, John Jacob: 242, 244-5, 249-50, 257, 260-1.
Asuncion Bay: 65-6.
Athabasca Pass: 175, 247, 253, 256-7, 259, 266, 269.
Athabasca River: 173, 218, 247, 252-3, 266.

B

Baffin, William: 38.
Bakers Bay: 101-2, 105-7, 211.
Baker, Mr.: 105.
Balboa, Vasco: 21-2.
Banff: 172.
Barkley, Charles: 80-2, 93.
Bates, Fredrick: 267.
Beaver Indians: 152.
Beaverhead River: 201.
Bella Coola: 143, 266.
Bella Coola Indians: 156.
Bella Coola River: 158-9.
Bennet Dam, W.A.C.: 148-9.
Bering Island: 57-8.
Bering Sea: 46, 49, 57, 77.
Bering Strait: 49-50, 52, 78.
Bering, Vitus: 47-51, 54-60, 73-4, 78.
Biddle, Nicholas: 268.
Big Bend: 253-8, 261.
Big Hole River: 199, 201.
Bitterroot River: 199, 207.
Blackfoot Indians: 193-4, 200-1, 203, 205, 214.
Blaeberry River: 224, 226-7, 229, 254.

Boit, John: 89-90, 100.
Bonner's Ferry: 246-8.
Boone, Daniel: 188-9.
Boston Bar: 232, 237.
Bow Indians: 126.
Bow River: 166, 174-5.
Brazeau River: 247, 251, 254.
Broughton, Lieutenant William: 104-8, 218.
Brulé Lake: 252, 255.
Bullfinch's Harbor: 100.
Bullfinch, Charles: 100.
Burke Channel: 158, 160.
Burrard Inlet: 98.

C

Cabot, John: 29.
Cabot, Sebastian: 29-30.
Cacafuego: 35.
Calgary: 166.
Campa, Father: 65.
Canal Flats: 174, 246.
Cape Blanco: 41, 60, 63, 74, 81, 91, 109.
Cape Conception: 40.
Cape Disappointment: 64, 66-7, 84, 96-7, 105-7, 210-11, 257.
Cape Flattery: 38, 63-4, 75-6, 80, 82, 91, 96, 99, 156.
Cape Frondoso: 65-7.
Cape of Good Hope: 35
Cape Horn: 24, 35, 85, 183, 245, 257.
Cape Prince of Wales: 49, 78, 81.
Cape San Roque: 65-7, 83.
Cape San Sebastian: 40.
Cape Shoalwater: 64, 83, 96, 107.
Carrier, Indians: 151.
Castlegar: 247-8, 258.
Chancellor, Richard: 30.
Charbonneau, Touissant: 193-4, 205.
Charlevoix , Francois-Xavier: 116-7, 142, 184.
Chatham: 95, 98, 104-7.
Chilliwack: 232, 239.
Chimney Creek: 230, 232, 234.
Chipewyan Indians: 167-8.
Chirikov, Alexei: 48, 50, 56-7, 59, 73-4, 76.
Chukchi Peninsula: 47-54,

78, 81.
Churchill River: 167-8, 170.
Clark Fork River: 199, 207, 247-8, 254, 256, 258, 262.
Clark, Anne Rogers: 185.
Clark, George Rogers: 185-6.
Clark, John: 185-6.
Clark, William: 112, 181, 185-94, 197, 199-212, 214, 219, 223-4, 233, 243-5, 250, 262, 266-8.
Clayoquot Sound: 64, 80, 89.
Clearwater River: 199, 208-9.
Clerke, Charles: 68.
Columbia: 85, 87, 89-92, 97, 99-103, 106, 108.
Columbia Lake: 10, 246-7.
Columbia River: 10, 38, 41, 64, 67, 75, 84, 96, 99, 101-2, 104, 106-9, 144, 163-4, 171, 174-5, 180-90, 194-5, 200, 206-11, 213, 216, 218-9, 224, 226-31, 233, 236, 241, 243-6, 247-50, 253-64, 266, 268-9.
Columbian Enterprise: 164, 170-1, 223, 241, 265.
Columbus, Christopher: 16-8, 20, 26.
Continental Divide: 127, 149-50, 152, 170-1, 173, 175-8, 183, 188-9, 194, 199-200, 202-4, 206-7, 214, 221-5, 228, 249, 251, 253-4, 257-9, 262, 264-5.
Convention of 1818: 262.
Cook Inlet: 77, 137-8, 189, 217.
Cook's River: 77, 136-8, 140, 149, 217.
Cook, James: 12, 68-82, 85, 93, 95-6, 102, 136, 142, 145, 149-50, 156, 179, 189, 262.
Coppermine River: 165.
Cree Indians: 120-1, 125, 129, 176.
Crooked River: 150-1, 217, 221-2
Crosse Road: 133, 135, 168.
Crowsnest Pass: 175.
Cumberland House: 132-3, 135, 166.
Cusick: 247, 257.

D

da Gama, Vasco: 19.
Davis Strait: 39.

Davis, John: 38.
de Aguilar, Martin: 40-1,
60, 67, 74-5, 109, 140, 144.
de Beauharnois, Marquis:
117-9, 125-6, 128-9.
de Eliza, Francisco: 87-8,
95, 98.
de Fuca, Juan: 39, 65, 76,
80, 82, 93.
de Hezeta, Bruno: 62-7, 74,
82, 84, 101, 157, 180.
Delisle, Joseph: 56-7.
Delisle, Louis: 56-7 .
de la Vérendrye, Francois:
122, 125.
de la Vérendrye, Jean-
Baptiste: 120.
de la Vérendrye, Louis-
Joseph: 121-3, 125-7, 129.
de la Vérendrye, Pierre:
112, 118-30, 132, 193, 243.
de la Vérendrye, Pierre Jr.:
120, 124-5.
de Legazpi, Miguel: 27-8.
de Maurepas, Comte: 117,
128-9.
de Noyelles, Nicolas-
Joseph: 128-9.
Dean Channel: 158, 160.
Dean River: 158-9.
Deception Bay: 84, 91, 96,
100.
Destruction Island: 81.
Devil's Canyon: 258.
Diaz, Bartholomew: 16, 19.
Diomede Islands: 49, 52.
Discovery: 68, 78, 95, 97-9,
104-6, 108.
Dorchester, Lord: 163.
Doughty, John: 33.
Drake, Sir Francis: 32-8,
102, 262.
Drouillard, George: 188,
201, 203-5, 214.
E
East India Company: 180.
Enterprise: 245.
Eric the Red: 13.
Ericsson, Leif: 14.
Experiment: 198.
F
Federov, Ivan: 52-4.
Felice: 82.
Fidler, Peter: 174.
Field, Joseph: 214.
Field, Ruben: 214.
Finlay & Gregory: 134.
Finlay River: 144, 149, 217,
221.
Finlay, Jaco: 224, 227-8.
Finlay, James: 217-18.

Flatbow Indians: 246, 248-9.
Flathead Indians: 207.
Fletcher, Francis: 35, 38.
Floyd River: 192.
Floyd, Sergeant Charles:
192.
Fond du lac River: 167.
Fort Astoria: 64, 247, 257,
262.
Fort Augustus: 171.
Fort Chipewyan: 133, 139-
44, 162, 164, 178, 231, 241.
Fort Clatsop: 211-2, 214.
Fort Edmonton: 171.
Fort Fork: 143-7, 149, 157-
8, 222, 231.
Fort Fraser: 221-2.
Fort George: 221, 223,
230-1, 237, 241.
Fort la Reine: 117, 120, 122-
5, 127.
Fort Mandan: 190, 193-6,
210, 216.
Fort Maurepas: 120-1.
Fort McLeod: 221-3.
Fort St. James: 221-3.
Fort William: 271.
Fraser Lake: 222.
Fraser River: 64, 88, 98,
150, 152-3, 155, 158-9, 163,
178, 217-8, 221, 223-4, 231,
234-6, 238-9, 240-1, 247,
249, 255, 260, 263, 266, 269.
Fraser, Simon: 112, 219-24,
230-1, 233, 235-41, 249, 255,
262-3, 270-2.
Friendly Cove: 82.
Friendly Village: 158-9.
Frobisher, Joseph: 133.
Frobisher, Joseph &
Thomas: 135.
Frobisher, Martin: 36, 38.
Frobisher, Thomas: 133.
G
Galiano, Captain Dionisio
Alcala: 98.
Gallatin River: 199-200.
Gass, Patrick: 188.
Giscombe Portage: 222.
Golden Hind: 33.
Grand Portage: 134-6, 140,
145, 163, 170-1, 224, 250,
265, 271.
Grant, Isabella: 220.
Grays Bay: 101, 106.
Grays Harbor: 63-4, 100-1,
107.
Gray, Robert: 85, 87, 89-92,
97, 99-106, 109, 144, 179-
80, 188, 244, 250, 254, 259,
262.

Great Falls: 197, 199-200,
212, 214.
Greenland: 13.
Gregory & McLeod: 135-6.
Gulf of Anadyr: 48-9, 74,
57.
Gulf of California: 39.
Gwosdef, Michael: 49, 52-
4, 73-4.
H
Hancock, Judy: 267.
Haswell, Robert: 90.
Hawaii: 257.
Hearne, Samuel: 132, 165.
Hector, James: 259.
Hell's Gate: 232-3, 237-8,
255.
Henry the Navigator: 14-5.
Henry, William: 251-2.
Herjolfsson, Bjarni: 14.
Herodotus: 15.
Herrick Creek: 153-4.
Hinton: 247, 252.
Hope: 232, 234, 239, 241.
Horse Indians: 125-6.
Hoskins, John: 91.
Howe Sound: 98.
Howse Pass: 173-4, 175-6,
224, 226, 228-9, 247, 252,
254, 256, 259, 269.
Howse River: 173, 225, 226-
8, 250.
Howse, Joseph: 229.
Hudson House: 166.
Hudson Bay: 10, 72, 76, 94,
97, 113-6, 118-9, 122, 124,
132-3, 136, 140, 164-8, 170.
Hudson's Bay Company:
114, 132-4, 141, 164-8, 170,
174, 229, 242, 259, 266.
Hudson's Hope: 149.
Hudson, Henry: 38, 113.
Hughes, James: 171, 176-7,
223.
Hyperborean Sea: 139.
I
Ile-à-la-Crosse: 135-6, 138,
169.
Imperial Eagle: 80, 82.
Iron Rapids: 232, 234.
Iroquois Indians: 243, 252.
J
James Creek: 152-3, 217,
222.
Jasper: 252-3.
Jefferson River: 199-201.
Jefferson, Thomas: 178-85,
187, 189, 194, 216, 219, 244.
Jenny: 104-7.
Jervis Inlet: 98.
John II of Portugal: 15-8.

286

K

Kamchatka Peninsula: 46, 48, 55-7, 59, 74, 179.
Kamchatka River: 48.
Kendrick, John: 85, 87, 89, 91, 97.
Kettle Falls: 247, 257-9.
Kicking Horse Pass: 172, 175, 247.
Kolyma River: 48, 55.
Kootanae House: 223, 228-9, 231, 233, 242-3, 246-9, 251-2, 255-6, 261.
Kootanie River: 175, 227, 231, 254-5, 257-8.
Kootenae House: 223, 228-9.
Kootenay Indians: 171, 173, 176-7, 224, 227-8, 257.
Kootenay Lake: 175, 246-7, 250.
Kootenay River: 171-2, 174-6, 246-9, 254, 256, 258, 262-3.
Kootenay Plain: 224-6, 229, 251.
Kotzebue Sound: 49- 50.
Kullyspell House: 247-8.

L

La Croyère, Louis: 56, 59.
La Gasse: 173-6, 224, 228.
Lake Louise: 172.
Lake Manitoba: 122, 124.
Lake Winnipeg: 118-9, 122, 128, 132, 134-5, 165.
Large Country: 47, 52-4.
Lauridsen, Peter: 56.
Le Blanc: 173-6, 224, 228.
Ledyard, John: 179.
Lemhi Pass: 199, 203, 209, 214.
Lemhi River: 199, 204, 207.
Leon Creek: 232, 235, 241.
Lewis, Meriwether: 112, 179-81, 183-216, 219, 223-4, 233, 243-5, 250, 262, 266-7.
Lewis, William: 181.
Lillooet: 232, 234-5.
Livingstone, Robert: 183-4.
Lock, Michael: 38.
Lolo Pass: 199, 207-8, 214.
Lolo Trail: 207, 212.
Louisiana: 131-2, 178, 180, 182-4, 187-8, 190, 196, 243, 267-8.
Lytton: 155, 232, 236.

M

Macdonell, Catherine: 271.
Mackenzie Pass: 158-9.
Mackenzie River: 139, 141.
Mackenzie, Alexander: 77, 112, 130, 134-64, 166-7, 170-1, 173, 178-9, 182, 189, 217-20, 222-3, 228, 241, 249, 259, 262-3, 265-6, 270, 272.
Mackenzie, Charlotte: 270.
MacKenzie, Geddes: 266.
Mackenzie, Roderic: 138, 145, 163, 272.
Madison River: 199-200.
Magellan, Ferdinand: 22-7, 33, 37.
Malacca Strait: 20, 43.
Maldonado, Lorenzo: 39.
Manchester House: 166.
Mandans: 119, 121-8, 132, 180, 182, 187, 192-3, 195-6, 216, 243.
Maria's River: 214.
Marks, Captain John: 181.
Martinez, E. J.: 86-7, 95.
Master of the Northward: 167-8.
McDonald, Finan: 224, 227-8, 251, 257-8.
McDonald, John: 223-4, 272.
McDougall, James: 221, 223.
McGillivray's River: 246, 248.
McGillivray, Duncan: 170-1, 173, 176.
McGregor River: 153, 155, 221.
McLeod Lake: 217, 222.
McLeod's Fort: 142-3.
McTavish, Frobisher & Co.: 220, 265.
McTavish, Simon: 133, 223, 265-6.
Meares, John: 79-84, 86-7, 91, 93-4, 96-7, 102, 104, 156.
Meriwether, Lucy: 181.
Metaline Falls: 247-9.
Mexicana: 98.
Michaux, Andre: 179, 181.
Middle Road: 222.
Miette River: 252-3.
Missouri River: 122, 128, 132, 179-80, 182-4, 187, 189, 191, 193-4, 199-201, 203, 214-6, 243-5, 269.
Mistaya River: 225-6.
Mohawk Indians: 129.
Moluccas: 20, 25, 37, 43-4.
Monroe Doctrine: 264.
Monroe, President James: 184, 264.
Moyie River: 247.
Muller, S.: 73-5.
Musqueam: 240.

N

Narvaez, J. M.: 88, 98.
Nechako River: 221, 223.
Nelson: 247-8.
New Albion: 36, 72, 74, 81, 102, 104.
New Westminster: 240.
Nez Perce Indians: 208-9, 213.
Nootka Sound: 64, 76, 79-80, 82, 85-7, 89, 95, 98, 102-4, 163, 179, 189.
Norsemen: 13-4.
North West America: 86-7.
North West Company: 133-6, 141, 168, 170, 217, 219-20, 223, 241-2, 245, 248-50, 257, 261-2, 266, 271.
Northeast Passage: 17, 30-1, 36, 47, 78.
Northward Country: 166-8.
Northwest Passage: 17, 30-1, 36, 38-9, 48, 71, 78, 93-4, 97, 104.

O

Old Toby: 206-9.
Ordway, Sgt. John: 188.
Oregon Territory: 102, 262-4, 267.
Oregon Trail: 263.

P

Pacific Fur Company: 245, 250, 260.
Pacific Lake: 152-3.
Pacific Northwest: 9, 11, 38, 41, 64, 68, 71, 79-80, 82, 85, 88, 95, 103-4, 109, 219, 245, 249, 260, 262, 264, 266, 269.
Pack River: 150-1, 217, 221.
Palliser, John: 248, 259.
Palliser, Sir Hugh: 70.
Parsnip River: 144, 149-50, 152, 217, 221-2.
Pavlutski, Dimitri: 51, 53-4.
Peace River: 142-5, 147-50, 152, 164, 173, 178, 217-8, 221-2, 228, 231, 263, 266.
Peace River Canyon: 147.
Pelican: 33-7.
Pend Oreille Lake: 248, 256.
Pend Oreille River: 247-50, 254, 258, 262.
Perez, Juan: 62, 67.
Phoenicians: 15.
Piegan Indians: 166, 171-2, 174, 176, 214-6, 223-4, 251, 256, 259, 261.
Point Adams: 64, 66-7, 106-7, 211-2.
Point Atkinson: 88.
Point Grey: 64, 98, 104, 232, 240.

Point Hope: 49-50.
Point Roberts: 88, 98.
Polk, James: 264.
Polo, Marco: 31-2.
Pond, Peter: 135-40, 142, 166, 217, 266.
Popoff, Peter: 47, 52-3.
Portage la Prairie: 122.
Portage Lake: 152-3.
Portage Mountain: 147.
Portage Stream: 227.
Prince George: 223, 234.
Prince William Sound: 79, 86.
Princesa: 86.
Princess Royal: 86
Puget Sound: 98.
Puget, Peter: 97-8.

Q

Quadra, Juan Francisco de la Bodegay: 62-3, 67, 81.
Queen Charlotte Islands: 62, 76, 87, 90, 94, 102.
Quesnel, Jules: 230.

R

Ram River: 176, 247.
Rascal's Village: 158, 160, 162.
Red Deer River: 172, 174-6, 247.
Red River: 120, 122, 269.
Red Rock River: 199, 202, 205.
Reindeer Lake: 167-8.
Reindeer River: 167.
Resolution: 68, 72, 76-7.
Revelstoke: 247, 258.
Rio de San Roque: 82-4, 91, 101.
River of the North: 140.
River of the West: 38, 41, 67, 74-5, 81, 101, 109, 118-9, 121, 123, 127, 130, 140, 142, 144, 157, 163, 218, 241, 254, 258.
River Oregan: 94.
Rocky Mountain House: 171-8, 223-4, 227-8, 231, 251.
Rocky Mountain Indians: 146, 194.
Rocky Mountain Portage House: 221-2, 231.
Ross, John: 136, 138.
Ross, Malcolm: 167-8.

S

Sacagawea: 193-4, 197, 200-2, 205-6, 268.
Saleesh House: 247-8, 256.
Salish Indians: 207.
Salmon River: 204, 206-7.
San Carlos: 86, 88.

San Lorenzo: 49.
Sandwich Islands: 78, 95, 104.
Santa Saturina: 86, 88.
Santiago: 62, 64, 67.
Sargeant Bluff: 192.
Saskatchewan: 261.
Saskatchewan River: 112, 128-30, 132, 166, 171, 173-4, 176, 223-6, 229, 231, 233, 247, 250-1, 254, 256, 259.
Sekani Indians: 151-2, 154.
Semple, Robert: 271.
Serrao, Francisco: 22.
Seven Years War: 60, 130.
Shestakof, Afanase: 51.
Shoshone Indians: 126, 193-4, 199, 201-7.
Simcoe, John Graves: 163.
Simpson, Sir George: 101.
Sioux Indians: 116, 120, 125, 191-2, 195.
Small, Charlotte: 169.
Small, Patrick: 170.
Smoky River: 142, 144-5, 231.
Snake River: 142, 190, 199, 204, 206, 209, 247, 257, 263.
Sonora: 62-4, 67, 81.
Souris River: 122.
Southeast Passage: 17, 19, 22, 29.
Southesk, Earl of: 110.
Southwest Passage (Strait of Magellan): 17, 24, 26, 29.
Spangberg, Martin: 48, 50.
Spanish Banks: 98.
Spice Islands: 20-2, 26.
Spokane House: 247, 257-8.
Spokane River: 247, 257-8, 262.
Spuzzum: 232, 238.
St. Gabriel: 48, 52-3.
St. Lawrence Island: 49, 52.
St. Paul: 56-7, 59.
St. Peter: 56, 58-9.
Steller, George: 56, 58.
Stinking Lake: 152.
Strait of Anian: 32, 35-6, 38-41, 47-8.
Strait of Georgia: 39, 64, 88, 98, 104, 232, 239-40.
Strait of Juan de Fuca: 39, 64, 74, 76, 80-2, 86-8, 93, 95-7, 99, 264.
Strait of Labrador: 39.
Strait of Magellan: 26, 33-5.
Stuart Lake: 222.
Stuart, John: 221-3, 230, 271.
Summit Lake: 150-1, 222.
Sutil: 98.

T

Talleyrand, Charles: 183-4.
Texada Island: 88.
Thomas: 252.
Thompson River: 232-3, 236-7, 231-2, 247.
Thompson, David: 112, 165-73, 176-7, 214, 223-30, 233, 242-3, 246-58, 261-3, 266, 268-70, 272.
Thomsen's River: 233, 255.
Three Forks: 199-201.
Tonquin: 245, 250, 257.
Tordesillas: 17-9, 21-2, 26.
Treaty of Ghent: 262.
Treaty of Paris: 120-2, 130, 132, 134.
Treaty of Utrecht: 114-5, 130.
Turnor, Philip: 141-2, 166-8, 269.
Tyrrell, J. B.: 270.

U

Unimak Pass: 77.

V

Valdes, Captain Cayetano: 98.
Valerianos, Apostolos: 39.
Vancouver Island: 65, 76, 80, 82, 94, 102, 264.
Vancouver, George: 93, 95-9, 102, 104-6, 189, 195, 262.
Vermilion Pass: 172, 175-6, 247.
Vizcaino, Sebastian: 40-1.

W

Wadin, Etienne: 135, 138.
Washington, Lady: 85, 87, 94-5, 97.
Wayne, General Anthony: 186-7.
West Coast River: 156.
West Road River: 143, 155, 157-9.
Western Sea: 113, 116-9, 121-8, 130, 137, 184, 219.
Weymouth, George: 38.
Whirlpool River: 252-3.
Willapa Bay: 83.
Williams Lake: 230, 232.
Willoughby, Sir Hugh: 30, 36.
Windermere Lake: 228, 246-7.
Winnipeg: 122, 271.
Winnipeg River: 118.
Wollaston Lake: 167-8.
Wood River: 254-5, 258.

Y

Yale: 155, 232, 236, 238.
York Factory: 122, 167.
Youens, Captain: 211.

288